THE LABYRINTH AS SACRED COSMOS

RITUALS OF UNITY AND DIVERSITY

LILAN LAISHLEY, PH.D.

Copyright © 2023 Lilan Laishley

All Rights Reserved

Year of the Book
135 Glen Avenue
Glen Rock, PA 17327

ISBN: 978-1-64649-367-8 (paperback)
ISBN: 978-1-64649-368-5 (ebook)

This book or parts thereof may not be reproduced in any form, stored in any retrieval system, or transmitted in any form by any means—electronic, mechanical, photocopy, recording, or otherwise—without prior written permission of the publisher, except as provided by United States of America copyright law.

Cover digital collage image by Catherine Anderson
www.creativepilgrimage.com

I dedicate this book to my family for providing me roots, and my husband Bill Harman, for giving me wings.

Contents

Chapter 1: Origins of the Labyrinth Movement 1
    Introduction 2
    Classical and Christian Labyrinth..3
    The Labyrinth Movement's Two Branches 5
    Rituals on the Labyrinth 13
    Conclusion 17

Chapter 2: The Labyrinth as a Reflection of Religious Diversity 19
    The Labyrinth and American Religious Diversity...............19
    The Labyrinth as Popular and Lived Religion.....................27
    The Labyrinth and America's Quest Culture.......................34
    Spiritual but not Religious 38
    Conclusion 44

Chapter 3: The Adaptation of the Classical and Christian Labyrinth .47
    The Classical Labyrinth...49
    Chartres Cathedral Labyrinth 55
    Conclusion 71

Chapter 4: Rituals that Connect to a Sacred Cosmos 73
    The Sacred Cosmos 75
    Connection to a Sacred Cosmos 79
    Time and Space in Ritual 81
    Ritual and a Sacred Cosmos 93
    Conclusion..101

Chapter 5: Church-based Liturgical Rituals 103
    The Liturgical Calendar...104
    Incarnation Cycle: An Advent Ritual 112
    An Epiphany Ritual – The Magi's Journey 123
    Ordinary Time 130
    Resurrection Cycle: An Ash Wednesday Ritual................130

    Holy Week Ritual – Stations of the Cross 134
    Conclusion.. 139

Chapter 6: Nature-based Labyrinth Rituals 141
    The Labyrinth and Nature Religion 144
    Environmental Trend 148
    Metaphysical Trend.. 157
    Mind/Body Healing Trend 168
    Conclusion.. 172

Chapter 7: Beginnings and Endings... 175

Notes 183

Bibliography 201

List of Figures

Fig. 1 Classical seven-circuit labyrinth, design c. 1200 BCE 3

Fig. 2 Chartres eleven-circuit labyrinth, design c. 1200 CE 3

Fig. 3 Hedge maze, design 1820 CE. 4

Fig. 4 Classical seven-circuit labyrinth built in Vermont by Sig Lonegren in 1986, Winter view Winter view. Photo by Sig Lonegren. 6

Fig. 5 Labyrinth at Chartres Cathedral, built c. 1200 CE. Photo by Sonia Hallida. 10

Fig. 6 Portable labyrinth at Grace Cathedral Episcopal Church, 1991. Photo by Cindy Pavlinic. 11

Fig. 7 Open walk on labyrinth at ELPC, 2002. Author's photo. 15

Fig. 8 Scripted ceremonial on labyrinth in Dayton, Ohio, 2000. Photo by Dianna DeLong. 16

Fig. 9 Theseus and Minotaur in Cretan maze, Vienna, c. 300 CE. 51

Fig. 10 Girl in labyrinth from a wall painting from Sibbo church, Finland, Fifteenth century CE. 54

Fig. 11 Earliest Christian labyrinth, Algiers, dated 324 CE. 56

Fig. 12 Chartres Cathedral with labyrinth. 57

Fig. 13 Labyrinth at Chartres Cathedral, built c. 1200 CE. Photo by Sonia Halliday. 57

Fig. 14 Minotaur as Devil in a manuscript dated 989 CE from the monastery of St. Germain–des-Pres, Paris. Earliest Chartres-style labyrinth. 62

Fig. 15 Situs Jerusalem Map, Brussels, thirteenth century CE. 69

Fig. 16 Diagram of Borobudur. 74

Fig. 17 Liturgical Year.. 106

Fig. 18 Program for Advent ritual, ELPC. Author's photo. 116

Fig. 19 Shrine to Mary at Advent ritual, ELPC. Author's photo.......... 117

Fig. 20 Baptismal font at Advent ritual, ELPC. Author's photo. 118

Fig. 21 Labyrinth path, ELPC. Author's photo. 126

Fig. 22 Holy Week – Stations of the Cross, ELPC. Author's photo..... 136

Fig. 23 Pinecone seven-circuit labyrinth in Massachusetts, 2001. Photo by Sara Penn-Strah. 142

Fig. 24 Rock seven-circuit labyrinth in California, 2003. Photo by Jan Bradley. 143

Fig. 25 Alex Champion's dowsed Classical seven-circuit labyrinth in CA. 1987. Photo by Cindy Pavlinic. 160

Fig. 26 Alex Champion's illustration of labyrinth energy.................... 161

Fig. 27 Prairie Labyrinth outside of Kansas City, MO. Photo by Toby Evans. 164

Fig. 28 *Chakra* post at Prairie Labyrinth. Photo by Toby Evans.......... 166

Fig. 29 Labyrinths for Peace in Washington, D.C................................ 172

1
Origins of the Labyrinth Movement

Introduction

Millions of people in recent years have been captivated by the mystery and beauty of a 4000-year-old geometric form called the "labyrinth." They have walked, prayed, meditated, and engaged in ritual on the labyrinth's winding and circular pathway that guides the walker with absolute sureness toward the center. Labyrinths are located in parks, schools, museums, prisons, hospitals, memorial gardens, retreat centers, and churches.

There are two main labyrinths found in this labyrinth resurgence. The first is considered "Classical" since its origins are from Egypt and Crete over 3000 years ago. Relatively simple in design, it is easy to construct, is often made outside in nature, and is sometimes thought of as a "pagan" labyrinth. The second is "Christian" since it originated in medieval Catholicism, with the beautiful stone labyrinth at Chartres Cathedral, a 12th century gothic church, considered the quintessential expression. The Chartres labyrinth's complicated design is based on sacred geometry and is more difficult to construct. It is often found in churches built of stone and brick, or painstakingly painted on canvas.

Since the late 1990s some Protestant churches have included labyrinth rituals in their worship, a rather surprising ecumenical move since over 450 years ago, Protestants vehemently condemned both Catholicism and ritual during the Protestant Reformation. Many churches are using labyrinths in their church service to reach out to Christians who have strayed away from the more traditional approaches to worship, but still state a belief in God. Others, who consider themselves "spiritual but not religious," use the labyrinth as an expressive way to connect to the divine.

There is a growing movement around the world of people walking the labyrinth for prayer, introspection, and healing.[1] The *San Francisco Chronicle* in February 2003 reported that millions of people had walked over 1800 labyrinths located in the United States.[2] In 2011 there were over 2800 labyrinths in the United States, and over 3740 labyrinths total have been documented in seventy-five countries around the world. In 2023, there are over 4,611 labyrinths documented in the United States and 6250 in ninety countries around the world.[3] The Labyrinth Movement connects people to each other through conferences, newsletters, and the internet to create an international community.

The labyrinth has become a unifying symbol and ritual structure that attracts people from a broad spectrum of religions and belief systems. In this way the labyrinth has become an excellent window from which to view the growing trend of religious diversity and the importance of ritual as a means of connecting to the sacred.

The Classical and Christian Labyrinth

A labyrinth is usually a circular form with a single path that begins at the perimeter and winds in the most convoluted, circuitous route to the center. Labyrinths can be any size, but the ones used in the Labyrinth Movement are large enough to walk, ranging from 12 to 160 feet in diameter. Labyrinths are described by the number of rings, called circuits, one walks through to get to the center. Though there are many styles of labyrinths that date back as far as 3000 BCE, the two labyrinths used most frequently today are the Classical seven-circuit and the Chartres eleven-circuit.

The Classical seven-circuit labyrinth comes from Minoan Crete and can be accurately dated to 1200 BCE though it may be older (see fig.1).[4] Because of its association with the classical Greek and Roman civilizations it is sometimes called a pagan labyrinth. It is a relatively easy labyrinth to make and typically has seven circuits to the center, though it can be made with more or less, such as three-circuits or thirteen circuits.

Figure 1: Classical seven-circuit labyrinth, design c. 1200 BCE.

Figure 2: Chartres eleven-circuit labyrinth, design c. 1200 CE.

The second labyrinth is the Chartres labyrinth (see fig.2). This labyrinth design dates to 989 CE in manuscript form and c. 1200 CE as a forty-two foot pavement labyrinth built into the floor at *Notre Dame de Chartres* in Chartres, France. Due to its association with a Catholic cathedral it is sometimes called the Christian labyrinth. Built on the medieval principles of sacred geometry it is a more complicated labyrinth to make than the Classical.

Until recently it was common practice to refer to a labyrinth and maze as synonymous terms, though today it is standard to make a distinction between them. The labyrinth is uni-cursal in that it has a single path which leads to the center through the most circuitous route. Following that same path in reverse will lead back out of the labyrinth. A maze is multi-cursal in that it has multiple paths leading to the center, some of which have dead-ends and others which branch out to other paths (see fig. 3). The most common maze type is a hedge maze that was built as part of formal gardens in Europe beginning in the fifteenth century.

Figure 3: Hedge maze, design 1820 CE.

One of the major differences between a labyrinth and a maze is the type of logistical and psychological experience involved. A maze, with its multiple paths, is an intellectual puzzle with many dead-ends that requires the walker to constantly choose which way to turn. This on-going decision making process results in many wrong decisions, leading the walker to constantly retrace one's steps until the goal of the center is reached. The mind puzzle continues on the journey back out of the maze as the walker must continually decide which way leads to the exit. The constant decision making of a maze stimulates the left-brain which rules logical thought. By contrast, in a labyrinth the only decision one makes is whether to enter or not, for once the walker is on the path all he/she needs to do is put one foot in front of the next to arrive inevitably at the goal of the center. There is no puzzle, no choices on which direction the path might take, no intellectual decisions required. Hence the focus can be directed toward individual inner processes. The labyrinth stimulates the right brain, which rules emotional and intuitive thinking. The Labyrinth Movement uses mostly labyrinths and labyrinth-like uni-cursal forms due to its more interior and reflective nature.

The Labyrinth Movement's Two Branches

The current Labyrinth Movement grew from two different roots, the first associated with the Classical labyrinth and the second associated with the Chartres labyrinth. These two roots grew over the years, at first distinct, but now wound together in such a way that at times their distinction blurs. But in order to understand the popularity and broad reach of this blended labyrinth, it is best to re-visit the Labyrinth Movement's dual origins through a glimpse of two very dissimilar people, Sig Lonegren and Lauren Artress, who were there at the beginning and unknowingly set the labyrinth trajectory in two different directions.

Beginning in the U.S. east coast in 1986, a pagan, dowser, and geomancer named Sig Lonegren quietly began the revival by building a seven-circuit Classical labyrinth in a field outside his Vermont home (see fig. 4).[5] A dowser, sometimes called a "water witch" or "diviner," has been associated historically with rural people who use a stick or rod to intuitively sense water in order to locate the best placement for a well. Dowsing was taught to Lonegren when he was twenty-one by his mother using a metal coat hanger to practice on the underground water pipes of their house. But it was not until ten years later when Lonegren went to watch the sunrise at Summer Solstice with a group of people involved in ancient power centers (places of raw earth energy), sacred sites (a power center that has been modified by the activity of humans), archeo-astronomy (the orientation of ancient sacred sites to astronomical events such as the position of the sun), and ley lines (straight alignments connecting sacred sites) that he became fascinated with power centers and the energies of the earth that are associated with them.[6] Lonegren's interest in the spiritual dimensions of the earth led him to a Master of Arts in Sacred Space from Goddard College in Vermont and "twenty-five years studying ancient tools that enhance intuition," which he found time to do while being the selectman in Vermont and teaching English, Anthropology, and Ancient Sciences.[7]

Figure 4: Classical seven-circuit labyrinth built in Vermont by Sig Lonegren in 1986. Winter view. Photo by Sig Lonegren.

Lonegren used dowsing not only to sense water, but also to locate and measure the earth energies present at sacred sites, making dowsing "a tool that works as a bridge that can take you from the physical to the spiritual realms."[8] In the early 1970s he joined the *American Society of Dowsers* (ASD) which at that time consisted of "sixty-five year old male water-dowsers wearing coats and ties."[9] Now the ASD Annual Convention has a younger membership of more women than men with workshops on healing, earth energies, and labyrinths, in addition to water dowsing. He has been part of ASD's evolution including being a Trustee, founding their first Earth Mysteries Group, and heading their dowsing school. The ASD began building labyrinths in the mid 1980s at their meetings and used dowsing to experiment with the types of energies labyrinths produced. Dowsers use rods or pendulums to find the correct alignment on the earth to place a labyrinth so that it will be in greatest harmony with its surroundings and therefore most effective, not only for the person using the labyrinth, but also for the earth. In finding the right "place" for a labyrinth, dowsers may also include sacred geometry and astronomical alignments in order to harmonize the physical and spiritual environment. This art of placement is called Geomancy, similar in ways to the Chinese method of placement, *feng shui*. Dowsers often prefer outdoor locations and are more typically interested in the Classical seven-circuit labyrinth due to its antiquity and simplicity of form which makes it easier to build outside than the more complicated eleven-circuit Chartres labyrinth which requires exact mathematical measurements.

For Lonegren, sacred space is created by three qualities. The first is the powerful energy it emanates; the second is its particular astronomical alignment; and the third is its geometrical design. These same three qualities can be present in a labyrinth. He describes the labyrinth as a type of sacred space that needs to be located in harmony with the earth so that it can be "a tool to aid the seeker not only in contacting the numinous, but also in helping the intuitive side of the seeker's being to come to the fore."[10] For this reason he will "dowse" where to put a labyrinth by asking the Spirit of that place for permission to put a labyrinth in a particular spot.

Lonegren wrote *Labyrinths: Ancient Myths and Modern Uses* (1991), one of the first popular books on the labyrinth where he focuses on the "magical" seven-circuit Classical labyrinth. Lonegren has also written *Spiritual Dowsing* (1986), *The Pendulum Kit* (1990) and *The Dowsing Rod Kit* (1995). He is currently living in rhythm with the Wheel of the Year by celebrating the Solstices, Equinoxes, and Cross Quarter days of the pagan and Celtic calendar.[11] He moved from Vermont and now lives in the town of Glastonbury, England, which is acknowledged as a New Age center partly due to its connection to the Arthurian legend as the island of Avalon and the resting place of the Holy Grail.[12] Lonegren was a founding member and former Webmaster of *The Labyrinth Society* (TLS), which from its very beginning had a strong contingency of dowsers, with twelve of the forty-three founding members involved in dowsing.

A point of reference for this early labyrinth interest was *Caerdroia*, a non-profit organization in England founded in 1980 by Jeff Saward, arguably the world's leading expert on labyrinth history. *Caerdroia* maintains an archive of labyrinth photographs and other resources and has published a journal since 1983 which provides a forum for researchers and labyrinth enthusiasts worldwide. By 1995 there were enough people working with labyrinths in areas as diverse as education, art therapy, metaphysics, religion, psychology, ritual, business, medicine, and history that the first national labyrinth conference was held, followed by conferences in 1996, 1997, and 1998, all of which were the nexus for TLS. In 1999 TLS was incorporated as a non-profit organization with forty-three founding members, at least partially to counter the widely held belief that all labyrinths were the eleven-circuit Chartres design and used exclusively in churches. TLS has an international Board of Directors and membership that is joined together through the website, e-mails and yearly Gatherings.

Meanwhile the second branch of the Labyrinth Movement was developing on the west coast when in 1991 an Episcopal priest named Lauren Artress was going through a personal transition in her job at Grace Cathedral Episcopal Church in San Francisco where she was Canon for Special Ministries and director of *Quest, Grace Cathedral Center for Spiritual Wholeness*. Artress received her master's degree in religious education from Princeton Theological Seminary and her doctor of ministry from Andover Newton Theological School. She is also a licensed psychotherapist in the state of California. Feeling the need for inner reflection Artress went to a Mystery School seminar by Jean Houston. Houston is known for her work in the human potential movement and author of eighteen published books (some with her husband Dr. Robert Masters). At the Mystery School Houston had taped an eleven-circuit labyrinth, similar to the one at Chartres Cathedral, on the floor, calling it a powerful spiritual tool whose path would lead each person to their own center.[13] As Artress walked the winding path she was so moved by the experience that on returning to Grace Cathedral she decided to go to Chartres, France, to walk the original, a stone labyrinth forty feet in diameter built into the floor of the nave around 1200 CE (see fig. 5). She soon realized that just being in Chartres Cathedral did not guarantee seeing, much less walking the labyrinth, as it is normally covered with over 250 folding chairs, which Dr. Artress and her companions, including Alan Jones, the dean of Grace Cathedral moved in order to be able to walk. Once again her experience walking the labyrinth was profound and after attaining the accurate measurements of the Chartres labyrinth she had a replica made for Grace Cathedral out of canvas (see fig. 6). The labyrinth was opened to the public in December 1991 and response was so positive that in 1994 a second labyrinth, woven into a carpet, was purchased for $45,000 and placed in the nave of the Cathedral. In 1995 a permanent terrazzo stone labyrinth was installed as part of a two million dollar restoration project in the outside courtyard and available to walk by the public twenty-four hours a day. By winter of 1996 the Grace Cathedral labyrinths had been walked by over a million people.[14] Artress's book *Walking a Sacred Path: Rediscovering the Labyrinth as a Spiritual Tool* was published in 1995, igniting interest in the labyrinth, particularly in churches. She began to take the canvas labyrinth, which was portable, to conferences and events worldwide including one in 1996 at the Washington National Cathedral in Washington, D.C., which is where I first saw the labyrinth in a photo in the *Washington Post*. Since then the original canvas labyrinth has logged over 200,000 miles around the world and has been walked by over 500,000 people.[15]

In 1996 Artress started a non-profit organization housed at Grace Cathedral called Veriditas, which means "greening," a vision of the flourishing growth of the "healing and meditative powers of the labyrinth."[16] In order to accomplish this vision Veriditas has a variety of outreach and marketing strategies that include workshops on the labyrinth at Grace Cathedral and pilgrimages to Chartres, France. They sell portable canvas Chartres-style labyrinths and "seed kits" that have instructions on how to make a Chartres labyrinth for those who want to do it themselves. Veriditas also trains "labyrinth facilitators" to bring a labyrinth into their church or community and by 2003 eleven-hundred people had been trained.[17] In addition to a print newsletter called *Source*,

Veriditas has an extensive website which offers labyrinth information, merchandise, music, and a "Labyrinth Locator" which is an internet search engine that brings up the location of labyrinths throughout the United States. Though Artress is personally open to various types of labyrinths throughout the world, Veriditas has almost exclusively used the Chartres labyrinth since it is a "Christian" labyrinth and more amenable to work within the church.

Figure 5: Labyrinth at Chartres Cathedral, built c. 1200 CE. Photo by Sonia Halliday.

Figure 6: Portable canvas labyrinth at Grace Cathedral Episcopal Church, 1991. Photo by Cindy Pavlinic.

The popularity of Artress's book *Walking a Sacred Path* and the sizeable support that Grace Cathedral could give to Veriditas led to the church-based part of the Labyrinth Movement receiving most of the attention of the press, including the *New York Times* article. The sophisticated marketing of Artress and Veriditas to meet its mission of "reintroducing the labyrinth, which had been dormant for centuries, as a spiritual tool" led to the false impression that the Labyrinth Movement was mostly

Christian and that it began in the mid 1990s. But when one goes more deeply into the story it becomes clear that the labyrinth has been used for over 5,000 years in ritual and myth, has never been entirely dormant, and that the current movement began in the United States in non-church settings. However, Veriditas appears to have legitimated the use of the labyrinth in Christian settings and has added to a new impetus in the Protestant church of using ritual as a means of worship.

I employ this distinction between the Classical seven-circuit branch and the Chartres eleven-circuit branch of the Labyrinth Movement as a central organizational device.[18] I henceforth refer to these two branches as the Classical nature-based, which I examine more fully in Chapter 5, and the Chartres church-based which I examine in Chapter 6. Utilizing this distinction I limit my inspection of the Labyrinth Movement to rituals associated with these two widespread labyrinth types, even through variations of these, as well as new designs altogether, are being used as well. Since the beginning of the Labyrinth Movement in 1986 the boundaries between the two branches have blurred and the separations between them are less apparent as they have grafted together. For example, Lauren Artress is a frequent speaker at TLS Gatherings, and TLS and Veriditas have officially joined together to create a World-Wide Labyrinth Locator, an internet search engine for labyrinths worldwide. Labyrinths other than the Chartres-style are being seen in churches, and the Chartres-style labyrinth is being built in outdoor locations. Yet the early differences still exist and are easy to distinguish. To acknowledge these distinctions can help explain how the labyrinth is used in such diverse rituals as Epiphany at a Protestant church and Summer Solstice on a hilltop sheep farm.

My entry into the labyrinth culture was relatively straightforward since when I first started my research in 1996 the core people involved were relatively small in number and very enthusiastic, pleased that there was someone who was interested in studying the experience. Since 1996 I have documented labyrinths in churches, prisons, hospitals, elementary schools, universities, conferences, parks, retreat centers and backyards. I have witnessed them used for walking, dancing, praying, meditating, anointing, and weeping. I have read about them in everything from major daily newspapers, new age publications, church bulletins, and gardening magazines to mortuary advertisements.

I began to find out everything I could about the Labyrinth Movement and discovered the two main branches. In order to learn about each branch I researched two groups that represented the movement's two divisions. For the church-based branch I chose East Liberty Presbyterian Church (ELPC) in Pittsburgh Pennsylvania, the first church in Pittsburgh to have a labyrinth. ELPC was part of Veriditas in that they made their labyrinth from a Veriditas "seed kit" and had a pastor go to Grace Cathedral to train as a "labyrinth facilitator." At the ELPC field site my first event was in September 1996 at the dedication of their first labyrinth. In November 1997 I was trained by them as a labyrinth facilitator and from December 1997 until August 1999 I was a volunteer once a month at their weekly walks. In January 1999 I was invited to join the Labyrinth Committee at ELPC, which met approximately every two months to facilitate the use of the labyrinth at the church, consider requests from groups to borrow the two canvas portable "loaner" labyrinths, and to plan larger events which took place about four times a year.

The second group was The Labyrinth Society (TLS), an international organization of labyrinth builders, facilitators, and enthusiasts which was officially created in 1998, but had been loosely formed since 1995. At the TLS field site my first event was in November 1997 when I went to an "invitation only" conference of key labyrinth workers who had gathered in St. Louis, Missouri, to form a labyrinth organization. At this meeting I joined the Board of Directors of the new organization to work on a directory of labyrinth sites around the world. I was on the Board until November 2000, and then again from 2004-2007 as chair of Research. I went to conferences open to the general public in November 1998 (St. Louis), 1999 (Denver), 2000 (Arkansas), and 2002 (England).

Rituals on the Labyrinth

Regardless of whether the labyrinth used is the Classical nature-based or the Chartres church-based, the rituals that occur are of two broad categories. I refer to them as the "open walk" and "scripted ceremonial," each of which can have countless variations.

The open walk is the most basic ritual and involves the simple act of walking the circuitous path of the labyrinth from the circumference to the center, where the walker might pause for reflection, and then walk back out again. It is a private, internal, self-motivated act done by an individual, either alone or with others. Even if other people are walking the labyrinth at the same time (the maximum number of people recommended to be on a forty-foot labyrinth at one time is thirty-five) they are not doing so in concert or pre-arranged agreement with each other. It is simply that they are all doing the same thing at the same time, like jogging in the park while other people are also jogging. It is an individual act in the company of others. The labyrinths where people engage in open walks may be located anywhere—a park, beach, field, backyard or the church social hall.

At an open walk there is no ritual script, professional leader, or predefined action. These open walks have no rules, are free-form, and follow the recommendation to "trust the labyrinth," which means to accept whatever happens on the labyrinth to be exactly what should occur. There may be guidelines for walking that are written on a poster or flyer which include recommendations to remove one's shoes, and some suggestions for visualizations or prayers. But for the most part the decision to walk is self-motivated and the intention for the walk is self-chosen. Walking can be very slow, like a Buddhist walking meditation, or combined with yoga, dance, bowing, pausing, kneeling, praying, or prostrations. For this reason one person may be walking very slowly and crying, while another person may be dancing to the center. This photo of an open walk shows one person walking, another doing yoga, another journaling, and another contemplating (see fig. 7). J.Z. Smith says that ritual is a means of paying attention and this is especially true with the open labyrinth walk.[19] The mindset of the walker is like a lens through which all activities become focused and other people on the labyrinth and events that happen on the open walk become significant to the walker as a metaphor for his/her life. For example, if the walker finds herself behind a very slow person on the path and feels frustrated and held back, she will often view it as a metaphor for some issue in her life where she has felt constrained.

Figure 7: Open walk on labyrinth at ELPC, 2002. Author's photo.

The time when labyrinths are available for an open walk may differ according to where they are placed. Many of the labyrinths at churches are canvas and this portable quality means that they will be available to the public at those times when it is convenient to the church to unfold them, for example at ELPC it was Wednesdays from 9 AM to 9 PM and Mondays 12 PM to 9 PM; others may be available twenty-four hours a day, like the outdoor labyrinth at Grace Cathedral or one that is situated in a park. There is usually no charge for walking a labyrinth at an open walk though a donation may be requested.

The second type of labyrinth ritual is the "scripted ceremonial" (see fig. 8). The scripted ceremonial is an event that is pre-planned, or scripted, on the labyrinth for some specific purpose and then executed in such a way as to meet that purpose. The scripted ceremonial is often a complex ritual that might include any combination of symbols, music, adornments, scents, icons, and activities, all to elaborate the basic ritual of walking from the circumference to the center and back out.

Figure 8: Scripted ceremonial on labyrinth in Dayton, Ohio. 2000. Photo Dianna Delong.

Usually there is a ritual leader and people attending the event are directed as a group, rather than acting independently. The scripted ceremonial rituals that can be constructed on the labyrinth are varied depending on what group or person is involved. In the church-based branch the scripted ceremonial may be a liturgical ritual, such as marking the forehead with ashes during Ash Wednesday, or providing a reflective journal for the four weeks of Lent. For the nature-based it may be a Summer Solstice event or Earth Day commemoration. The scripted ceremonial rituals are often offered by donation, though certain events can cost hundreds of dollars such as the "Theater of Enlightenment" offered by Veriditas that spans three days and combines the labyrinth with natural settings, music, drama, and journaling. The labyrinth rituals in Chapter 5 and 6 are scripted ceremonials in that they are more elaborate pre-planned events that were designed for a specific purpose.

Though rituals on the labyrinth range from private open walks to more elaborate and public scripted ceremonials, I am directing my attention to the analysis of scripted ceremonials. In these more elaborate rituals the themes that are being enacted are more readily discernable than in the more subjective and personal open walks. The types of rituals that people construct and enact on the labyrinth are indicative of what matters to them. People create and attend labyrinth rituals by choice, not by dictate or tradition. For this reason labyrinth rituals provide an excellent window into the beliefs and practices of the segment of American people who are actively seeking spiritual notions of the world, both inside and outside the confines of institutional religion.

Conclusion

The labyrinth is emerging around the country and the world as an arena for ritual that is apparently unbounded by the types of rules and limitations that often accompany religious expressions. It belongs to no one religion, has no single leader, no absolute ritual, no authoritative text, and no localized placement. Labyrinths are popping up everywhere, from backyards to cathedrals, and can remain in place from a single hour to hundreds of years. They are used by individuals for reasons known only to themselves and by churches to teach religious doctrine. Yet this vast array of labyrinth rituals does not imply spiritual anarchy, rather there is a sense that labyrinths and the people who use them are interwoven. The image associated with the labyrinth was articulated at a March 2000 labyrinth exhibit at the House of Representatives in Washington, D.C., where the Labyrinth Movement was described as a network, with each labyrinth linked to every other as if by connect-the-dots, developing a communication grid that crosses the world. All these connections are held together virtually through the internet, e-mail, websites, and forums, and physically through conferences, pilgrimages, books, and trainings. It is a nascent movement consciously defining itself, literally, from the ground up.

Two questions drove my research. First, what does the Labyrinth Movement say about the current state of religious diversity, especially in America? And second, how is it possible that the labyrinth can be used in so many ways by peoples of diverse religious beliefs and practices? To answer these questions I examined the rituals enacted on the labyrinth in nature-based and church-based settings. From this I developed the hypothesis that the labyrinth can be used by people with diverse beliefs because its geometrical form acts as a template upon which people overlay their idea of a sacred world, or cosmos, with which they can then engage through ritual. People's understanding of a sacred cosmos varies greatly from well developed, clearly articulated ideas that are part of institutional religions such as Christianity, to ideas that are self-consciously created and privately held, yet still have coherence and meaning.

2

The Labyrinth as a Reflection of Religious Diversity

Many elements found in the Labyrinth Movement are a reflection of religious diversity, particularly as seen in America. The labyrinth therefore provides an opportunity to examine several key themes current in American religion and to consider such questions as: Is America more religiously diverse than it was in the past, and if so, what caused this shift? In what way is the Labyrinth Movement part of America's identity as a pluralistic nation? Does the Labyrinth Movement constitute a popular religiosity? And finally how does the labyrinth exemplify those people who are "spiritual but not religious"?

The Labyrinth and American Religious Diversity

There is no question that the American religious landscape is changing. *The Yearbook of American and Canadian Churches* states:

> The religious landscape in North America is in constant motion. It is axiomatic to note that the contours of the religious landscape are in perpetual flux as befits a continent in which religious tolerance abides. As the close of the millennium approaches, this rate of change appears to have picked up momentum. . . Such a dizzying array of traditions raises new questions about the religious composition of the U.S. society in particular.[1]

The changing religious composition of the United States has been attracting the attention of scholars who have speculated on what is causing such a trend and what it could mean. The changing trend is evidenced by a decline in the Christian faith in America while at the same time there is an increase in other religions. For example in 1900 96.4% of Americans defined themselves as Christians; in 1979 the number had decreased to 90.1%; in 1997 that number was 85%.[2] At the same time there has been an increase in Muslims, Hindus, Sikhs, Baha'is, and Buddhists. There are also religions newly introduced to the United States such as Chinese folk religion, Shamanism, and Jainism, not to mention an increase in atheists and those nonreligious.[3] And while mainline Protestant groups such as Methodist, Presbyterian, and United Church of Christ have declined, Conservative Christian groups have been rapidly increasing. From 1970 to 1996 the Pentecostals and Evangelicals had a combined increase of 13.5%. Often these conservative Fundamentalist groups see various other religions as moving into what had once been their exclusive domain, leading them to take a hard line against multi-culturalism and religious diversity.[4]

Robert Wuthnow, Diana Eck, and Wade Clark Roof all agree that the increase in religious diversity began after the 1950s though they differ on the reason, citing education, immigration, and generational causes, respectively. The 1950s were seen as a period of social and religious stability and there was a general consensus that religion was a positive component of society. During the 1950s religion served as a central means with which to define identity both for the individual and the nation, for example denominationalism was strong, there was prayer in the schools, and the line "One Nation under God" was added to the Pledge of Allegiance. When there were conflicts in religion they were usually limited to major divisions between Christians and Jews, Protestant and Catholics, and various Protestant denominations.

But the religious stability of the 1950s deteriorated in the 1960s when the social unrest that rocked the nation also led to changes in religion. Issues such as the civil rights movement and war in Southeast Asia led to a division in the churches between the liberals and conservatives. This division was based not only on what particular views were espoused, but even more so on the fundamental question of whether the church was to fulfill its role by taking part in direct activism (social justice) or by addressing itself to public values that lead to a change in an individual's behavior (evangelism).[5] This conflict led to many denominational schisms and mergers. At the same time there was growth of other religious groups that included various sects seen as deviant Christian groups, such as the Mormons and Seventh-Day Adventists; many "new religions" that were not Judeo-Christian such as the Zen Center in San Francisco, Unification Church, and Transcendental Meditation; groups that were a syncretic blend of psychology, esotericism, and mysticism such as EST, and Silva Mind Control; as well as thousands of small communes each with their own particular belief. By 1970 there were approximately 3,000 new groups and religions, of which one-tenth of the population had some type of participation, pushing the outer limits of religious respectability.[6] The 1960s had brought such an array of religious diversity that the pretense of a consensus in religion could no longer be maintained. Robert Bellah's 1966 writings on *Civil Religion* made an attempt to say that even if the country appeared to be pluralistic on the surface, that there was an over-arching belief in God and country that cemented public opinion and provided unity within the fragmentation.

Robert Wuthnow attributes this "restructuring" of American religion largely to an increase in the percentage of people who received higher education. This was due to two main factors. The first was that youth between the ages of 18 and 24 increased from 15.2 percent to 19.6 percent of the population (from 16.2 million to 24.4 million). The second was an increase in participation in higher education helped in part by the GI Bill following WWII. From 1960 to 1970 the increase in people enrolled in higher education was 139% (from 3.5 million to 8.6 million) and expenditures on higher education went from 5.6 billion in 1960 to 23.4 billion in 1970.[7] Wuthnow credits this increase in higher education with influencing changes in cultural attitudes such as an appreciation of egalitarianism, greater acceptance of religions other than one's own, more equal recognition for women and homosexuals, an increase in civil liberties, and an acceptance of lifestyle choices such as pre-marital sex and divorce. Wuthnow states that "virtually every study showed that the growing liberalization of American culture in these years was closely related to the rising influence of higher education," and that higher education was the greatest single indicator in polls to differences in values, with the better educated being more liberal and the less educated as more conservative.[8] College educated people were twice as likely to be religious liberals as conservatives, for example over 50% of those who had only a grade school education considered the Bible the literal word of God compared to 20% of college educated people. Religious liberals were likely to support the ordination of women and homosexuals as well as changes in the Second Vatican Council. Liberals also showed a difference in style of religious expression, with more emphasis on a compassionate and forgiving faith and the belief that one can be a true Christian without believing in the divinity of Christ.[9] This brought a more open, tolerant approach to other religions. Religious liberals worked to incorporate meditation, mysticism, and holistic health into their beliefs while conservatives took an antagonistic attitude to new religions by participating in anti-cult work and issuing warnings against the "New Age."[10]

Diana Eck in *A New Religious America* takes an approach different from Wuthnow's to explain changes in the American religious landscape. Rather than an increase in higher education, Eck cites the 1965 Immigration and Naturalization law as the major factor. The 1965 Immigration and Naturalization Act signed by President Johnson had been inspired by the Civil Rights Act of 1964. It was acknowledgment that racism extended further than Black Americans to the overall national attitude toward immigrants. The 1965 Immigration and Naturalization Act reversed a restrictive quota system that had been in force since 1924, leading to an influx of foreign religions being transplanted and taking root in American soil. The 1965 law opened up a wave of immigration including Hindu, Sikh, Muslim, Buddhist, Jain and others who brought their own religious traditions with them. By 2002 there were over thirty million immigrants in the U.S., with one million more arriving each year. Unlike earlier immigrant groups who were cut off from their home country, these new faiths are getting replenished by maintaining cultural customs and staying in contact with people from their homelands through internet, e-mail, cable television, and telephone.[11]

Wade Clark Roof attributes the changing complexion of American religion neither to education nor immigration, but rather to the generation known as the "baby boomers," those born between 1946 and 1964. According to Roof's definition there are seventy-six million baby-boomers, about one-third of the American population. Due to this large percentage they have had a major influence on American society.[12] Roof finds it significant that baby boomers came of age during the turbulent and expansive 1960s, a period that offered a rich variety of religious choices. He believes that the opportunity to experience these choices transformed the spiritual life of many, turning them into "a generation of seekers." Many baby boomers "reacted against the bland religious establishment of their youth" and dropped out of traditional religious institutions to search for a new spiritual style, from fundamentalism to New Age.[13]

Wuthnow, Eck, and Roof all agree that the increased diversity in American religion occurred after World War II, though their main causal factors differ. But Laurence Moore, Jon Butler, and Robert Ellwood take a different stance, and might declare that none of these theories of the recent increase in religious diversity can be correct since America has always been diverse. Their critique points to the fact that America has not suddenly changed its composition, but rather that it has historically held widely diverse beliefs that were ignored in an academic study of American religion that tended to consist of white Anglo-Saxon Protestant males researching their own history, leaving the "fringes" that were not considered relevant undocumented. Moore contends that this earlier scholarship which overemphasized America's Protestant past made the current diversity seem more nascent that it really is. In examining the historiography of religious scholarship, Moore points out those early religious scholars had a vested interest in showing that America's formation was both inspired and directed by God through Manifest Destiny, particularly as it was expressed in New England. As such, historians ignored or downplayed anything that did not support that contention. Moore questions why religious movements that were very visible and viable in their time, such as Spiritualism in the 19th century, were areas often ignored by academics.[14] He attributes this partially to the fact that "other" religions challenged the Protestant hegemony, and were therefore labeled as "outsiders" and hence outside the purview of serious research.

Robert Ellwood supports Moore's argument that scholars ignored religious movements that did not fit what they considered the mainstream. Ellwood attributes elite academics who did not want to study the common folk to the lack of academic scholarship on the activities of lay people, called "popular religion."[15] Robert Wuthnow agrees that there has been a lack of research on America's diverse religious past, but attributes the late arrival of popular religion as an area of study to the fact that religions that are textually based, such as Protestantism, are more directly accessible for study, whereas the practices of the common folk are not easily found outside of extensive ethnography or archival work.

Jon Butler also contends that America has always been religiously diverse but that American scholarship made it appear otherwise. Butler attributes this skewed perception of a solid Protestant past to the fact that Puritanism was historically given too much importance, while not enough importance was given to concurrent, eclectic, religious practices. For example, in 1650 only 33% of adults ever belonged to a church and in the period of the American Revolution it was far less at only 15%.[16] Butler focuses on the occult traditions, such as astrology and alchemy that were used across society by the wealthy and literate elites as well as the poor and illiterate peasants.[17] Historians generally shunned such "fringe" topics as alchemy and astrology. For instance, it is not common knowledge that the sale of astrological almanacs outsold Bibles in Puritan America. And Isaac Newton's study of alchemy was more dominant than any other of his areas of research including mathematics, if the number of books on alchemy found in his library is any indication. And the Harmony Society (1805-1905), a wealthy and educated German Lutheran community, had three alchemical laboratories in their town of Economy, Pennsylvania, as well as a labyrinth, but they are usually referred to only as a Lutheran sect with millennial tendencies.

Moore, Ellwood, and Butler all agree that religious diversity was present in America's history from the beginning; Wuthnow, Eck, and Roof all state that diversity began in the 1960s. While it may appear as if these scholars offer two opposing views on the development of American religious pluralism, I see them as complementary approaches that together explain the current religious landscape. I contend that the recent increase in immigration, education, and number of baby boomers has led to a greater acceptance of diversity while at the same time causing a decline in the Protestant dominance. This decline has created cracks in the Protestant veneer that has exposed an underlying pre-existing pluralistic composition of America, which makes diversity much more visible and the subject of increased scrutiny.

These changes in the religious composition of America have not occurred without a struggle. In order to study the growing religious diversity in the United States Harvard University in 1991 started *The Pluralism Project* to research new houses of worship, legal challenges to religious freedoms, and continuing conflicts that occur as Americans struggle to find common ground with new religious practices. One of their publications indicates that: "How Americans of all faiths begin to engage with one another in shaping a positive pluralism is one of the most important questions American society faces in the years ahead."[18] As nations, states, cities, and neighborhoods become more diverse in culture and religion, it becomes necessary for differing religious groups to work together.[19] Diana Eck, head of *The Pluralism Project*, believes that it is crucial that a definition of religious pluralism entail more than just an acceptance or tolerance of the many different faith groups. Instead pluralism should involve an active engagement with diversity so that a real understanding and appreciation of various faith groups can be developed. This engaged appreciation does not mean that all religions are being melted into one to create a bland universality; rather, pluralism is a process by which each religion is fully seen so that it can stand in contrast with other religions, allowing a genuine dialogue of differences and similarities.[20]

Building bridges between religions to allow for a genuine dialogue can be a difficult task. This is all the more so since the American religious landscape is in such flux. Wade Clark Roof states that lines of religious understanding need to be regularly redrawn since "no one map can serve well for long."[21] Though the labyrinth is not a clearly defined map of religious topography, it does reflect the shifting terrain of religious pluralism in America through the diversity of the rituals enacted upon it.

The labyrinth is amorphous and not exclusively tied to any particular religious belief or practice. I have documented participants in labyrinth rituals from religious and spiritual traditions that include Brahma Kumari, Buddhist, Christian (Catholic, Episcopalian, Methodist, Non-denominational Fundamentalist, Presbyterian), Goddess, Hindu, Jewish, Kriya Yoga, Kundalini Yoga, Muslim, Native American, Pantheism, Paganism, and Twelve-Step Programs. Perception of the labyrinth's topography changes with the beliefs of the individual or group, reflecting such diverse territories of Mecca, Jerusalem, Trail of Tears, and the Womb of the Mother. The labyrinth is also not tied to any particular locale or site of worship. I have documented its use in churches, prisons, retreat centers, backyards, mountains, beaches, government buildings, memorial gardens, hospitals, elementary schools, colleges, and parking lots. The labyrinth is a liminal object that moves across the borders of religious traditions.

Participants acknowledge the liminal quality of the labyrinth as being important, even essential. One informant said that: "Anyone may come to walk the labyrinth. It knows no creed, no color or culture. We are all one on this path." Another said: "The labyrinth is open-ended. It doesn't require any particular prayers, and no particular faith, tradition, and creed. There are no boundaries or limits on its spirituality." Another informant stated: "The labyrinth expands the notion of religion. It's not just an institutional form, historical form, or individual history. It resonates within you and is a religious experience more than a religion. It's not an ideology, but taps something within you."

The more data I collected the more it became evident that the labyrinth was being used in ritual by different people, in different places, and for different reasons. I wanted to know how this one ritual form—the labyrinth—could accommodate such a broad range of beliefs and practices. I developed the hypothesis that the labyrinth acts as a template upon which participants engaged with their idea of a sacred cosmos. For example, a medieval Christian saw it as a substitute pilgrimage to Jerusalem, a nineteenth-century Lutheran as an enactment of *Pilgrim's Progress*, a modern day Jew as the Tree of Life, a Buddhist as the practice of a walking meditation, a Muslim as circumambulating the

Ka'ba, and so on. The labyrinth acts like a spiritual Rorschach test where people see in it a reflection of their deeper beliefs. The labyrinth has the same characteristics that John Eade and Michael Sallnow attribute to the essential and universalistic character of a shrine:

> The power of a shrine derives in large part from its character almost as a religious void, a ritual space capable of accommodating diverse means and practices. . . its capacity to absorb and reflect a multiplicity of religious discourses, to be able to offer a variety of clients what each of them desires. Universalism is ultimately constituted not by a unification of discourses but rather by the capacity of a cult to entertain and respond to a plurality. The sacred centre, then, in this perspective, appears as a vessel into which pilgrims devoutly pour their hopes, prayers, and aspirations.[22]

In this paper I contend that the iconographic form of the labyrinth has this same quality of a shrine to "absorb and reflect a multiplicity of religious discourses." Rather than using Eade and Sallnow's terminology of a "void," I prefer to discuss the iconographic form of the labyrinth as a "template," or generalized pattern, on which a cosmos, or meaningful world, can be overlaid. The labyrinth functions as a spatial canvas that through ritual can become transformed into the meaningful world of the participants, allowing them to become actively engaged in their own universe. In this way it provides an arena for the religious diversity that is so much a part of American contemporary religion.

The Labyrinth as Popular and Lived Religion

The American religious landscape is diverse and the fringes once underrepresented in the study of religion are now a legitimate area of research known as "popular religion." Popular religion is how people practice their faith outside of institutional parameters. In order to situate the Labyrinth Movement as part of popular religion it is first necessary to fully examine the term. However trying to find a generally agreed upon definition of popular religion is as difficult as creating unanimity on the terms "religion" or "ritual." Scholars approach the debate from their own corners and direct their understanding of popular religion based on their own particular theory, methodology, geographical setting, historical focus, and research subject.

Within this debate most scholars agree that popular religion is religion as it is practiced outside of the doctrines, texts, dogmas, and rituals that are part of an established and institutional religion. Popular religion is religion of the lay people and not as dictated by the religious specialists, such as priests. Popular religion is also defined by its syncretic nature. Folk traditions, myth, magic, holy places, diet, and more, all combine in an eclectic and myriad way, sometimes in association with the official religion of the region, and sometimes in a form all its own. Wade Clark Roof refers to it as "multi-layered," Charles Lippy as a "smorgasbord," Robert Wuthnow as "syncretic," and Laura Stark as "innovative." Whatever the term used, the idea is that popular religion is not concretized in texts and dogma, but is a fluid, flexible, and constantly changing expression of the people.

Disagreement arises however on how closely associated the practices of popular religion are to institutional religion. Keith Thomas, Peter Williams, and Laura Stark support the view that popular religion needs to be considered in juxtaposition to institutional religion and includes a tension between how the doctrines prescribed by religious elite are put into practice by lay people. They describe popular religion in terms of differences in class structure between the "popular" and the "elite," including social inequality based on wealth, prestige, and power. This concept of popular religion is influenced by Bronislaw Malinowski and Robert Redfield.[23] Malinowski made a distinction between popular magic and religion. He equated popular magic with a functional approach to problem solving, and considered religion a more highly evolved moral and philosophical doctrine. Keith Thomas was influenced by Malinowski's distinction between magic and religion as seen in Thomas's seminal study of popular religion, *Religion and the Decline of Magic*. In it Thomas examines the magical rites of a superstitious peasantry by placing them in contrast to the more educated Christian elite.[24]

Redfield created a "folk/urban" typology as he defined folk religions as homogenous practices that came out of small, isolated, rural communities, and compared them to the practices of a more normative urban population. This led him to the "little/big tradition" dichotomy where the "little tradition" is the poor, common, peasant folks who are illiterate and distort in practice the "big tradition," which consists of the theological teachings of rich, literate, elite, religious priests and professionals. The "popular," that is rural, lower class religion, is seen as an expression of "the people" rather than the "elite" doctrine imposed by the more urban, ruling church professionals. Peter Williams, influenced by Redfield's typology, examines popular religion in this fashion in *American Popular Religions*. He describes popular religion as an extra-ecclesiastical, symbolic activity engaged in by less educated non-elites outside of formal church structures.[25] Laura Stark views popular religion as one component of a dialectic process that occurs when priestly authorities work to accommodate the beliefs and practices of the "people," practices which are often physical in their expression.[26]

However, other scholars disagree that the definition of popular religion should be seen as a lower class form of orthodox (often Christian) worship. Natalie Davis points out that while it is necessary to examine class distinctions, the reliance on the definition of popular religion as a differentiation between magical/Christian and peasant/elite is unhelpful. It creates a misunderstanding of religious practice, a misunderstanding that discredits innovation among the subordinates by labeling popular practices as distortion of doctrine, while at the same time minimizing the extent of "supernatural aid" in Christian services.[27] Catherine Albanese questions the entire concept of "the people" as a way to discuss popular religion. She wonders how it is decided who exactly are "the people," for example what about the working-class, lower-middle class, or even the upper-class.[28] William Christian's study of "local religion" in Spain breaks down class division all together as he documents the worship of local shrines and patron saints which are stylistically shared across all classes.[29]

In contrast, Robert Fuller and Wade Clark Roof contend that the study of popular religion should not be tied to its relationship with institutional religion at all, either by its acceptance, rejection, or integration of orthodox ideas. Robert Fuller refers to the category of popular religion as too limiting since it revolves around practices that while unsanctioned by church authorities, are "in some way connected with formal religious institutions and are thought of by laypersons as acts of piety consistent with these traditions."[30] He suggests instead the term "unchurched spirituality" as a distinctly different category that involves beliefs and practices originating outside of religious institutions. While Fuller's attempt to remove popular religion from its association with institutional religion is understandable, using the category of "unchurched spirituality" still keeps the concept of "church" as the central arbiter. This makes "church" the point with which other practices are somehow in tension, inadvertently keeping Christianity at the center of the discussion.

Wade Clark Roof defines a popular religious culture as including aspects that may or may not be associated with traditional institutions, for example metaphysics, new thought, reincarnation, angels, astrology, New Age, Neo-Paganism, and so on. Roof shifts the focus of popular religion from an association with religious authority to an association with individualism and people's private actions. Religious individualism is not new in the United States nor has it been regarded without controversy, since individualism in religion has been seen as a threat to religious authority and social identity. The issue of individualism versus authority was the center of Robert Bellah's *Habits of the Heart*, which examined individualism as a possible disruption of community life. The Baby Boomers were seen to have metamorphosed into the "me generation" whose focus was on the self, even to the point of worship of the self. This internal focus was epitomized by Bellah in his description of a woman named Sheila, whose self-created and self-directed collage of religious beliefs was termed "Sheilaism."[31] Roof points out that the concerned dialogue that "Sheilaism" raised about the problems of individualism was all about the individual's threat to authority. It failed to note that "Sheilaism" was an early example of spiritual reflexivity, and that for Sheila it may have been a spiritually rejuvenating journey toward personal wholeness. Roof chooses not to focus on the threat to religious authority that individualism may engender, but rather to witness its changing developments in the religious milieu.

This debate about what constitutes popular religion has scholars engaging in a fundamental rethinking about what constitutes religion. They realize the individual spiritual practices that people engage in while living their daily lives are indicative of what matters to them, and therefore merit serious attention, whether these practices are part of institutional religion or not. These daily actions are the basis of "lived religion." Lived religion is an alternative to the term "popular religion" in that it expands the scope of beliefs and actions beyond the limitations of what is considered extra-ecclesiastical. Lived religion recognizes any activity or practice that people engage in that expresses their religious sensibility.

When the labyrinth is used as an extra-ecclesiastical activity in the churches it is a movement in tension with orthodoxy and fits the categorization of a popular religion. When it is used on the spiritual frontiers where just about any belief or practice is acceptable it fits the categorization of a lived religion. To more clearly distinguish between these two terms I will explicate the labyrinth within both contexts.

To begin an examination of the labyrinth as a popular religion I return to Peter Williams. He states that there are three qualities of popular religion—that it is an extra-ecclesiastical activity, that it is transmitted through channels outside the institutional religion, and that it has a supernatural element.[32] The labyrinth meets the first criterion in that it is an extra-ecclesiastical activity that occurs outside of the parameters of official church structures. The labyrinth is not part of church text, doctrine, or liturgy, nor do these dictate its use. And while labyrinths are used in the churches, it is usually not during the main Sunday service. Additionally, the labyrinth is met with disapproval by some church hierarchy and members. For example, the labyrinth revival has been viewed with some skepticism at Chartres Cathedral in France and regardless of the Chartres labyrinth's growing popularity the Chartres Cathedral labyrinth it is still usually covered with chairs and unavailable for the public to walk. There is some concern at Chartres Cathedral that it will become a New Age pilgrimage site, and the gaze that shifts toward the labyrinth will be at the cost of the liturgy and message of Jesus Christ. Closer to home, I heard a man use passages from the Bible to protest the labyrinth arguing that it was only through Jesus Christ, and not a labyrinth, that one finds God. At ELPC the labyrinth is not part of the main Sunday service, but is usually set up in the gym or social hall on Mondays and Wednesdays. Additionally the labyrinth has encountered opposition from some ELPC members. In 2001 some members formally protested the church's decision to build a permanent stone labyrinth, stating that it was too New Age and not Christian enough.

The labyrinth meets the second criterion in that information regarding the labyrinth is communicated outside of the formal church structures. The labyrinth used in most of the Protestant churches is a religious icon from a medieval Catholic cathedral. And many people gain an understanding of the labyrinth by reading the mass-marketed book *Walking a Sacred Path*, which is written by an Episcopal Priest. Other modes of transmitting knowledge include workshops, trainings, and conferences that are open to the public, a far cry from official seminary instruction. At ELPC the open walks and special events are often advertised to the larger community through flyers sent by bulk mailing, and advertisements in a New Age publication and alternative street newspaper. Additionally, communication about the labyrinth cuts across denominational lines as Episcopal, Presbyterian, Catholic, Methodist and even Fundamentalist churches borrow the loaner labyrinth from ELPC to introduce it to their congregation.

The labyrinth also meets the third criterion in that it often deals with the element of religion that is beyond an intellectual or scholastic understanding. As a type of walking prayer or meditation it engages the participant in a bodily experience. Often considered private and internal, the labyrinth provides an opportunity to focus on interior, even mystical states rather than doctrine or texts. Informants have reported mystical types of experiences during their walk, including seeing Jesus, visits from ancestors, inspired ideas, and healings.

But outside the churches the labyrinth is used in ways that have no association with institutional Christian religion, for example in hospitals for healing, the desert to attract UFOs, and the prairie to calm disembodied spirits. In these contexts they do not meet Williams's definition of an extra-ecclesiastical popular religion but instead fit into Wade Clark Roof's three-part description of lived religion. First, there is a symbolic system that explains the world; second, there is a practice performed within that system; and third, there is a person who actively performs that practice within the symbolic system.[33] The basic geometric form of the labyrinth—a circle with a path to the center—is a template upon which people can juxtapose any number of different symbolic systems. In scripted ceremonials various ritual "sets" are constructed through the selective choice of props, symbols, adornments, music, lighting, and scents. The chosen set is combined with a ritual "script" that comes from a variety of textual references or imaginative sources. The set and the script join together to transform the labyrinth from a blank canvas to a symbolic system rife with meaning. Chapters 5 and 6 give multiple examples of how the labyrinth can represent symbolic systems ranging from the Native American Trail of Tears to the Christian journey to Bethlehem.

Upon the symbolic system of the labyrinth a practice or an activity occurs. The simple act of walking the path to the center and back out is the most basic and frequent action performed on the labyrinth. But there can be many variations on this basic walk depending on the symbolic system that is perceived. For example, two women who viewed the labyrinth as Persephone's descent to the underworld walked the concentric paths of the labyrinth in a darkened room while holding candles. As they circled the concentric paths to the center they imagined themselves moving downward to the depths of the earth. Once they arrived at the center, which to them symbolized the lowest point of the subterranean region, they sat in the near dark and shared in a deep and reflective manner. On the other extreme, seventy people were directed by a leader to dance lightly through the paths of the labyrinth, two by two, weaving in and out to lively Celtic music. Variations on the types of ritual action engaged in on the labyrinth seem to be limited only by the imagination of the participants.

The labyrinth's circumference provides the symbolic system and the path provides the practice of walking. But the labyrinth is empty, both literally and figuratively, without people who transform the blank slate of the labyrinth into "the religious worlds they create."[34] On the labyrinth people first construct and then engage in their idea of the world.

The Labyrinth and America's Quest Culture

It is often the task of a religion to construct a coherent and sacred world of meaning. It does this by using a combination of doctrine, text, revelation, and ritual. Members of a religion establish their identity in part, by participating in that world through an adherence to the religion's beliefs and practices. However, for many of today's baby boomers these worlds of meaning are coming less from organized religion, which many view as dogmatic, and more from a personal and self-directed approach to their spiritual life that has meaning for them alone.[35] Many baby boomers are following a personal spiritual path that Roof refers to as a "quest" and he calls baby boomers who are defined by this attitude of seeking as being part of a "quest culture."[36] He estimates that up to fourteen percent of baby boomers are on a personal spiritual quest and states that "the current religious situation is characterized not so much by a loss of faith as a qualitative shift from unquestioned belief to a more open, questing mood."[37] This questing mood can be seen in the religion section of large chain bookstores as they include topics on healing, esotericism, and channeling. There are also changes in traditional religious institutions as they include new programs to appeal to these seekers. Offerings at ELPC include Mary as the Feminine Face of God, Twelve-Step Programs of "recovery religion," and a Seekers Class where the idea of getting a labyrinth was first introduced by congregants who were reading Artress's book *Walking a Sacred Path*.[38]

Individuals and groups self-consciously construct their own worlds of meaning through the act of "reframing" religious language and symbols. Reframing occurs when people actively and provocatively engage with religious symbols and language to create a new religious identity, and no longer passively accept the traditional connotations. Roof states:

> Rather than looking upon symbols as fixed realities in some objectivist manner, they become negotiated and situational, used to construct a set of meanings in the face of serious human dilemmas

and existential concerns... Implicit is the assumption that it falls on the individual, or small groups of individuals, to weave a coherent narrative of meaning and life, and that religious symbols and practices are at their perusal and disposal.[39]

This construction of personal religious identity occurs by an eclectic mixing of traditions, religions, beliefs, and ethnic practices that cross religious boundaries. People combine anything from Buddhist meditation, Catholic Mass, and UFOs into a meaningful approach to understanding life.[40] The importance is not on whether practices are consistent with traditional beliefs, but rather that the collage that is created is coherent to the individual, even if to an outsider it may look questionable.[41]

The enterprise of reframing religious language is central to the popularity of the labyrinth, for the labyrinth is a symbol that can be negotiated and re-negotiated, both by individuals and groups. One informant stated that the labyrinth is "open-ended," another that "it contains all symbols." The labyrinth has no fixed interpretation connected to it, but rather it entails different narratives depending on its context. The labyrinth has been an arena for a wide variety of events, each with its own mix of symbols from many traditions. During a Spring Equinox labyrinth ritual in 1999 there were Native American, Tibetan, and Pagan elements for a group of participants that included Jain, Buddhist, and Christian. Labyrinths have been used for liturgical events such as Epiphany, to balance the aura, for healing Native American injustices, as UFO landing sites, art therapy for children with cancer, for connecting to the *chakras* of Indian religious symbology, a place for prayer for women incarcerated, emotional healing for parents of AIDS patients, and for celebratory dance. These are only a few of its uses that cross borders, boundaries, faiths, traditions, and professions. Additionally this multi-layered quality is found in the people who participate in labyrinth rituals. In one survey over 50% of my informants described themselves as being more than one tradition–for example both Jewish and Buddhist—with some people combining up to five traditions to make up their multifaceted identity.

It is perhaps easier today than in the past to create a personal spirituality since people are exposed to a broad range of spiritual choices. Religion is being packaged and marketed to appeal to the public and a wide array of religious specialists—therapists, astrologers, guides, workshop leaders, and publishers—have replaced the religious authorities of the past. Boundaries between religion and other services are becoming blurred as therapy, exercise, and environmental issues become interwoven with religion. Symbols are no longer the purview of any one religion but are sometimes marketed as fashion accessories. For example *malas* used in Buddhist meditation became a fashion statement among the youth as "Buddha beads." People find their spiritual texts at Barnes & Nobles and get their religious experience through weekend workshops at Omega Institute.

Wuthnow refers to the "religion industry" and points out that churches are not sought out as safe havens, but rather as suppliers of goods and services.[42] Roof terms it a "spiritual marketplace" to describe how religion competes for the consumer.[43] People can shop for their beliefs from a vast array of alternatives, mixing and matching symbols and practices at will. The Labyrinth Movement is a prime example of these concepts.[44] The labyrinth is literally a material product being offered in the marketplace; a canvas labyrinth can range from $2000 to $4000 depending on size. The experience of walking the labyrinth is marketed through flyers, newspaper articles, internet sites, workshops, and conferences. The 2003 TLS Gathering was priced at $525 not including lodging or airfare, and pilgrimages for a week at Chartres Cathedral can be as expensive as $4000. Supplementary labyrinth items such as music, books, jewelry, table-top labyrinths, and t-shirts are for sale. Veriditas's entry into the spiritual marketplace is clearly demonstrated in their newsletter *Source* which in the Spring of 1998 advertised products, promoted events, and requested donations on 17 of its 23 pages, a full 74%.[45]

Roof speculates that individuals who construct their own religious identity may have less ties to ethnic, family, religion, and community than other subgroups he characterizes.[46] This rootless nature in some of the baby boomers fits with the temporary nature of labyrinths. Although some labyrinths are permanent, more are made for short-term use, such as those scratched out of sand or shaped out of leaves. Other labyrinths are made from canvas or a cloth light enough to be portable, and moved from place to place. There are personal labyrinths small enough to fold up and put into a suitcase, so that they can be available anytime, anywhere. And if someone has relocated to another part of the country, an internet search will locate a labyrinth near to the new location, along with times it is available for use.

Just as people are negotiating religion in a conscious manner, they are also negotiating a new kind of community. They join women's groups, Twelve-Step Programs, and stay connected through e-mail and the internet. The internet has been a key part of building the labyrinth community and has become one of the central ways that members of TLS stay in contact. It also makes it possible to run the organization since in 2003 the fourteen people on the Board of Directors were from two continents and ten states. The annual conference of TLS is called a "Gathering" to emphasize that the central focus is not just on learning new labyrinth skills, but on building community. This is accomplished at the Gathering through networking by regions (Northwest, Central, etc.) and by interest groups (corporations, health, education, etc.). Regional Representatives act as a focal point by listing labyrinth events in their area. A central tool for the Labyrinth Movement is the "Labyrinth Locator" which has an online listing of labyrinths around the country and the world. There is the sense that the labyrinth is a community. One informant writes: "The Labyrinth IS the Living Church. We are, above all else, a community, finding community, recreating what ancient peoples have done before us, and standing in our own lives in the present, to guide those who are seeking the finding of their peace with the support of this symbol."

This personal quest for religious identity is a trend encouraged by a more educated populous, an increase in cultural diversity, and influence of mass media. From being passive recipients of religious doctrine, individuals have instead been making active efforts to become "co-creators with God" and re-enchant the world based on their own spiritual needs and inclinations.[47]

Spiritual but Not Religious

In America many people are seeking spirituality outside of institutional religions which they view as limiting. These changes in America's religious proclivities are seen in the distinction being made of people who are "spiritual but not religious." The Latin root for the word spiritual comes from *spiritus* which means "breath" and often refers to the internal, invisible, fluid, and experiential aspect of one's connection with the sacred. Religion, on the other hand, comes from *religare* which means "to tie" and refers to that which binds people together and is often perceived as that which is external, institutional, fixed, and doctrinal. These two words have come to represent the tension that can exist between personal spirituality and institutional religion, between the private and public realms of religiosity. Robert Fuller, in his book *Spiritual but not Religious*, estimates that twenty percent of Americans fit this category. He believes that this group's influence is becoming widespread and is gradually changing the shape of mainstream American religion beyond what their numbers would indicate. As an example Fuller cites that fifty-five percent of all church members believe in some aspect of spirituality, such as astrology or reincarnation.[48]

Robert Wuthnow also describes an increase in people who are spiritual but not religious in his study of spiritual "seekers," which he contrasts to religious "dwellers." Wuthnow describes dwellers as part of the religious establishment that was most visible in America in the 1950s. At that time the majority of those religious were Christians or Jews and their "habitation" was the congregations or temples which were located in a solid community and supported by family rituals. Dwellers have a solid sense of their own place, suggested by such stories as the Garden of Eden and the Promised Land, and see God and themselves as fixed within the solid boundaries of the Sacred. Dwellers are settled in traditional institutions such as churches or temples, and guided by religious authority. Conversely, spiritual seekers are on a journey to find the Sacred which can exist in any number of spiritual landscapes. Instead of being protected in the safe haven of the fortress they live in the unsettled territory of the desert. Instead of a fixed sense of the Sacred they experience spirituality as fluid, transit, and constantly in flux.

Instead of clear boundaries, seekers have the open road, and instead of finding God in a fixed place, they actively pursue Him.[49]

Wuthnow suggests that both the dweller and the seeker exist in all of us, but that circumstances can emphasize one aspect more than the other. Dwellers live a life that is more organized, stable, and community-based; their cosmology, like their community is stable, orderly and systematic. Seekers, on the other hand, are those who are most influenced by the transient and mobile society where like their life, their spirituality is constantly changing, a matter of choice, and unpredictable. Dwellers are more connected to the institutions of society which are hierarchal and have "proscribed behavior through formalized rules," rules that are reflected in roles that are clearly defined.[50] Seekers are involved in diffuse networking in a complex secular world where identities and religious beliefs are negotiated by choice. There is also a relationship of dwellers and seekers with the American economy as it moves from the production of goods to provider of services. Wuthnow says that where houses of worship provide a safe haven for dwellers, they become a place of spiritual production and consumption for seekers, who will shop for a church that can provide them anything from a Twelve-Step Program to meditation exercises.

Some scholars view dwellers as a positive influence providing the stable root of community, and seekers as negative and self-serving. But Wuthnow perceives that distinction as too simplistic to provide a full understanding of the American religious sensibility, for while dwellers are more connected to community they often depend on institutions that are undependable, for example the sexual molestation scandal in the Catholic Church; and while seekers can be part-time dabblers and too individualistic, they often revitalize churches with their new ideas, such as labyrinths.

The labyrinth has some of the characteristics that appeal to seekers, especially the metaphors often associated with it including pilgrimage, journey, search, and quest. Yet the labyrinth more fully fits with Wuthnow's description of a third group he refers to as "practice-oriented spirituality." Those in this group are people who practice a deeper mode of spirituality outside of religious institutions with commitment and intentionality through activities that deepen their relationship to the sacred.[51] It is called a "practice" because it includes activities such as mental prayer, devotion, meditation, and contemplation that take time and effort to become skillful in the same way that other practices do, such as playing the piano. Practice-based spirituality combines qualities inherent in both dwellers and seekers. Wuthnow states:

> Practice-oriented spirituality preserves some of what has always attracted people to a spirituality of dwelling, for it too requires the setting aside of a space in which to meditate, to pray, and to worship, and in the confusion of everyday life such a space may be possible only by carefully demarking it from its surrounding. Yet these spaces are negotiable, changeable, and the point of engaging in spiritual practice is not merely to feel secure in a sacred space but to grow increasingly aware of the mysterious and transcendent aspects of the sacred as well. Practice-oriented spirituality makes full use of the opportunities of exploration that are available in a complex market society, but it is also a way of imposing discipline on personal explorations. Above all, practice requires responsibility on the part of the individual practitioner rather than on the part of some community or marketplace.[52]

The labyrinth meets Wuthnow's criteria for a practice-based spirituality by providing a deeper, more disciplined form of spiritual practice for some. Although many people walk the labyrinth at random intervals, there are others who treat it more as a practice. For example, TLS has the *365 Club* whose members have committed to walk the labyrinth every day for a year. Their website states that "many of the *365 Club* believe that walking a labyrinth on a daily basis is a deepening commitment to spiritual development in their daily lives."[53] As another example, two women have gone to ELPC at their lunch break every Wednesday for the past two years to walk the labyrinth. And in November of 2003 Lauren Artress gave a talk entitled "The Labyrinth as Spiritual Practice."

In addition to being a discipline, the labyrinth combines both dwelling and seeking. The path provides the course of action that one takes in a search for the sacred and a journey toward deeper understanding. The labyrinth is a moveable and changeable space. At ELPC the labyrinth is a canvas tarp that travels to various locations in the church including the social hall, main sanctuary, gymnasium, music room, schoolroom, and an outside courtyard. Since the labyrinth can be found at a different place from week to week, signs are placed at the church entrance to guide a walker to its current residency. The circumference provides the separation from the chaos of the rest of the world and provides a container for dwelling. The labyrinth's circular form creates a consistency of space that is familiar and even considered by many to be sacred. Signs and brochures ask walkers to take off their shoes before walking the labyrinth in order to honor the "sacred space" as well as encourage people to pause at the entrance, which is considered a portal into a protected world.

Wuthnow gives five other characteristics of a practice-oriented spirituality besides commitment to the discipline, engaging in a personal spiritual quest, and demarcating a sacred space. These are: 1) rules of conduct that are considered necessary to conduct the practice, 2) enough mastery of the skill that the focus shifts from the external technique to the internal transcendent self, 3) a technique usually embedded in a broader community of tradition even if practiced on one's own, 4) an interpretive spiritual narrative and deep reflection of self, 5) and often a connection to service.[54]

Responding in order, first, there are certain rules of conduct to walking the labyrinth. The most obvious rule is established by the path itself, which implies following it to the center and back out. The basic rule for labyrinth walking is "to trust the labyrinth" which means that whatever happens on the labyrinth will be the right action. But there are also guidelines for the walk that are provided on posters or flyers at the site. These guidelines include: how long to wait before entering the labyrinth behind another walker, how to pass a slower walker, and what to do when you meet another walker on the path. While any movement, from dance to walking meditation is allowed, certain conducts are expected. Most people walk slowly, keep their head down (either in prayer or trying to watch the path), and tend to avoid eye contact with other walkers. Only once have I heard that there was no need to stay on the path and this was at a New Age Center where the labyrinth was to represent "The Hero's Journey," a place where individuality and each person following his/her own path, rather than a prescribed one, was considered the hallmark. The only "breaking of the rules" I have heard about is the man who hugged everyone he passed on the path, which felt like an intrusion to some other walkers.

The second characteristic, mastery of the technique, also applies to the labyrinth. While walking the labyrinth is not a hard skill to learn, mastery of it can mark a change from focus on the external walk to an awareness of internal transcendence. At first the novice is often confused and disoriented by the path. While there is only a single path that goes both to the center and back out, it is not uncommon to get misplaced in the journey and end up at back at the entrance instead of the center. I have heard beginners describe themselves as getting dizzy, lost, confused, and disoriented. The first time I walked both a Chartres and a Classical labyrinth I was relieved to be following someone who appeared to know the way. However, the more one walks the less one pays attention to doing it right; this allows one to relax into the rhythm of the twists and turns of the path, moving from carefully watching each step to paying attention to internal bodily sensations and insights.

The labyrinth walk meets the third characteristic of being embedded in a larger community of tradition that suggests a rationale for its use, even if it is practiced on one's own. Though the labyrinth has a long history, the Labyrinth Movement is relatively new and has no overarching tradition which directs its application. It is found in a variety of communities, each which might suggest a different use for the labyrinth. For example a labyrinth situated in a church context suggests that it be used for prayer; a labyrinth situated in hospital suggests that it be used for healing; a labyrinth situated in a memorial park suggests it be used for dealing with the grief over deceased loved ones.

The fourth characteristic of a spiritual practice is that it has an interpretive spiritual narrative and provides a deep reflection of self. This also fits the labyrinth, for even when the walk is done in the presence of others, it is a highly personal experience. One of the appeals of the labyrinth is its highly interpretive nature as people bring to it their own beliefs and symbolic systems. It can be walked at the same time by dissimilar people who are expressing different beliefs. In addition to the different beliefs the walkers may hold, they may also have particular methods of practice that work specifically for them. For example one person may respond more to body and movement and dance through the labyrinth, while another may be more connected to solitary prayer and spend time prostate in the center. A discussion among the Labyrinth Committee at ELPC tried to put this quality of diverse methodology into words.

> The labyrinth is a very individualistic experience and the experience in each of us is so unique. You may be there with other people but it's what's happening within you that matters. What comes to my mind is consciousness, inner consciousness. The experience of walking the labyrinth is the external thing—the changes are the internal thing.

This access to inner consciousness brings to the practice a deeper sense of self-awareness and reflection. Walking the labyrinth can be a personal inner journey of transformation, which is a reward unto itself. And while the labyrinth can be used as a means to an end, for example as a tool for community building in corporations or a geometry lesson in the schools, for those who walk it as a spiritual practice the rewards are more internal and personally measured.

The sixth and last characteristic is that a spiritual practice is often connected to service. At TLS there is a group of over 100 labyrinth walkers who are termed "energy keepers." Energy keepers are spread across the world but are connected by e-mail. They have volunteered to send energy for healing to those people who request such help, much like a prayer circle. Once a request for healing is received the energy keeper may walk a labyrinth while sending healing energy to the person requesting aid. Additionally, labyrinths are also suggested as an outreach for peace and healing to communities struck by tragedy. For example, designs centered around labyrinths were submitted for a "Peace Labyrinth and Meditation Garden" in the aftermath of the 1999 Columbine High School shootings and for the World Trade Center

"Ground Zero" memorial to commemorate the September 11th terrorist attacks. Walking the labyrinth is a practice, not only in Wuthnow's theoretical definition, but also in the broader sense of "how people choose to act" in relation to their religious and spiritual beliefs.

Conclusion

The American religious landscape is changing. Several factors have combined to create a more religiously diverse population including an increase in immigration which has brought many new faiths to this country, a more educated and liberal populous, and a whole new generation of baby boomers who are redefining the nation as they redefine themselves,. This new diversity has led to cracks in the Protestant hegemony to reveal types of religious behaviors that have been present since the founding of the nation, like folk rituals, astrology, alchemy, dowsing, and spiritualism, but were largely ignored by scholars of religion as "fringe" topics that were not considered the subject of serious study.

These practices of the people have been referred to as "popular religion" and at first were considered mostly in relationship to established and institutional religions. But it is becoming more evident that people are practicing religion beyond of the perimeters of religious institutions and are finding their spiritual salvation in a growing marketplace that includes books, workshops, shamans, angels, and labyrinths. It is estimated that up to twenty percent of Americans fit this category of "spiritual but not religious," and their influence extends even further since many of them are the influential generation of baby boomers. These spiritual seekers have been largely overlooked as a serious religious force since they lack the continuity and organization of those who dwell in strong faith communities. They seek their worlds of meaning on a spiritual frontier where religious beliefs and symbols can be combined to create a personal world of meaning. People in America are searching for the sacred in ways that are as individual as themselves.

The labyrinth has become an arena where many of these individual spiritual seekers are meeting to journey the path together. Its origination goes back at least 4000 years yet it has shown up in our current times unattached to any single religion and without any defining ritual, providing a place for people to practice their spiritual and religious beliefs in any manner they want. It supplies the simplest of structures—a path to the center and back out—and can be utilized alone or with others, at any place, and at any time. It is as transient as the American society and provides a moving site of worship. The labyrinth is a mirror where the shifting religious terrain of America can be viewed, one ritual at a time.

The next chapter will examine the labyrinth's use in history with an emphasis on its amorphous quality to represent the different views of the world of those who use it.

3
The Adaptation of the Classical and Christian Labyrinth

The relative newness of the Labyrinth Movement and its characterization as a popular religious expression means that the rituals associated with the labyrinth tend to be less influenced by orthodoxy (the correct belief in theological doctrine) or orthopraxy (the traditional expectations of behavior). Instead, labyrinth rituals are part of an emerging paradigm in the study of ritual, that is, invented rituals that are consciously constructed by those who participate in them.

This is due partially to a religious pluralism in America that deemphasizes practices that are associated with a single tradition in favor of cultural relativism. This is especially true as new organizations work to create rituals that are inclusive, and older religious groups seek to adapt their traditional rites to the changing spiritual and social times.[1] But the invented nature of labyrinth rituals is mostly due to the fact that the labyrinth was not linked solely to any single ritual tradition when it was introduced to the American public in the mid 1980s. This meant that there were no constraints to what rituals could occur on it. This is not because the labyrinth had no tradition. Quite to the contrary, its history dates back to 3000 BCE. Yet despite this lengthy history there is not a clear record of a text or liturgy so completely connected to the labyrinth that it tied the labyrinth's current use exclusively to any religion or specific rite.

There was speculation, which arose from physical evidence and stories of Christian and non-Christian use, but no formal set of rules came from the past to dictate the type of rituals that should be performed with the labyrinth in contemporary America. Since the labyrinth came from the past it is what Tom Driver refers to as a "received ritual," but since it was received with no instructions, the ritual acts and their meanings are being constructed by those who currently participate in them.[2]

The fact that the labyrinth did not come with a defining ritual is not to imply that the past is not important to those who currently use the labyrinth. Traditionalism, the linking of activities to the past in such a way as to suggest that the past is important is a powerful form of ritual legitimation. This is true whether events from the past are repeated perfectly, adapted to a new setting, or only vaguely alluded to in new settings.[3] Linking the labyrinth to its historical roots legitimates this new spiritual expression with an ancient past and a sense of tradition.

An interest in labyrinth history led two TLS founding members, Jeff Saward and Robert Ferre, to translate the monumental work on labyrinths by Hermann Kern entitled *Labyrinthe: Erscheinungsformen und Deutungen: 5000 Jahre Gegenwart eines Urbilds*. *Labyrinthe* was first published in 1982, and with 492 pages and 666 illustrations it was the most comprehensive book on the history of the labyrinth, and still holds that distinction today. The translation *Through the Labyrinth*, published in 2000, was updated with new material including a chapter on the current "labyrinth revival." In the foreword to the English edition Ferre says the "English edition was born from sheer enthusiasm within the American labyrinth community."[4] Labyrinth researchers and enthusiasts are still uncovering the history of labyrinths. Older labyrinths like the one at Chartres Cathedral are a particular point of interest and provide a destination for labyrinth tours and pilgrimages. John Kraft, a labyrinth researcher from Sweden searches and restores labyrinths along the Baltic Coast, some of which are 1,000 years old.

At ELPC the history of the labyrinth was considered particularly relevant after some members of the church opposed building a permanent stone labyrinth. They objected by stating that the labyrinth was non-Christian, even pagan, and did not belong in a Christian ministry. At an open meeting called by the Labyrinth Committee to discuss this opposition a defense was established which linked the ELPC labyrinth to the past, citing that the Chartres labyrinth and Presbyterianism both had Catholic roots. Conversely, churches use traditional Christian prayers and liturgical rituals as a way to link the newly introduced labyrinth to solid theological ground. The introduction of the labyrinth to newcomers includes a discussion of its medieval history, and a photo of the Chartres labyrinth has been part of the church's labyrinth display.

Labyrinth history is not limited to Western Europe and labyrinths are found in India, Africa, North America, Brazil, and other countries.[5] But since the Classical and Chartres labyrinths are most central to the Labyrinth Movement I will limit my historical focus to these labyrinths with two main goals in mind. The first is to show how labyrinth myths and rituals have been selectively appropriated from one group to the next. To illustrate I use the adaptation by the medieval Christians of the Cretan labyrinth story of Theseus and the Minotaur as an early typology of Christ and the Devil. A secondary goal is to illustrate how the labyrinth is used as a template upon which a sacred cosmology can be overlaid. For illustration I use the Christian tri-partite world of Hell, Heaven, and Earth. This analysis will set the groundwork for Chapters 4, 5, and 6 which examine how different groups today use rituals to construct their own idea of the cosmos.

The Classical Labyrinth

Some of the earliest research on the labyrinth was done by Samuel Hooke who in 1935 dated the labyrinth form as far back as 3000 BCE on Egyptian mortuary seals. This links the early labyrinths to the labyrinthine architecture of Egyptian tombs and mortuary temples, associating them with the death of Osiris, the Egyptian god-king.[6] The legend tells of Osiris who was a good and just king of Egypt. He was killed by his jealous brother Set who dismembered Osiris and spread the pieces of his body far and wide. The Goddess Isis was the wife of Osiris, and in great grief she searched the land and found his body parts and with the help of other gods restored him to life. After the resurrection Osiris departed the earth and ruled as god of the dead, where he enjoyed even greater popularity.[7] The story of Osiris's death and rebirth was reenacted yearly using ritual, art, music, and dance in the Osirian Mystery Drama in the temple of Amenemhet III, circa 2000 B.C.E.

The death of Osiris was represented by the slaying of a bull. The temple, a complex and confusing array of rooms, was the labyrinth which provided protection and safety for the body of Osiris during his time in the underworld, where he was kept for three days for the re-membering that led to his triumphant resurrection.[8] Though the labyrinthine layout of Egyptian tombs has been interpreted as a form of protection against grave robbers, these tombs were initially designed before there was any indication of plunder. This leads to an alternative explanation, namely, that the intricate mortuary design had a religious, rather than practical, significance, thereby connecting labyrinths with ritual for over 4,000 years.[9]

Egypt was in close commercial and cultural contact with Crete and it seems likely that the myth of the Cretan labyrinth was adapted from Egyptian sources.[10] It also included the slaying of a bull and the saving of a king by the intervention of a goddess. In the Cretan myth, the Minotaur, half-man and half-bull, was killed by Theseus with the help of Ariadne. Since parts of this Cretan myth get appropriated by medieval Christians into the story of Christ's resurrection, it is worth reviewing the central points. The great architect Daedalus (Daidalos) built a labyrinth in Crete, a powerful kingdom in the Aegean Sea, around the year 2000 BCE.[11] The labyrinth, an immense maze-like structure of many confusing and dead end paths, was built by the order of King Minos to contain the Minotaur, a flesh-eating beast that was half-man and half-bull[12] (see fig. 9).

The Minotaur was the result of an unfortunate and illicit love affair between King Minos's wife, Pasiphae, and a magnificent white bull given to King Minos by Poseidon.[13] Every nine years Athens had to make a tribute to Crete of seven virgin maidens and seven young men taken from the best families of Athens. They would be taken to Crete by ship and sacrificed to the Minotaur, who lived in the labyrinth. One year Theseus, the son of the King of Athens, volunteered to be one of the fourteen youth to go to Crete vowing to kill the Minotaur, end the tribute, and return to Athens with the rescued youth.

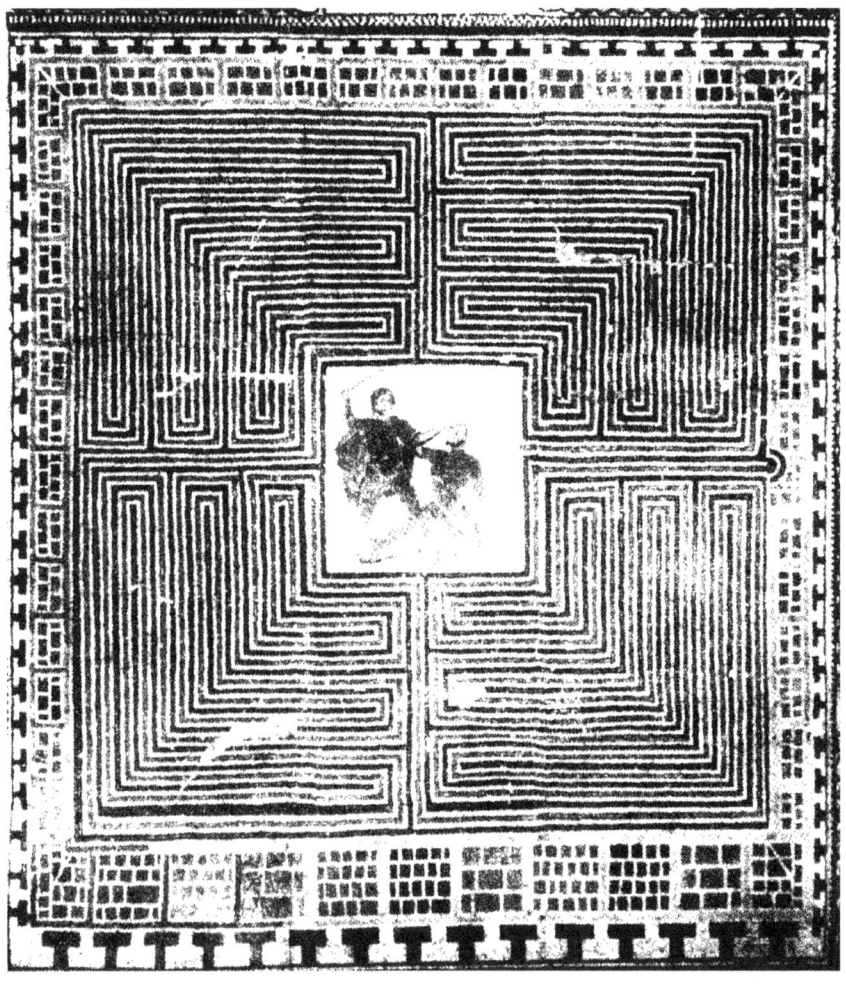

Figure 9: Theseus and Minotaur in Cretan labyrinth, Vienna, c. 300 CE.

Once the Athenians arrived in Crete, Ariadne, daughter of King Minos, immediately fell in love with Theseus. Unable to bear the thought of his death in the labyrinth she went to Daedelus and asked for help. Daedelus gave Ariadne two balls. The first was a ball of thread for Theseus to unravel as he went to the center of the labyrinth to find the Minotaur, enabling him to find his way back out of the maze. The second was a ball of pitch to shove into the Minotaur's mouth to keep him from biting Theseus, allowing Theseus time to kill him.[14] All went as planned as the Minotaur was killed and Theseus followed his trail of thread to freedom accompanied by the youth of Athens that he saved. Theseus departed

Crete with Ariadne, but then abandoned her on the island of Naxos before returning victorious to Athens where he became a national hero, king, and even a demi-god to the Greeks. His tomb was seen as a sanctuary and it was said that he could visit the underworld and return. King Minos was so furious with Daedelus for helping Theseus that he imprisoned him and Daedelus's son, Icarus, in the labyrinth. Fearing for their lives, Daedelus made wings so that he and Icarus could fly out of the labyrinth to their homeland and freedom. Daedelus made it safely and went on to serve as an architect in Sicily, but Icarus flew too close to the sun, which melted the wax on his wings and caused him to fall to his death.[15]

Like the Osirian drama, this myth was also celebrated in a yearly festival that included the slaying of the divine bull and ritual dancing.[16] And just as Isis played a central role in the restoration of Osiris, Ariadne was vital to Theseus's success by providing Theseus his means of escape from the labyrinth. The myth downplays Ariadne's role and portrays her as a love-struck princess who was first used and then left by Theseus. Catullus (c. 84-54 BCE) gives an emotional telling of how Ariadne was abandoned by Theseus on the island of Naxos to weep in loneliness and despair, while Theseus danced in glorious celebration on the island of Delos.[17] Ariadne was later rescued by Dionysus, who made her his bride. The importance of Ariadne to the story has been long lost in the retelling, for Ariadne was no ordinary princess, but a goddess in Crete, a culture known to worship the Goddess. The name Ariadne was originally a Cretan goddess, which meant "all-holy," who was only later adopted into Greek mythology.[18] Robert Graves says that Ariadne was the Cretan Moon-goddess and that the fact it was the god Dionysus who first rescued and then married her, further supports her status as a goddess.[19] John Chadwick has deciphered texts of the Cretans that confirm they not only worshiped some of the Greek Gods, like Zeus and Poseidon, but also a goddess.[20] He states that the most curious divine title found is *Potnia*, which means "Our Lady." It is a word that can stand alone as a title for any goddess but usually is associated with a place, in this case the offering of a jar of honey to "Our Lady of the Labyrinth." Chadwick states that "Our Lady of the Labyrinth" is the most striking dedication to come out of Knossos and goes on to say that: "We know from Minoan and Mycenaean monuments that a female deity played a prominent part in their religion, and I have therefore suggested identifying *Potnia* with this figure."[21] Since Ariadne is the main female figure in association with the labyrinth it is possible that she was "Our Lady of the Labyrinth."

Cretan myths, including the one about the labyrinth, were later incorporated into Greek mythology and rituals involving labyrinths continued in Greek culture.[22] Sir Arthur Evans, who excavated Knossos, says that the story of the Minotaur and the maze was added later by the Greeks to make their exploits in conquering the Minoans even grander. He states that the "labyrinth" was not a prison maze, but instead the Palace of Knossos, which was the sanctuary of the *labrys*, or double axe, which was the symbolic weapon of Minoan divinity.[23] If the goddess Ariadne is the "Lady of the Labyrinth" this myth of Theseus killing the Minotaur, Ariadne's half-brother (and perhaps the crown prince), and snatching her away from her home to then abandon her, could be a Greek tale describing a patriarchal culture forcing a goddess culture into submission.[24] Herman Kern doubts there was a building called the labyrinth at all and suggests rather that it was an outline of a dance given to Ariadne, perhaps even a dance floor.

As a dance, palace, or prison, the physical form of the labyrinth was clearly associated with the Cretan civilization by the fact the labyrinth is on many of their coins dating from 500 to 100 BCE. Plutarch writes that after Theseus abandoned Ariadne he went to Delos. In celebration of his victory he danced the *geranos,* the crane dance, which Plutarch describes as "an imitation of the circling passes in the labyrinth, and consisting of certain rhythmic involutions and evolutions," and may have included linking the multiple dancers together with a rope known as "Ariadne's thread."[25] A similar dance is still done on Delos today and the importance of a "lady in the labyrinth" has survived in common folklore throughout Northern and Western Europe. John Kraft in his 1985 book *The Goddess and the Labyrinth* documents folktales in Sweden and Finland of a woman in the center of the labyrinth and young men who run the path as fast as possible to claim her as their prize, sometimes in competition with other men (see fig. 10).

There are over 500 labyrinths in Nordic countries, some over 1000 years old. They are built mostly along coastlines in stone and therefore do not disintegrate as do the grass or turf labyrinths more common in England. Some of the 150 labyrinths in Finland are called *Jungfrudanser* (Virgin dances) which is descriptive of the dance through the labyrinth to the young woman in the center.[26] A similar story of a dance to win the woman is connected with a turf labyrinth at Saffron Walden in Essex.[27]

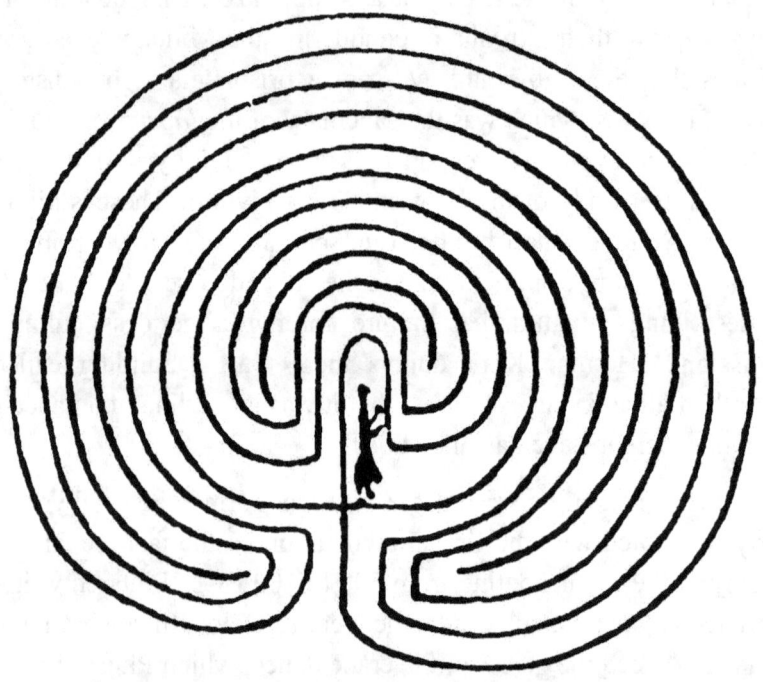

Figure 10: Girl in labyrinth from a wall painting from Sibbo church, Finland fifteenth century, CE.

To carry this idea of the woman in the labyrinth even further Kraft states that many of the labyrinths in Scandinavia are called *Trojeborg* (castle of Troy) and in England are called *Troy-town, The Walls of Troy, Troy's Wall's* or *City of Troy,* referring to the story of the Trojan battle. While it was common to refer to labyrinths as the name of towns (Jerico and Jerusalem were two of the most frequent) the reference of the labyrinth with Troy brings to mind Helen of Troy, who, like the woman in the labyrinth, was held in the center of Troy while the Greek men battled to get her back. Kraft believes these many references to rescuing, abducting, or winning the woman in the center of the labyrinth shows the labyrinth's ancient relationship with the Goddess, since not only Ariadne, but also Helen was born divine, being the daughter of Zeus and Leda.[28]

Chartres Cathedral Labyrinth

The Cretan story of a king, a bull, a goddess, and a daring rescue was selectively appropriated by the Christians in the Middle Ages. The Minotaur of the labyrinth who ensnared and destroyed sacrificial victims was changed into the Devil who lived in Hell and entrapped sinners. And the hero figure of Theseus who defeated the Minotaur, set the victims free, and then became a King and god, was altered to Christ, who defeated the Devil in Hell, released the sinners, and ascended to Heaven.

Not only was the story of the labyrinth changed to meet medieval religious beliefs, but the actual shape of pagan labyrinths, which include both the Roman mosaic type and the Classical seven-circuit, were also transformed to a Christian style.[29] Though some scholars believe that labyrinths were introduced in Northern Europe by Christian churches, there is evidence that the labyrinths in Europe existed prior to the influence of Christianity and in fact, that pagan labyrinths probably inspired the church labyrinths.[30] The earliest example of a pagan labyrinth changed by Christian influence is seen in the fourth-century labyrinth in Algiers Cathedral in Algerian, north Africa (see fig. 11).[31] A Roman mosaic type, it has the words "Sancta Ecclesia" (holy church) at the center, and the thread of Ariadne can be seen wound as far as the second turn. Kern states that during the ninth and tenth centuries the seven-circuit Classical style that was associated with pagan Europe was purposely Christianized in the Chartres model by making it eleven paths, the number associated with sin and excess. Additionally the design was overlaid with two axes which create a cruciform image, showing that the path out of the sin is salvation through Christ.[32] Some evidence exists in England that the Classical turf-style labyrinth was widespread throughout the countryside until it was re-cut into the form of the eleven-circuit Christian style.[33]

Figure 11: Earliest Christian labyrinth, Algiers 324 CE.

The earliest example of the eleven-circuit cruciform Christian style labyrinth is a manuscript drawing in the tenth century. From that time until the sixteenth century, nearly forty Christian-type manuscript, tile, stone, and pavement labyrinths were created.[34] It was in the eleventh century that labyrinths came into full flowering within Christianity as pavement labyrinths large enough to walk were built in eleven cathedrals in France between 1160 and 1495.[35] Though there are some variations between the medieval church pavement labyrinths, the Chartres Cathedral labyrinth is the oldest extant medieval labyrinth and the exemplar of Christian labyrinths; for this reason the terms Chartres labyrinth and Christian labyrinth are considered interchangeable. The Chartres labyrinth is the medieval style most commonly used in the Labyrinth Movement today.

DIVERSITY AND UNITY ON THE LABYRINTH 57

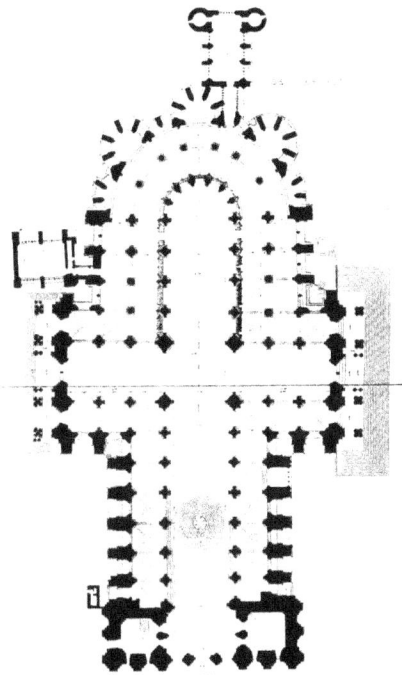

Figure 12: Diagram of Chartres Cathedral with Labyrinth at west nave.

Figure 13: Labyrinth at Chartres Cathedral, built c. 1200 CE. Photo by Sonia Halliday.

The Chartres labyrinth is a stone pavement labyrinth nearly forty feet in diameter built into the floor of the nave at Chartres Cathedral in Chartres, France (see fig. 12 and 13). Researchers dispute when it was actually installed with dates ranging from 1194 when the Cathedral began to be rebuilt after a devastating fire, to c. 1230 when it was copied in Villard de Honnecourt's (Wilars de Honecort's) sketchbook.[36] The article "The Enigma of the Labyrinth" in the Chartres Cathedral publication *Notre-Dame de Chartres* states four possible interpretations of the labyrinth.[37] These are: a substitute path to Jerusalem used as a penance; a model for Heavenly Jerusalem which is the hoped for destination after death; a tribute to the builders of Chartres who were compared to the master architect and first labyrinth builder, Daedalus; and as a mathematical and geometrical positioning point for the construction of the cathedral.

In addition to these four theories Penelope Doob speculates it could allude to Neo-Platonic cosmology and the zodiac.[38] For the medieval theologian, who was often the same as the natural philosopher, cosmology was a combination of biblical descriptions of the world, mostly from Genesis, and of pagan Greek ideas, particularly Plato and Aristotle.[39] The works of Plato were especially influential at the Cathedral School at Chartres, which flourished from the eleventh century to the middle of the twelfth century. Teachers or Chancellors at Chartres Cathedral in the twelfth century who were Christian Platonists were Bernard of Chartres (c. 1114), Thierry of Chartres (c. 1119-1151), William of Conches (c. 1125), Gilbert of Poitiers (c. 1126), Bernard Silvestris (c. 1147) and John of Salisbury (c 1176).[40] Although the works of Aristotle became the predominant influence in the universities of Europe in the thirteenth century, the school at Chartres was a holdout of the Platonic tradition.[41] Thierry of Chartres (d. c. 1156) compared Plato's *Timaeus* to Genesis, and Macrobius's *Commentary on the Dream of Scipio* was known to be in the school library. Plato's view of the world soul, as well as his idea of a divine but natural order, linked humans integrally to the greater universe by a microcosm/macrocosm analogy. Plato's contention that planets had souls supported an astrological world view common during the twelfth and thirteenth centuries.[42] The Chartres labyrinth is eleven circles and a center, providing an astrological link with the cosmology in *Commentary on the Dream of Scipio* which noted twelve divisions: earth, the seven planets, the fixed stars, the world-soul, Mind, and God.[43]

While the Neo-Platonism that was integrated into Christianity by the intellectual elite of Chartres Cathedral School likely had some influence on the ideas depicted in the architecture and iconography of the Cathedral, I have been unable to draw any direct connection between the school and the labyrinth, though it is a task that still holds potential. Conversely, there is evidence that links the labyrinth to lay Christians and the more standard theological doctrines to which they would have been exposed. The labyrinth encompasses the entire width of the nave which makes it the first thing pilgrims and parishioners would encounter as they entered the cathedral. This very public location would require crossing to continue to the altar and indicates that the labyrinth was meant to be accessible to the lay people who would have had little interest in the Platonic Christianization of the Chartres School. For them a basic understanding of the medieval Christian cosmos was that God created the world which was divided into Heaven, Earth, and Hell. Heaven and Hell existed in eternal time; Earth was in linear historical time. Heaven was populated by God and his angels and was the holy place of eternal reward; Hell was populated by the Devil and his demons and was the evil place of eternal punishment; Earth was the battleground in-between where God and the Devil vied for the souls of humans who struggled between living in grace and living in sin. Christ was God's son who came to Earth to save humans from their sin and lead them to Heaven. After Christ's death he descended to Hell and released the enslaved souls that resided there before he returned to Heaven to be with God. The Church continued to do Christ's work on Earth of redeeming souls from the perils of sin so that humans might have eternal salvation with God in Heaven.

In the early thirteenth century few men and women knew how to read, so the churches used symbolism as a didactic tool to guide the layperson to an understanding of the glories of the Christian world. Otto von Simson describes the medieval mind as being preoccupied with "symbolic vision," or the ability to see the spiritual world that lay beyond the material, where everywhere the "visible seemed to reflect the invisible."[44] Art and architecture, especially as seen in the cathedrals, were designed to represent this ultimate reality. They depicted in physical form the highest thinking regarding the grandeur of God's creation and the teachings of the Church. The cathedrals, including Chartres Cathedral, were essentially symbolic images of the cosmos.[45] Edward Grant states that "the medieval cosmos is sometimes characterized as a metaphor of a gothic cathedral whose separate elements flow together rationally and logically to form a splendid, intelligible whole, soaring upward toward the Deity himself."[46] Architecture, which included mathematics and geometry, was used as a way of linking the physical world to the invisible world of God.[47] God was seen as an architect who used geometry in his creation. When architects used mathematics and geometry in building the cathedrals, God's work was imitated and the harmony of the cosmos could be recreated. Simson points out that once the importance of geometry as an expression of God is comprehended, then the cathedral is understood not so much as a metaphor, but more so as a model of God's creation, the cosmos.[48]

Sacred geometry was used not only in the creation of the cathedral, but also in the creation of the labyrinth, and just as the cathedral represented a model of the Christian cosmos, I contend that the labyrinth represented a smaller version still.

Emile Mâle, author of *The Gothic Image*, gives three rules of Christian art that can also be applied to the labyrinth in Chartres Cathedral.[49] First, it is like an alphabet with particular signs representing certain objects in the physical world. This is seen in the eleven paths of the labyrinth which represent a sinful world, and the cruciform shape representing Christ as the way out of sin. Second, it follows the rules of sacred mathematics with an emphasis on placement and symmetry. The labyrinth, just as the cathedral, was designed based on sacred mathematics and may have been used as a geometrical positioning point for the building of the cathedral.[50] Third, it is a symbolic code representing spiritual meaning. I believe that the labyrinth acted as a representation of the Christian tri-partite world of Hell, Heaven, and Earth.[51] Like most symbols, the labyrinth is multivalent and allows for such multiple interpretations. To fully understand the labyrinth as a representation of Heaven and Hell it is important to revisit the story of Theseus and the Minotaur on the ancient island kingdom of Crete. The realm of Earth will be analyzed following the story of Theseus in a description of the labyrinth as the city of Jerusalem.

Hell

According to the Chartres Cathedral publication *Notre-Dame de Chartres*, a copper plaque was once in the center of the Chartres labyrinth that had on it an engraving of Theseus and the Minotaur. Such an engraving would provide a clear link between the pagan Classical labyrinth and the Christian Chartres labyrinth. The studs that held the plaque are still plainly visible, and the plaque along with the cathedral bells was melted down in 1792 to provide cannons for the Napoleonic wars.[52] Although Kern disagrees that there is a connection between the Cretan myth and the Chartres Labyrinth—he thinks the plaque honored the cathedral architect as does the Amiens labyrinth—there does seem to be enough documented and contextual evidence to provide a link.[53] Medieval Europe had high regard for Classical Greece, as seen in the use of Plato and Aristotle to illuminate Christian theology. Additionally, the figure of the Minotaur is the most frequently encountered character depicted on classical mosaic, medieval manuscript, and medieval pavement labyrinths. He is often seen with Theseus, as he was at Chartres, who is portrayed as the victorious assailant. The medieval Christians saw the combat between Theseus and the Minotaur as a prefiguration of the battle between Christ and the Devil. This further links the labyrinth to the Christian cosmos, particularly the tripartite world of Hell and Heaven.

Kathyrn Woodward examines the allegorization of Theseus and Christ looking specifically at the Christian labyrinth as a symbol of submission and deliverance. The earliest Christian example that clearly allegorizes Theseus as Christ is a labyrinth in a manuscript of Servius's commentary on the *Aeneid* found in the Freising Cathedral dating c. 1000 CE.[54] Though the figure is almost illegible, traces of a Minotaur are visible in the center with a statement that translates from the Latin as: "See here, the Minotaur devours everyone enveloped by the labyrinth; this represents Hell and that is the devil."⁵⁵ Surrounding the labyrinth's perimeter is an inscription explicitly comparing the Minotaur to the Devil and Theseus to Christ. It states: ". . . the devil, to whom the world was the labyrinth. . . confined in this cleft like the Minotaur. Until Theseus was sent to this [world] as Christ by the Father. Conquering thus by force of divinity as [that] by Ariadne."⁵⁶

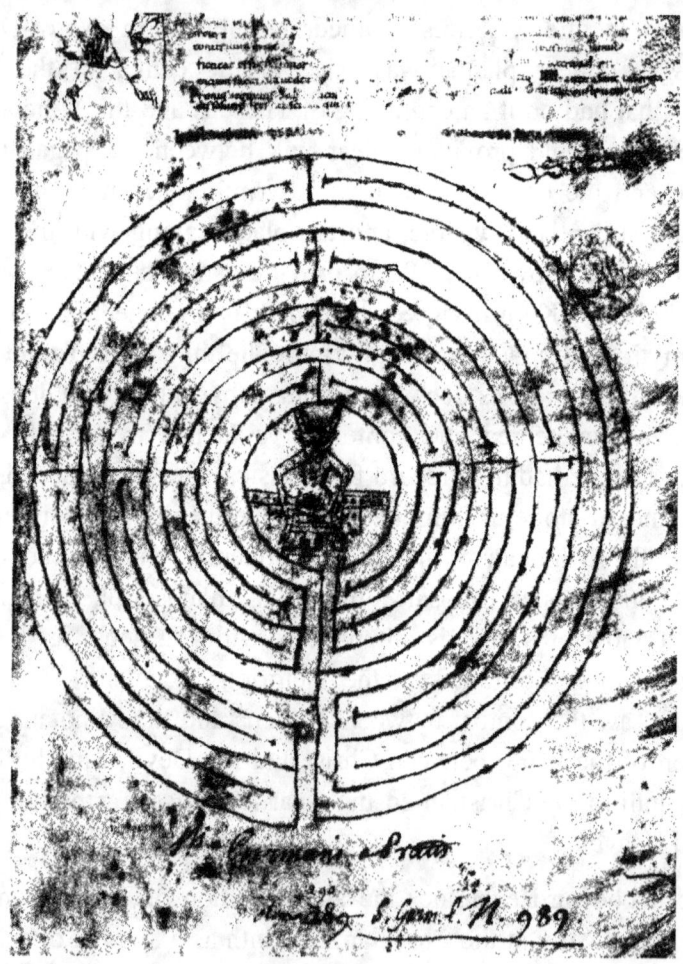

Figure 14: Minotaur as Devil in a manuscript dated 989 CE from the monastery of St. Germain-des-Pres, Paris. Earliest Chartres-style labyrinth.

A manuscript labyrinth dated 989 CE, the oldest surviving depiction of a Chartres-type labyrinth, has the Minotaur depicted as the Devil, the "prince of the world"[57] (see fig. 14). Another early reference to the Minotaur and Theseus as analogous to the Devil and Christ is on a fifty-centimeter wall labyrinth located on the west narthex of the Cathedral of San Martino in Lucca, Italy. Dated to c. 1200 the center originally had a battle scene between Theseus and the Minotaur which has been worn off by the fingers of people tracing the path. Next to it is a Latin inscription that translates as: "Here is the labyrinth that Daedalus from Crete built, and which no one can exit once inside; only Theseus was able to do so thanks to Ariadne's thread." [58] Though there is no reference to Christ, its appearance at the Cathedral certainly implies a Christian connotation. Additionally there are two Italian church pavement labyrinths from the twelfth century that show Theseus battling the Minotaur in the center. Based on these examples of Christian labyrinths with Theseus and the Minotaur there is little reason to doubt the documentation that places them in the center of the Chartres labyrinth.

Christ's descent into Hell, defeat of the Devil, and rescue of the souls entrapped there, known as the "Harrowing of Hell," was analogous to Theseus's passage into the labyrinth, defeat of the Minotaur, and rescue of the Athenian youth. The Harrowing of Hell is not in the canon, but is found in the fourth-century apocryphal *Gospel of Nicodemus*, also called the *Acts of Pilate,* and is referred to in the Apostle's creed where it states Christ "...was crucified, died, and was buried. He descended to the dead. On the third day he rose again. He ascended into heaven. . ."[59] The story in the *Gospel of Nicodemus* explains what Christ was doing during those days of descent: Christ breaks the gates of Hell, tramples on Death, defeats Satan, and leads Adam, the Patriarchs, and others from the human race into Heaven. The Harrowing of Hell has been called the story of Christ that most impressed the Middle Ages, being one of the most popular sequences from the tenth century to the fourteenth century in drama and vernacular literature. *The Gospel of Nicodemus* was translated at least three times in the thirteenth century and was known all over France, including being the standard fare in the stories of entertainers.[60] Two such examples were told in the popular poems of the *Ovide moralise* (c. 1291-1328) and *Ovidius moralizatus* (1340).

The *Ovide moralise* is an anonymous poem of over 70,000 lines where the analogy between Christ's Harrowing of Hell and Theseus's storming of the labyrinth is clearly articulated with the poem shifting back and forth between the two stories. First there is the telling of the myth of Theseus, followed by an exposition of the story by referring to Christ and the Devil. The Devil is described as a fallen angel who tried to elevate himself above God, only to end up entrapped by God in a horrible place. From this vile jail he ruled over all the souls of the human race who had been damned by Adam's sin. In the poem it is Christ who is sent by God to save humanity. After his death on the cross he too goes to Hell, since he is partly mortal, but he saves the souls who were forsaken there by overcoming Death and defeating the Devil in a victorious battle. " . . .His soul went to darkest hell; he destroyed the devil and vanquished powerful death by his divinity. . . He broke down the infernal prison and put his troops at the gates. Then he returned in great victory."[61] The poem finishes by reminding the reader of Theseus, "full of goodness who by his submission discharged this grave debt and conquered the monster."[62] In the poem, Hell is not just a place from which one needs to escape, but also the state of humanity in bondage until set free by the way of Christ.

Heaven

This freedom from death, which Christ accomplishes in the Harrowing of Hell, brings the reward of Heaven. Christ and Theseus can go to the realm of death and return. They bring back those who had already been given up for lost to escape the confines of bondage and be set free. In the story of the Cretan labyrinth, Daedalus also becomes free from confinement and death. After his assistance to Ariadne was discovered by King Minos he was entrapped in the labyrinth with his son, Icarus. To escape to his homeland Daedalus made wings and flew away. The winged flight of Daedelus was seen in medieval Christianity to represent the soul, who could rise above confinement and find freedom in Heaven, the homeland of God. Ambrose (c. 339-397) used wings as a metaphor for the soul, and flight as the journey of the soul to God. Augustine (354-430) in his commentary on Psalm 149 states that the celestial realm is not found by land or sea, but by winged flight.[63] Daedelus may have become imprisoned after Theseus set the captives free, but he could still escape the confines of the prison by transcendent flight; likewise, even though Christ is not still fighting the battle in Hell, the soul can still be released from death, with the way to Heaven shown by Christ through the resurrection. The *Ovid moralise* states that Christ "flew straight to heaven and ascended in order to show how those who wish to come after him may fly upward. And what way must they take if they want to go to heaven: With the aid of two wings they must fly who wish to go there. . ."[64]

The labyrinth as Hell and Heaven is seen most clearly in the Easter ritual enacted from at least the early fourteenth century to 1535 on the labyrinth at Auxerre Cathedral in France. The Easter ritual at Auxerre is the only known documented use of the labyrinth in medieval Christendom. While there is no mention that such a ritual occurred at Chartres Cathedral, there is evidence that similar activities occurred in other towns and churches and Penelope Doob says there may have been such rituals at Reims, Sens, Chartres, and Amiens.[65] The Auxerre labyrinth was built sometime in the fourteenth century, possibly as early as 1309, which was when construction of the nave began. The labyrinth lasted until 1690. Documents state that the labyrinth at Auxerre was similar to the one at Sens, so it was most likely circular and thirty feet in diameter, situated in the nave.[66]

Documents in the fourteenth, fifteenth, and sixteenth century recount a ceremony performed on the labyrinth each Easter when the dean, who was the head of the chapter (body of clergy responsible for the cathedral), received a ball (*pilota*) from the most recently accepted canon (member of the chapter). The dean danced to the center of the labyrinth while members of the chapter danced around, or possibly through, the path of the labyrinth as they tossed the ball back and forth to the dean while singing the Easter song *Victimae paschali laudes* (Praise to the Paschal Victim). Woodward surmises two themes associated with this labyrinth ritual: allegiance and deliverance.[67]

The theme of allegiance is seen in the fact that the newest canon would provide and pay for the ball and present it to the dean or the senior dignitary present, symbolizing the new canon's submission and acceptance by the chapter. Ball games, played mostly on holidays, were extremely popular in the Middle Ages. The rights to ball games were given to nobility as part of their feudal privilege, thereby linking them to control and acceptance of a hierarchal allegiance. In addition to ball games in the secular arena there were also ball games associated with churches. Providing balls to church chapters was accepted and in some cases the omission of the balls led to a fine. Although it was understood the priests needed exercise after hours of prayer, their participation in ball games was discouraged since it was unseemly for a priest to be disheveled and engaged in such a frivolous activity. Hence, the presence of a ball game at a cathedral would not have been without controversy. In 1165 the *Rationale officiorum divinorum* stated that although ball games are played in many large churches such as Reims, it is better to refrain. In 1286 the Bishop of Mende in his *Rationale* agreed. In 1325 a statement from the Cathedral of Paris stated clerics should be excommunicated if they played these games at any time except when specific approval was given.[68]

This disapproval of the games was what led to the end of the Easter ritual at Auxerre. In 1471 and again in 1531 the new canons who were to provide the ball refused, stating that although other large cathedrals played such games, they thought Auxerre should refrain. In 1472 the canon relented and provided the ball, but in 1531 the civil authorities agreed with the dissenting canon and told the chapter to alter the ceremony. The chapter appealed and in 1535 after a bitter dispute, a ruling by the courts ended the ball ritual completely. The new canons were told to pay a sum of money, termed the *pilota,* to substitute for providing the ball.[69]

Whereas the allegiance shown between the new canon and the dean can relate to the submission to Christ, it is the theme of deliverance that more clearly aligns Hell and Heaven to the symbolism of the labyrinth. Both Doob and Woodward describe the Easter ball ritual at Auxerre as a reenactment of the Harrowing of Hell and the victorious resurrection of Christ.[70] The central figure of the dean is the Christ/Theseus figure. The rest of the canons represent those who Christ saved by the Harrowing of Hell, and are subsequently brought into Heaven. The ball is the ball of pitch that Theseus took with him into the labyrinth and used to defeat the Minotaur or the ball of thread given to Theseus by Ariadne to lead him back from the depths of the labyrinth. The song *Victimae paschali laudes* refers to Christ's battle with death and offers the promise of Salvation.[71]

To the medieval mind, music and dancing were methods to bring the universe into the cosmic harmony which was promised by the resurrection. The dancers, if they were following the circuitous path, which is likely since the dance was described as "garland like," would be following Ariadne's thread to freedom. In some labyrinths, both Christian and pagan, the threaded path is marked as a reminder of its importance (see fig. 11). Neither the exact dance nor its correct interpretation are known, but the elements of the Easter ritual dance certainly appear to be celebrating Christ's triumphant return from Hell and movement into Heaven. The labyrinth's association with Easter and Christ's resurrection is further supported by two labyrinths that are placed in manuscripts that contain computational tables to calculate the date of Easter.

Earth

It has generally been taken as a fact that the labyrinth was used as a substitute pilgrimage to Jerusalem, where the same graces and indulgences could be obtained from walking the labyrinth as an actual pilgrimage, and that it was done frequently by the faithful on their knees. This use of the labyrinth has been taken as historical fact to the point that it is one of the standard explanations provided by Chartres Cathedral.[72] The argument is largely based on the name for the labyrinth at Chartres and the labyrinth at Reims Cathedral as "*chemin de Jerusalem*," which means "road to Jerusalem." The labyrinth at Reims was built in the nave between 1287 and 1311, and was thirty-three feet in diameter. An article published in 1856 stated that while proceeding along the path believers said prayers from a special prayer book with the title which translated as "Stations along the Path to Jerusalem to be Found in the Cathedral of Our Lady in Reims."[73]

Labyrinth scholars Hermann Kern, author of the monumental *Through the Labyrinth,* and Penelope Doob, author of *The Idea of the Labyrinth*, state that no concrete evidence exists to support the notion of the substitute pilgrimage to the Holy Land and that it was an eighteenth-century creation. Doob is particularly adamant about dismissing the claims in her statement "...in the absence of the tiniest shred of evidence that pavement labyrinths were used for real or substitute pilgrimages, the hydra-like hypothesis should be dismembered for good."[74] However, it would appear Doob's insistence on the insubstantiality of this claim is overstated. There is some good contextual evidence that supports the use of the labyrinth as a substitute pilgrimage for those who could not go to the Holy Land for any number of reasons, whether economic, health, age, monastic vows, or servitude to the land.

First the Christian Crusade lost the Holy Land to the Muslims in 1187 which was approximately the same time as the accelerated building of pavement labyrinths in cathedrals. This loss of Jerusalem as an actual destination may have contributed to other types of metaphorical or visual pilgrimages, such as labyrinths. Daniel Connolly provides substantial research to support his premise that visually oriented meditational and bodily practices such as descriptive travel guides, maps, and pavement labyrinths were created in the high and late Middle Ages to provide "imagined pilgrimages" to Jerusalem.[75] Connolly shows that the labyrinth was a symbol of earthly Jerusalem by pointing out the relationship between *mappaemundi* and pavement labyrinths. Larger wall-sized *mappaemundi* were common at that time and portrayed the way the medieval mind shaped its spaces and viewed its history.[76]

Connolly investigates the parallel association between maps and labyrinths illustrating his point through manuscripts, for example Paulino Veneto's Italian *Chronicle* of 1334, which includes both *mappaemundi* and drawings of labyrinths, suggesting a related meaning. Veneto's map of the world is oriented with east on top and Jerusalem at the center, the same orientation as the labyrinth drawn above it and church pavement labyrinths. In the thirteenth century, after the loss of the Holy Land, the portrayal of Jerusalem as the center of the world increased to a point of primary significance in medieval cartography, as seen in Hereford *mappaemundi* (c. 1276) which was thought to guide pilgrims on the great circle pilgrimages from Mt. Sinai to Jerusalem to Rome.[77] The Hereford map is a circular image of the world with Jerusalem at the center, east on top, and shows Crete with the labyrinth drawn in the Christianized Chartres-style in the western part of the island. The western opening into the labyrinth is the same orientation as the labyrinth at Chartres, as well as most Church labyrinths. Kern also states that *mappaemundi* and pavement labyrinths are analogous visual metaphors since the labyrinth was oriented like a map and therefore suggestive of the world view.[78]

Second, it is common in labyrinth history for the labyrinth to be called the names of lost cities, for example Troy, Babylon, and Jericho. Kern relates a history of equating the labyrinth with Jericho that lasted for 1,000 years in the Greek Orthodox, Roman Catholic, Jewish, and Syrian traditions, and provides sixteen Jericho labyrinth illustrations. Most Jericho labyrinths were Classical seven-circuit, to represent Jericho's seven walls. The single exception is a Chartres-style Jericho labyrinth created in the twelfth century. Kern also notes that no Christian Jericho labyrinths were made after the twelfth century which is, perhaps significantly, the same time that the pavement labyrinths representing Jerusalem, the latest lost city, began to be built.[79] The connection to the Chartres labyrinth to Jerusalem can be seen in its similarity to the "Situs Jerusalem" maps (see fig. 15).

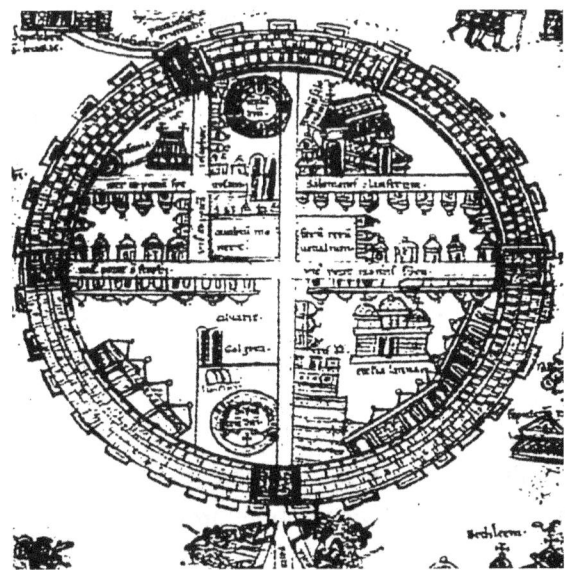

Figure 15: Situs Jerusalem Map, Brussels, thirteenth century.

In these twelfth- and thirteenth-century maps of Jerusalem the circular perimeter is surrounded by a brick-like wall and the city is divided by a cross created by the horizontal and vertical axis. Likewise the labyrinth's perimeter at Chartres Cathedral is surrounded by a scalloped pattern and divided into four quadrants by a cross-like dissection, showing marked similarity to these maps of Jerusalem.[80] Surrounding the labyrinth with a fortified wall was a feature seen in many Roman labyrinths.

Third, as Connolly suggests, essential in explaining the use of labyrinths is the fact that they changed in size from manuscripts, drawings, and mosaics too small to be walked, to large pavement labyrinths whose placement in the nave of the church almost demanded that they be walked. Labyrinths large enough and positioned such that they could be walked would most likely mean that they were specifically designed to be walked. They provided an imagined pilgrimage to Jerusalem for the laity in the same way as the written visualizations and *mappaemundi* provided imagined pilgrimages for the priests and monks.[81]

John Demaray's 1987 *Dante and the Book of the Cosmos* also relates the labyrinth as a pilgrimage that leads to the "spiritual-geographical" center of Jerusalem. As evidence he gives the strong pilgrimage tradition of the medieval church, with specific reference to the circle pilgrimage of Egypt, Jerusalem, and Rome as well as the pilgrimage to the Church of the Holy Sepulchre in Jerusalem. He cites many architectural imitations of the Church of the Holy Sepulchre, most of them built as circular, hexagonal, or octagonal structures. Worshippers would enter these circular cathedrals and basilicas, moving across the floor and through the ambulatory, to the high altar, which corresponded to the temple altars in Jerusalem. At the Church of the Holy Sepulchre in San Stefano, Bologna, a chain of pilgrimage stations was established from the tenth to twelfth centuries so that worshippers could experience a pilgrimage to Jerusalem without long distance travel. Demaray speculates that worshipers encountering the labyrinth in the nave of Chartres Cathedral would fall upon their knees, moving through it before they continued on to the altar where they found redemption through the Eucharist.[82]

Conclusion

Spiritual seekers of the twentieth century were not the first to selectively borrow from other traditions to construct labyrinth rituals. Such adaptations of the labyrinth began over 4,000 years ago with the Egyptian story of the death and rebirth of Osiris, which was transfigured by the Cretans into the triumph of Theseus, and further adapted by the medieval Christians as a typology for Christ. When symbols are selectively appropriated, some are kept as central to the story, while others downplayed or eliminated completely. The defeat of the Minotaur by Theseus was preserved as a prefiguration of the defeat of the Devil by Christ. But Osiris's three days spent in the underworld before his triumphant resurrection bypassed the Cretan story, only to resurface in the Christian, where Christ spent three days in Hell before his resurrection. The importance of the role of the Goddess, prominent in the Egyptian tale, was diminished first in the Cretan, as Ariadne's status as a goddess was downplayed, and later in the Christian adaptation where Mary is apparently missing altogether.

However symbols have a way of resurfacing on their own, and upon closer inspection the divine feminine may be present in the Chartres labyrinth after all. For if Theseus is Christ, and the Minotaur is the Devil, then perhaps Ariadne is analogous to Mary, Mother of Christ. Isis and Mary have been associated since early Christianity when the worship of Isis was a major competitor to the nascent Christian movement; the image of Madonna and Christ was drawn from similar images of Isis and Horus. Stories of Chartres told as early as the 1600s show Mary as prefigured by a local pagan goddess. These stories tell of a holy well in the caves underneath the current Chartres Cathedral which was the site of the druid worship of a *virgo paritura* (a virgin who was to give birth).[83] In addition to Mary's association with pagan goddesses, Mary's part in the Christian story also has some similarities to Ariadne's. For example, like Ariadne, Mary becomes a secondary player in a story that could not have occurred without her. The heroic deeds of Theseus subsumed Ariadne's role, and similarly the central importance of Christ's death and resurrection to Christianity made Mary's role as a mother ancillary. Ariadne ends up abandoned by Theseus, as Mary was left by Jesus. But in the end, Ariadne wed Dionysus, a god of death and rebirth, and Mary was assumed into Heaven, thereby linking both to immortality and divinity.

In the current Labyrinth Movement, Mary is strongly associated with the labyrinth at Chartres Cathedral. Chartres was a premier pilgrimage site to Mary in the Middle Ages as location of the holy relic of her birthing gown. For some people today the Chartres labyrinth is a representation of Mary. This is due in part to the six petals in the center of the Chartres labyrinth, often referred to as the "rose," the flower of Mary. The relationship between the labyrinth and Mary will be explored further in Chapter 5.

By looking at the historical use of the labyrinth it becomes clear that various cosmologies have been superimposed on its single form. In this broad examination of the use of the labyrinth in Western Europe we have found Isis and Osiris, Theseus and the Minotaur, Christ and the Devil, Heaven and Hell, plus the cartography of Troy, Jericho, and Jerusalem. By continued adaptation and selective appropriation, the labyrinth today continues to reflect the belief systems of those who use it. The next chapter will go further into how the labyrinth is a template for the cosmos and how ritual is used to construct cosmologies.

4
Rituals that Connect to a Sacred Cosmos

Chapter 3 demonstrated the selective appropriation of religious ideas and symbols from the Classical to the Chartres labyrinth using as a basic example Theseus who was an early typology for Christ. I demonstrated how the medieval Christian used "symbolic vision" to become aware of the unseen reality behind physical creation, particularly the art and architecture of Chartres Cathedral and the labyrinth. The only documented ritual on the Christian labyrinth was at Easter when the Harrowing of Hell was re-enacted. Using music, dance, and symbolism, part of the Christian cosmos was constructed on the labyrinth and the dean and canons became engaged in that cosmos by re-enacting the story through ritual. On labyrinths today, ritual is still being used as a means to construct a cosmos in which participants can become engaged.

The labyrinth is not the only architectural form used to represent a cosmos in which participants can engage in through ritual. For example, Chartres Cathedral is considered a model of the Christian cosmos, and the Egyptian mortuary tomb depicted the Egyptian view of the world through the ritual reenactment of Osiris's death and rebirth. Another example is the Buddhist temple of Borobudur in Java (see fig. 16), where walking up its labyrinthine structure is analogous to engaging in the three spheres of Mahayana Buddhism, the lower, middle and higher worlds.[1] Other examples of cosmic templates include the Tibetan mandala, Native American medicine wheel, Jewish Tree of Life, and Wiccan magical circle.

Figure 16: Diagram of Borobudur.

In addition to the purposeful construction of the cosmos on the labyrinth, as in the Harrowing of Hell ritual, the labyrinth can also "evoke" personal cosmologies, either spontaneously within the ritual or *ex post facto* upon further reflection. In each case the labyrinth acts as a template upon which individuals and groups engage with their beliefs of the world. The labyrinth rituals described in Chapters 5 and 6 are examples of purposeful constructions of a cosmos through scripted ceremonials. When a labyrinth ritual is purposefully scripted to reflect some part of the cosmos this does not necessarily mean that all the participants in the ritual accept the beliefs presented *in toto* or even in part, just as going to a Sunday worship service does not imply acceptance of the reading of the statement of faith. To begin my examination of ritual as it is used to construct and engage participants in their idea of the cosmos, I will define what I mean by cosmos and how I see ritual as a means of engagement.

The Sacred Cosmos

Norriss Hetherington, editor of the 1993 *Cosmology: Historical, Literary, Philosophical, Religious and Scientific Perspectives,* views cosmology not as an empirical fact but as a cultural creation that reflects its multiple sources across disciplinary boundaries.[2] While admitting that the idea of the cosmos can never be thoroughly separated from its cultural influences, I am directing my attention to the term as used in religion. According to J.Z. Smith:

> What we study when we study religion is an inextricably human phenomenon. In the West, we live in a post-Kantian world in which man is defined as a world-creating being and culture is understood as a symbolic process of world construction. . .What we study when we study religion is one mode of constructing worlds of meaning, worlds within which men find themselves and in which they choose to dwell.[3]

Within the realm of religion I am further narrowing my discussion of the cosmos to Peter Berger's notion that a cosmos is a socially constructed human enterprise.[4] Berger describes the cosmos as an immensely powerful overarching fabric of meaning that both transcends and includes humans, and locates a human's life in an ultimately meaningful order. Berger suggests that humans construct a cosmos because of the need for an all-encompassing system of meaning. He contends that in today's American society many systems can constitute a cosmos, with modern science being the most prevalent.[5] But ultimately it is religion that is the oldest and most all-pervasive explanation of the world. Religion is "the establishment, through human activity, of an all-embracing sacred order, that is, of a sacred cosmos that will be capable of maintaining itself in the ever-present face of chaos."[6] Berger describes the sacred as that mysterious and awesome force which is outside of humans and which "stands out" or is separate from the ordinary, everyday, profane life. In his words:

> Such a cosmos, as the ultimate ground and validation of human *nomoi* (order), need not necessarily be sacred. . . It is safe to say,

however, that originally all cosmization had a sacred character
...Viewed historically, most of man's worlds have been sacred
worlds. Indeed, it appears likely that only by way of the sacred was
it possible for man to conceive of a cosmos in the first place. It can
thus be said that religion has played a strategic part in the human
enterprise of world-building.[7]

Berger considers religion to be the most powerful system that constitutes a cosmos since it links the physical world to a divine structure. When humans participate in the institutional structures of their religion they, *ipso facto*, participate in the sacred cosmos.[8] I intend here to use the term "sacred cosmos" to differentiate my use of the term from other uses, such as scientific or philosophical.

There are cultural differences in what constitutes a sacred cosmos since there are different cultural notions of what is sacred. The sacred is believed to reside variously in objects, animals, people, ancestors, spirits, deities, forces of nature, and institutions, as well as sacred places and sacred times. Regardless of a society's specific perception of a sacred cosmos, the reality of that cosmos must be maintained. Berger states that: "The reality of the world as socially defined must be maintained externally, in the conversation of people with each other, as well as internally, in the way by which the individual apprehends the world within his own consciousness."[9] Berger points out that while definitions of a sacred cosmos may include explicit and coherent theoretical schemes and a fully detailed and articulated *weltanschauung*, or worldview, it is understood on this level by only a small group of people who are so intellectually inclined. Hence, even though details of a sacred cosmos can be clearly described in doctrine and texts, most ideas are pre-theoretical and are accepted *ipso facto* due to their integration in an accepted institution. For example, participating in the Eucharist maintains the Catholic sacred cosmos not because the deeper significance of transubstantiation is theoretically understood by the public, but because "this is the way it has always been done." In this way ideas of a sacred cosmos may not be consciously formulated or articulated by the general public. Instead they may be understood informally in myths, folktales, and experienced in social practices.[10]

Berger states that these more informal methods of explaining and legitimizing a sacred cosmos need to be taken seriously.

> The degree of theoretical elaboration of the religious legitimations will vary with a large number of historical factors, but it would lead to grave misunderstanding if only the more sophisticated legitimations were taken into consideration. To put it simply, most men in history have felt the need for religious legitimation—only very few have been interested in the development of religious "ideas."[11]

Cosmologies are often built up from a combination of minor sources and the basic principles of a sacred cosmos are implied even when they are not consciously formulated or articulated by the people themselves.

A sacred cosmos is not necessarily always collective, but can be individually constructed as a collage appropriated from multiple sources. In Chapter 2, I discuss Wade Clark Roof's description of a generation of "seekers" who are reframing religious symbols from many different traditions to negotiate their own personal worlds of meaning, some highly defined and stable while others are amorphous and changing. And as Roof points out, an individually negotiated sacred cosmos can be as personally meaningful as one that has been institutionally formulated and theoretically comprehensive. Jonathan Smith also discusses the idea of a personally constructed cosmos and illustrates this with a story of a farmer who created a world with "gestures and words in which he, his family and farm gained significance and value." Smith defines this world with its own ordering principles, rules of conduct, boundaries, and limits as a cosmology, "a locative map of the world. . . a map of the world which guarantees meaning and value through structures of congruity and conformity."[12]

Even though a personally negotiated cosmos may have importance to an individual, it will not have the stabilizing framework that an institution can provide. Berger defines this stabilizing framework as a "plausibility structure" and describes it as the reality base that supports the beliefs of a sacred cosmos, with the stronger the plausibility structure the stronger the accepted reality of that cosmos. The strength of a plausibility structure makes some versions of a sacred cosmos more acceptable to the general public than others. For example, in the 1950s Protestantism had such a firm plausibility structure in America that participation in its sacred cosmos was assumed. But in today's diverse religious landscape, various beliefs have set up competing plausibility structures, with some more pervasive than others.[13] Personally negotiated idiosyncratic worlds of meaning are often precariously based in a plausibility structure and are considered to be on the edge of religious respectability. However, the creation of new concepts such as "spiritual but not religious" and Roof's contextualization of a "quest culture" pulls within them people and beliefs that do not quite fit anywhere else. That in itself establishes the beginning of a plausibility structure that may eventually lead to a greater acceptability of such beliefs.

Although the term "cosmology" is sometimes used synonymously with "worldview" I am employing the distinction made by Kees Bolle between the two terms in his entry on "cosmology" in *The Encyclopedia of Religion*. He describes the difference thus: "Worldview is a more general term, less precisely delineated, but commonly accepted set of ideas (ideology) concerning life and the world. Cosmology refers to more consciously entertained images, doctrines, and scientific views concerning the universe."[14] Following his lead I may use the term "worldview" in a general sense, such as a "mechanistic worldview" or "naturalistic worldview." But I will use the term "sacred cosmos" when there are specific images, doctrines, or views such as temporal and spatial distinctions, deities, sacred objects, ancestors, forces of nature, and stories of creation. Another concept crucial here is Roof's term of "personal worlds of meaning." These worlds include beliefs that may be less clearly articulated, but still provide some of the same benefits as a sacred cosmos, including a sense of meaning and placement within the world.

In summary, I am defining a sacred cosmos as a socially constructed framework that explains and justifies the seen and unseen world, providing for humans a system of order, placement, and meaning. This definition of a sacred cosmos can exist along a continuum that goes from highly complex theories articulated in doctrines and texts, to general ideas embedded in folklore and social practices, to vaguely defined personally negotiated worlds of meaning.

Connection to a Sacred Cosmos

Berger makes clear that one of the most important qualities of a sacred cosmos is to "locate" or "place" humans in a cosmic frame of reference, providing meaning and order.[15] In ancient Greece the cosmos was the central concept by which people understood their world; they were part of a harmonious whole that was the universe in which they lived their lives. In the *Timaeus* Plato described the world and all the planets as having a soul, suggesting worlds that were alive and conscious, the macrocosm of which humans were microcosms.[16] With the advent of Judaism and Christianity this interconnection between humans and their cosmos deteriorated and was replaced by the bond between God and man. The cosmos was seen as a creation of God for the service of man and man's to govern. This changed man's relationship with the cosmos from being an integral part of life to an external tool to manipulate in order to survive and reach salvation.[17] The separation of humans from the cosmos continued as the Ptolemaic view of the universe, where earth and humans were the center, was replaced by the Copernican view, where the more impersonal sun took center stage. This "crisis of European consciousness" was characterized as the "destruction of the cosmos" where the concept of the world as a well-ordered whole shifted into a mechanized worldview.[18] The destruction of the cosmos continued as a quite unexpected consequence of the Protestant Reformation. At that time the multiple channels to the sacred that existed as part of the Catholic cosmos, such as symbols and sacraments, were replaced with a single avenue to the sacred, the Word of God.[19] Berger contends that eliminating all links to God except that single one made it more difficult for people to maintain their connection to the sacred. This caused an increase in secularization which Berger defines as the process by which "sectors of society and culture are removed from the domination of religious institutions and symbols."[20] The Enlightenment continued this disenchantment and metaphorically knocked the cosmos off its axis as rationality became the center of the world. With current advances in science it is now known that the solar system is not the physical center of our galaxy, and our galaxy is not the physical center of our universe, thereby displacing the concept of a solid and central fixed point of orientation.[21] In the field of science, cosmology brings together the natural sciences, particularly astronomy and physics, in a joint effort that aims at a critical and empirical comprehensive theory of the creation, evolution, and present structure of the entire universe. But the investigation of the physical universe separate from its divine creator is a development of the last half-century, and before that the natural world was closely intertwined with the religious.[22] Some scholars consider the separation between the world of nature and the world of supernature as a western intellectual concept that deconstructs an otherwise integrated whole, a whole that views the cosmos as a complete system, both seen and unseen, physical and spiritual.[23]

This separation of humans from their cosmos continues today in a rapidly changing technological world that is losing its interconnection with nature. People will forget about the sacred cosmos in which they live, especially in times of distress and chaos. They need to be reminded, a task which often falls to ritual. According to Berger, ritual is the human enterprise by which a sacred cosmos is re-established and provides the means by which a person or society is placed back into their sacred cosmos so that they are again located in that world of meaning.[24]

Labyrinth rituals have two main functions regarding their relationship to a sacred cosmos. The first is to provide an arena upon which a sacred cosmos can be constructed. The second is to provide actions through which an individual can engage with their sacred cosmos so as to locate their sense of "place." The simplest way to understand "place" as construed in ritual is to see it as the point where time and space intersect, a point which I call an "axis of placement." All rituals are done at a particular time and a particular place, for example Friday at the church sanctuary. Taking part in a ritual where this intersection of time and space occurs will establish an axis of placement that locates and places the participant in the physical world. To be placed is to be fully embodied, and like the quiet eye of a storm, a calm center is established that can provide stability in the chaos of life. But many rituals expand this notion of a physical time and space to create a historical, even cosmic, axis of placement. For example, the Friday ritual at the church sanctuary may be to commemorate the crucifixion of Christ on Good Friday in Jerusalem. Engaging in that ritual with its larger significance links the physical world of the participant with a divine structure, bestowing authority, power and a sense of being placed within a larger, sacred world. Since time and space are so central to being located within a sacred cosmos, further consideration is needed to more fully understand their role in ritual.

Time and Space in Ritual

My research in the field of religion on the use of time and space in ritual as a way to establish one's place in a sacred cosmos revealed few sources directly relevant to American contemporary ritual. Mircea Eliade's work as a historian of religion examined cosmology largely as the result of a manifestation of the sacred, an event he termed a *"hierophany."* The location of the *hierophany* established an *"axis mundi"* or central point around which a cosmos was founded. While this approach may be applicable in some contexts, I found it limited since my analysis of a sacred cosmos is as a social construction, rather than a religious manifestation. For Eliade ritual was largely as a method to renew and reenact this original creation of the cosmos through traditional stories regarding "the myth of the eternal return."[25] While the Christian liturgical rituals that I explain in Chapter 5 could fit into the category of "myth of the eternal return," I examine them as nascent social constructions rather than repetitive traditions.

It was in the cultural tradition of South Asian Hinduism, and indigenous traditions including South America, Native America, and Australia that I found the theories of ritual that were relevant to contemporary labyrinth rituals that engage a sacred cosmos. In indigenous religions, cosmology explains the basic ideological problems of any culture, such as death, society, and gender, and tells the story of origin as well as describes the world of the living and dead.[26] Emile Durkheim studied the cosmologies of totemic religious communities as cultural phenomena and found within them properties such as time, space, class, and substance that he considered universal. Gerald Weiss developed a theory of cosmology based on his studies of the Campa, a South American forest tribe, which I found relevant to contemporary urban culture. He described cosmology as "a set of ideas about the totality of reality, including both the world of appearances and the hidden reality" and stated that every cosmology explains the world through a set of ideas that contains both structure and content, including temporal and spatial realms, beings, forces, properties, myths, and ritual.[27]

While Weiss's theory brought many of the facets of cosmology together so that I could see the broader picture, I needed a clearer working definition of cosmology that would be helpful in the coding and analysis of the rituals I was documenting. I found such a working definition in the work of Archeologist Christopher Carr who reconstructs the cosmology of the Native American mound builders in Ohio by analyzing the objects contained in their burials.[28] In personal conversations he described cosmology as consisting of five elements that make up the Who, What, When, Where, and How of the world, a basic description that I expanded upon as follows: Who includes the inhabitants of the universe including gods, goddesses, deities, spirits, ancestors, or animals; What includes the myths and tales that describe the world including its origins and major events; When includes all temporal aspects including how time is viewed and ideas of time trajectories such as reincarnation or eschatology; Where includes all spatial considerations including the divisions of space and the distinction between sacred and profane, as well as spatial realms like heaven, hell, and the underworld; How includes methods to interact with the world including ritual, dance, devotion, and prayer. Taken together these five aspects—Who, What, When, Where, How—give a full understanding of the sacred cosmos of any given group or person. However, as Berger states, a fully articulated theoretical description of a sacred cosmos is rarely known by lay people and therefore a complete understanding of the entire system of belief is often lacking. But by using a *pars/pro/toto* approach, from a single part the entire system can be extrapolated and it becomes possible to investigate the sacred cosmos of participants through any one of the five elements.

Berger contends that one of the most important functions of a sacred cosmos is to "locate" or "place" a person within a world of meaning. Stephen Toulmin affirms that a central task of any cosmology is to place humans in the universal scheme of things, and goes further in stating that temporal and spatial elements are indispensable to this task.[29] Sam Gill, in his work with Native American tribes also refers to time and space as the most basic foundations from which humans orient themselves in reality. He encourages an examination of a culture's symbolic usage of time and space to lead to an understanding of their religious life, and states that "to focus our study on those most fundamental orientations may reveal to us the way in which a people view their world."[30] Since time and space are also central elements in any ritual, I will focus my examination of the sacred cosmos to the temporal (When) and spatial (Where) elements as they are enacted in ritual, referring to the other elements (Who, What, How) only peripherally.

Temporal Contexts for Ritual

I propose that there are four categories of time that are prominent in ritual in that they govern the context for the ritual and direct when the ritual will occur. These four categories are Ecological, Theological, Communal, and Convenience. The first category is Ecological time and it sets both the context and the occurrence of ritual in relation to the environment. It includes such events as Earth Day, Full Moon, Harvest Celebrations, or Summer Solstice, as well as dawn and dusk. Evans-Pritchard states that ecological time is based on relations to the environment and is cyclical, since planetary revolutions and seasonal changes repeat themselves again and again. Roy Rappaport makes a finer distinction believing it is important to distinguish ecological time from celestial time, since celestial time is connected to the movements of celestial objects that we cannot manipulate and therefore it is absolute and inexorable.[31]

Fred Clothey also presents a distinction as he separates astronomical time from seasonal/ecological. For Clothey astronomical time includes all astronomical moments including full/new moon, eclipse, solstice, equinox, and particular astrological alignments; whereas seasonal/

ecological time is based on the occurrences of nature such as planting, harvesting, and flooding.[32] I have combined all ecological, celestial, and seasonal factors into one category since seasonal events, such as planting and harvest, are also based on the astronomical occurrences such as movements of the sun. My concept of ecological time is very much like the timing that governs festivals referred to by Clothey as ecofests, in that it includes any celestial or terrestrial event that influences the timing or context of a ritual.[33]

The second category is Theological time and it sets the context and occurrence of ritual around any religious belief, whether that belief is based on a deity, doctrine, history, or practice, for example Christmas or Passover. Theological Time relates to Clothey's description of a theofest which includes any festivals or calendrical observances linked to the life, career, and death of a deity or sacred person.[34] Many commemorative or ritual events based on theological time were established as a result of religious adaptations and are interwoven with ecological time. For example, the birth of Christ, December 25th, was originally tied to the Winter Solstice, December 21st, a pagan holy day that literally celebrates the "birth of the sun." And Easter is adapted from the Anglo-Saxon spring goddess Eostre and the Jewish Passover, so it occurs at a different date each year, having been calculated as the first Sunday following the full moon after the vernal equinox.[35] However I refer to the timing or context of an event to be theological, regardless of its origins as ecological, if the main purpose is tied to a specific religious belief or to honor a deity.

The third category is Communal and relates to rituals that are significant to individuals and their community. This category is a combination of Clothey's Social and Personal types since I consider many personal events to be socially significant and difficult to separate from communal aspects. For example, a divorce effects not only the individual lives of the couple, but often the entire community. And what might be considered an extremely personal event such as first menstrual blood, is still a community event in that the young girl is taking her place as a woman within the society. Many personal touchstones such as birthdays, circumcision, and first menses are based on biological time and affirm that the continuing process of growth is proceeding correctly from stage to stage in the same way that ecological time affirms the celestial and natural rhythms of life.[36] In addition to personal and social events, Communal time contains institutional constraints including the division of the year according to the educational demands of school, such as semesters, and the division of the day according to work demands of corporations such as 9-5 Monday through Friday, a time frame so ubiquitous in the American society as to be one of the most determinant. It also includes civic rituals, such as July 4th, as well as rituals earmarking important cultural occurrences. An example of this would be Columbus Day, celebrated by many Americans as the day Columbus discovered the "new world," but more recently commemorated by Native peoples as the day Columbus stumbled onto their land and stole it.

The fourth category that determines the timing of ritual is Convenience. Many rituals are based largely on what is convenient for those involved. This can include choosing to be married on a particular date because it is a three-day weekend and relatives can more easily make the trip, or having the labyrinth ritual on Wednesday because it is the only day the needed space in the social hall is available.

These categories of time are not meant to be strict divisions, but rather to act as guidelines to better understand why a ritual is occurring and how the timing for the ritual was chosen. Often more than one type of timing will influence a ritual. For example, a marriage ceremony, which is a Communal event, may also be determined by Ecological time if the planetary alignments in the astrological chart are taken into consideration.

Time as Cosmic Rhythm

These temporal categories for ritual do more than just set the context for the ritual and define the time when it occurs. They also establish a rhythm to the world and those who live within it. Through rhythm humans get a sense of security and a belief that the universe is dependable and reliable. Ecological timing creates the rhythmic distinctions necessary for chronometry, the division of time into specific segments which can be measured, for example the rising and setting of the sun, and the full and new moon. Clothey discusses how chronometry in Hinduism divides the larger cosmic rhythm into small segments that makes the cosmos more understandable and establishes an important connection between humans and the cosmos.

> Each segment of time becomes a microcosm of the cosmic rhythm and appropriate junctures within that segment become "tempocosms" or points of access to the larger dimensions of existence. The beginning, apex, and end of various segments, for example, are such tempocosms since they serve as points of breakthrough to the larger process of the cosmic rhythm; they illustrate and reproduce on miniature scale the beginning, apex, and end of cosmic cycles. The measure of time and ritual observances which occur at important tempocosms thus reflect a basic cosmology or vision of the world, at least for those for whom the pattern is intelligible.[37]

I contend that cosmic chronometry can be as important an aspect in American contemporary rituals as it is in Hinduism. It can provide a link between humans and their cosmos, especially in those rituals based on nature and ecological timing, such as the Summer Solstice. The idea that cosmic chronometry can provide an important link between humans and the sacred cosmos leads to the speculation that the secularization of society could be related to the development of artificial chronometers, such as clocks. With artificial chronometers the measurement of time is taken out of the heavens and placed solely in the hands of man, creating another separation between humans and their cosmos. If this is true, the choice to stage rituals based on Ecological timing (Solstice and Equinox) as well as Theological (Christmas and Easter), could be construed as an attempt to keep the connection with the cosmos alive.

Humans need to connect to something greater than themselves and to establish an orientation that goes outside of daily living, into a larger, even sacred dimension. Lay people, especially in a secular society, can get so caught up in the insular rhythms of life that often it is the religious specialists who keep the connection between humans, god, and the universe alive through engaging in ritual. In the Tamil cult of Murukan the role of the priest is of "ritually maintaining the cosmos and assuring its constant renewal."[38] Anthony Good states that in the regular rhythmic repetition of temple liturgy in South Indian Hinduism "time is linked to cosmogonic processes of separation and reaggregation," and that worship is necessary to maintain cosmic stability and to keep the cosmos from falling into disorder.[39] While it is doubtful that most American laypeople think in terms of the consequences of cosmic disorder, they do seek ritual as a stabilizing force when social disorder occurs. This is evident in the ritual response to such national tragedies as the September 11th terrorist attack, where people participated in both spontaneous and planned rituals.

Time as Communal Rhythm

In addition to the cosmic rhythm established in ritual, there is also a sense of rhythm that connects humans to their own life and to the life of their community. Roy Rappaport remarks on the importance of a temporal rhythm that can unite a very temporally disparate society into a unified whole in the following statement:

> There seems to be no universal temporal sense guiding all humans through their lives at apparently uniform rates. Nor is there even subjective constancy of rate, for the chronicles of memory and anticipation are private and idiosyncratic, and they may be bent or reordered by regret, nostalgia, pain, delight, foreboding and hope, or disarranged by disease, age, and simple forgetfulness. The sense of passage that all normal humans possess, being idiosyncratic and unreliable, or at least subject to distortion, not only cannot itself serve as the ground for temporal ordering but may itself generate a need for the public ordering of time, not simply to coordinate social life, but to provide a well-marked road along which each individual's temporal experience can travel. Be this as it may, it seems safe to say that all societies recognize public temporal orders.[40]

Time in ritual can provide a roadmap for an individual's personal experience of time and for a community's temporal ordering. Deborah

Rose's research on Aboriginal dance ritual illustrates how one part of the function of ritual is to provide a connection not only to the cosmic rhythm, but also to the rhythm of oneself and community. Rose states that in ritual "the kind of time that separates living things is collapsed in favor of the kinds of time that connect them."[41] For the Aborigines, the cosmos is considered living and includes earth, sky, underground, ocean, and living creatures. For them the rhythmic repetition in ritual becomes "the pulse of continuous creation. . . and is itself a world generative action."[42] In the context of ritual, time shifts from being passive and absent to being active and focused. The participant becomes "the heartbeat of time" as their in/out movement in the space, and their connect/disconnect actions with other participants create a rhythm between "time, place, source, and living things."[43]

In a similar way, labyrinth rituals create a flowing motion that could be termed the "heartbeat" of the ritual. Participants establish an in/out rhythm as they walk first inward toward the center and then back out of the space, while at the same time connecting and disconnecting with others along the way. Even the ever-changing motion of walking first one direction and then another as the path twists and turns creates a rhythm like the ebb and flow of the tides. Rose states that "living things are coming and going, and, most importantly, returning. . . There is both movement away and movement toward, both the departure and the return."[44] Time in the ritual of walking the labyrinth becomes what Rose terms "embodied time," where time exists in the motions and movement of the actors. Time is not judged by artificial chronometers, but by the rhythm created by the departure and return that occurs in the ritual, and the focused interval between beginning and end. She states that Aboriginal ceremonies are meant to bring time and place into the body of the performers, a function of labyrinth rituals as well.[45]

Time in ritual accomplishes several tasks. It governs when the ritual will occur and sets the context for the event. It can also provide a cosmic rhythm through chronometry and tempocosms, and provide a communal rhythm through a temporal ordering that is shared by the individual and society. Part of the benefit of engaging in a sacred cosmos on the labyrinth is the connection to a rhythm that links humans not only to a communal temporal order that can provide constancy in daily life, but also to a cosmic order that provides a larger framework of meaning.

Spatial contexts for ritual

Space is as important as time in ordering the world and situating ritual. Sam Gill states that:

> ...human beings express and transmit their religious worldviews by making physical distinctions, by specifying the character of the place where they live. That is, we view the world in terms of fundamental distinctions that are projected upon the physical world—house, ceremonial and ritual structures, monoliths, mountains, homes, etc. Place distinctions are often extended into the imaginative world through oral traditions, ritual, dramas, and art. These distinctions support a system of values and ideas stated in terms of the relationships among respective places and characterization of being in or out of place. . . place distinctions are usually equivalent to ideological distinctions, so to consider categories of place and how they are characterized is one way of beginning the process of understanding and interpreting the religion of a particular culture or the significance of a particular religious event.[46]

One way to understand these distinctions in space is to consider where a ritual is being situated. In the same way that I suggest temporal ordering be considered through four categories, I also suggest four categories of space. I find the distinctions that Clothey makes in his work on Hinduism helpful in considering the spatial aspects of labyrinth rituals. His first category of space is historic/mythic and includes space made sacred by historical or mythical events, such as Jerusalem or the Cherokee Trail of Tears. His second category is ecographic space and includes natural settings that inspire wonder and have an aura of the sacred, such as mountains and rivers. His third category is architectural space which includes structures built for sacred purposes, at times even modeling themselves on the cosmos (*imago mundi*) such as the Cathedral at Chartres. And fourth is bodily space, where the body comes to have symbolic significance and is used as an arena in ritual, as in yoga.[47]

As in the categories of time, these categories of space are used as general guidelines to understand how space influences ritual, and there can be more than one type of space present in a ritual simultaneously. For example, the labyrinth is an architectural space in that it is a structure built as a container or arena for ritual. But it can also be situated in a natural setting, such as a mountain, and be used to represent a mythic-historic space such as Jerusalem. Regardless of where a labyrinth is located or what it represents, it is generally considered a sacred space in its own right. Rappaport points to the distinctions between ordinary profane spaces and the extra-ordinary sacred spaces that are part of religious ritual. In his words:

> "ritual may transform mere extent into ordered cosmos and that, as liturgical sequences distinguish mundane periods from the extraordinary intervals between them, so do they distinguish the extraordinary space at or inside loci of orientation—shrines, temples, mountain tops, caves, be they "center" or not—from the ordinary, or profane spaces surrounding or extending from them.[48]

The labyrinth's circular form transforms "mere extent into ordered cosmos" and the simple act of entering the labyrinth is considered moving into extra-ordinary space that is separate from the mundane space that surrounds it. This is indicated by the fact that people remove their shoes and often bow before entering.

In discussing rituals it is often difficult to make a clear separation between time and space, since rituals celebrate events that happen at specific times in a particular space. Rappaport gives an example of the close interrelationship between time and space using the Hopi, whose ritual calendar is based on the temporal occurrence of the rising of the sun at specific spatial points upon the horizon.[49] J.Z. Smith also relates the interconnection between time and space with his discussion of the transposition of the sacred space (*loca sancta*) of Palestine into a system that temporally structures the Christian year.[50] He demonstrates this overlay with the fourth-century document, the *Pilgrimage of Egeria,* where a woman describes her experiences, which probably occurred between 381 and 384 CE, as she traveled from Sinai to Jerusalem. In this journey she changed from what Smith terms a pilgrim, who journeyed from place to place at her own leisure, to a celebrant, whose prescribed movements to ten liturgical sites in and around Jerusalem were significant both in terms of the day and the place (*apta diei et loca*) of historical events relating to Christ. Smith states:

> It is at this point that formal, liturgical ordering takes hold, establishing a hierarchy of significance that focuses the devout attention, chiefly achieved by adding a temporal dimension to the locative experience. The pilgrim is free to be at whatever place he or she wishes to see, at whatever time; the celebrant must be at a fixed place, at a fixed time, to perform or participate in a fixed act that focuses the intended significance of this conjunction.[51]

Upon Egeria's visit to each place sacred to the story of Christ an appropriate scripture would be read, linking the *loci* of the text with the geographical equivalent. Added to this was the temporal dimension of reading the text at the appropriate time. For example, reading the scriptural story of the crucifixion, on the date of the crucifixion, at the site of the crucifixion. Smith describes the Stations of the Cross, developed by Crusaders in the Holy Land, as taking this link of scripture, time, and space to a fully articulated conclusion. Once the Holy Land of Jerusalem became lost during the Crusades and the proximity of topography to the *sancta loci* was unavailable, the temporal dimension superseded the need for a spatial one, allowing the Passion of Christ to be replicated away from the *sancta loci* of Jerusalem. Smith states:

> Outside Jerusalem, the relationship [between space and time] had to be sundered. While the *locus* was left behind, the system of "days" and the correlation of the *loci* of scripture to those days could be maintained. Through a concentration on the associative dimensions of place together with the syntagmatic dimensions of narrative, a system was formulated that could be replicated away from the place. In this case, unlike the Temple, it was not arbitrariness, but temporality, that guaranteed replicability. With few exceptions, the hymns, prayers, scripture, lessons, and gestures tied to particular places in the indigenous Jerusalem liturgy could be expropriated and

exported. The sequence of time, the story, and the festal calendar, have allowed a supersession of place. It is the *apta diei* that will be endlessly replicable, rather than the *aptus locus*."[52]

The narrative, time, and place combined through such multi-modal techniques as hymns, prayers, and gestures to replicate the event in Christ's life both temporally and spatially, establishing an axis of placement and locating Egeria in the sacred world of Christ.

The time/space created in *The Pilgrimage of Egeria* to compensate for the loss of the sacred space of Jerusalem is also seen in the sixteenth-century *The Spiritual Exercises* of Ignatius of Loyola. In *The Spiritual Exercises* Loyola directs the participant to first call forth the narrative of the event, and second to call forth a mental representation of the place, "as if" it were real. Smith states that for Ignatius: "Here, all has been transferred to inner space. All that remains of Jerusalem is an image, the narrative, and a temporal sequence." [53]

A third example of time/space mental representations more directly related to labyrinths is described by Daniel Connolly in his description of "imagined pilgrimages." Imagined pilgrimages are the visually oriented meditational and bodily practices, such as descriptive travel guides, maps, and pavement labyrinths that were created in the high and late Middle Ages to provide imagined pilgrimages to Jerusalem. Connolly draws primarily from Dom Jean LeClercq's study of fourteenth-century Italian imagined pilgrimages and his own in-depth research of the mid-thirteenth-century maps of English monk and historian Matthew Paris.[54] Both have detailed visual descriptions, multi-sensory depictions, and sensate body experiences, all operative elements of what Connolly describes as "translocative" techniques capable of transporting the practitioner spiritually and psychologically to another time and place.[55] A fourteenth-century Italian travel description states: "these are the journeys that pilgrims ought to make. . . and that every person can do, staying in his own house and thinking of each place that is written below …"[56] These visual pilgrimages are part of what LeClercq called *peregrinatio in stabilitate* (pilgrimages while stationary), interior meditative practices that initiated journeys of the heart and soul, instead of bodily travel. These interior pilgrimages addressed the two competing demands for the medieval monk—cloistered monasticism and religious pilgrimage. Bernard of Clairvaux (c. 1090-1153) solved the dilemma by uniting the pilgrimage to Jerusalem and the vow of monasticism as one spiritual journey, an earthly Jerusalem giving way to heavenly Jerusalem. He wrote: "For the object of monks is to seek out not the earthly but the heavenly Jerusalem and this is not by proceeding with [their] feet but by progressing with [their] feeling." [57]

Ritual and a Sacred Cosmos

The *Pilgrimage of Egeria*, *The Spiritual Exercises*, the "imagined pilgrimages" to Jerusalem, and The Harrowing of Hell as discussed in Chapter 3, are all historical examples of how ritual has been used to connect participants to a sacred cosmos, in these cases the Christian cosmos, by combining narrative, time, and space. Some rituals on the labyrinth today are being used in a similar fashion to connect participants to their idea of a sacred cosmos. The work of Ron Williams and James Boyd help explain how this can be accomplished. Williams and Boyd are two ritual theorists who direct their attention to an aesthetic approach of ritual interpretation by combining art and ritual theory. A large part of their approach is focused on how space is constructed and perceived in ritual.[58] The labyrinth is a type of space, a template, upon which people overlay various ideas of a sacred cosmos. Following an analysis of Williams and Boyd's theory of spatial construction, I will apply it to specific labyrinth rituals in Chapters 5 and 6.

Williams and Boyd refer to three types of space present in ritual—Physical space, Meaning space, and Virtual space. Physical space in ritual consists of "the material object or physical event in the space/time continuum it inhabits. Like any physical terrain, the physical space of an artwork [or ritual] can be photographed, measured, touched, or, in the case of dramas, walked through; it is in the realm of real objects."[59] The Physical space in a ritual or performance would be the stage, settings, actors, and movements and could include sounds, sights, smells, movements, and iconographic objects as they are objectively experienced rather than subjectively perceived.

Meaning space is a "complex dimension that has to do with what the work represents or expresses, its conceptual significance, and symbolic structure."[60] Each of the material aspects or events in the physical space such as music, language, actors, and settings, can have one or several meanings which lead to a multi-valent Meaning space. For example, in a performance such as Hamlet, the real-life components of the Physical space come to represent the life of a prince in Denmark during the Middle Ages.

Virtual space is a complex combination of the Physical space and Meaning space, a sort of "liminal space" that exists even though it is not real. Taken in part from optics "a virtual image, such as a mirror image or a rainbow, is visible even though it is not really there. It is opposed to a real image, like that produced on a screen by a slide projector: the latter can be intercepted by the screen; the former cannot."[61] A Virtual space in ritual creates a situation "as if" it was real, and is described by Williams and Boyd according to its relationship to drama.

> In a successfully performed drama, a separate "time-space" is created which we experience as virtually real in its own right. If, for example, the play includes a well-acted sword fight, we will experience the scene as real action in the present. It is perceived as actual behavior, though technically it is counterfeit. The attentive observer, capable of suspension of disbelief, becomes involved in the action and thus enters virtual space. A similar point can be made about the temporal duration of the play. The drama may actually require ninety minutes (physical time), it may represent events during an imagined time long ago (time meant), but we may also feel that we are perceiving a series of events presently occurring over a period of several days (virtual time)...Though virtual space is essentially related to both physical and meaning space, it is something separable from these two. It is a third kind of experienced reality...That this virtual, present violence is neither the physical nor the meaning space is apparent if we imagine the play poorly acted. For in that situation, we still know what the action being represented is and what it is purported to have happened, but we no longer feel present at a violent murder; rather

we are merely observers of bad acting. . .We are, in short, thrown back on the physical and meaning spaces, because the inept actors have failed to create a viable virtual space.[62]

Virtual space occurs in certain types of rituals and has been referred to in Smith's discussion of the Pilgrimage of Elgeria as "mental representations" and "inner space," and by Connelly in the imagined pilgrimages to Jerusalem as "translocative" and "interior meditative practices." As Williams and Boyd point out, Virtual time can be created as well as Virtual space. Since time and space are so often combined in ritual, I will henceforth refer to a Virtual time/space.

Williams and Boyd's discussion of Virtual time/space resonates with Ron Grimes's reference to ritual as an "enactment" which he describes as "not an ordinary action like changing a tire, nor is it an imitation of an action such as pretending to die on a stage. Rather, it is a kind of action which is in a category distinct from either of these. It is action thick with sensory meaning."[63] Grimes describes enactment as combining the literal and the symbolic, which is similar to Williams and Boyd's description of Virtual time/space as combining physical objects with the symbolic meaning.

I am describing the creation of a Virtual time/space in ritual as occurring through a three-step process. The first step involves setting the temporal and spatial context that is being enacted, such as first-century Jerusalem. This is done through a narrative which is given to the participant either verbally, such as in a sermon, or in writing, such as a scripture or handout. The second step is the development of the Physical space and its corresponding meaning space. The Physical space is constructed through a combination of material objects and events, such as icons, lighting, costumes, music, scents, physical props, and actions. The Meaning space is the symbolic representation of what these physical objects are supposed to mean. Sometimes the symbolic representations are clearly stated in the narrative, for example, describing the labyrinth path as the road to Jerusalem. At other times the meaning of the symbolic representations are not so clearly articulated, and may be evoked by the individual while in the ritual, or explained to them after the ritual. Since participation in ritual varies greatly from participant to participant, the level of comprehension of the meanings of the symbolic representations will also vary from a pre-cognitive or embodied sense, to a completely theoretical understanding of every nuance. The third step is the creation of the Virtual time/space, which is an integration of the Physical space and Meaning space. In Virtual time/space the participant engages in a sense of the ritual "as if" it were real. The Virtual time/space is a matter of perception and so will differ from participant to participant. Though it is closely connected to Physical space and Meaning space, it has a reality of its own. Virtual time/space is liminal in that it mediates between the known and unknown. It heightens experience and it is within Virtual time/space that participants feel power, openness, transcendence, and other transforming experiences and emotions.[64]

In describing Virtual time/space Williams and Boyd "portray ritual as a set of 'artworks' which represent, express, map, model, and otherwise symbolize features of the world and our experience of it."[65] This description of ritual as a model that symbolizes features of the world helps explain the varying reports I have received by informants of their experience on the labyrinth. These reports include descriptions of the labyrinth as Jerusalem, the womb of the Mother Goddess, the underworld, a vortex of energy, a walking meditation, circumambulating the Ka'ba, a path of peace, the brain, and more. All these descriptions imply some belief by participants of the world around them. They fall along a continuum that ranges from highly complex theories articulated in doctrine and texts (Jerusalem), to general ideas found in folk-lore or myths (underworld), to vaguely defined personal worlds of meaning (path of peace). Berger alleged that it is the ritual specialists and the theoreticians of ritual that have fully developed theoretical concepts of a sacred cosmos. Most lay people have pre-cognitive or embodied beliefs about their world. They may not become consciously aware of their beliefs until they are evoked during the ritual, or arise after the ritual in response to questions they are asked about the experience.

Though participants may experience some aspect of their sacred cosmos quite spontaneously during an open labyrinth walk, I am directing my attention to the more elaborate labyrinth rituals which I term scripted ceremonials. Scripted ceremonials, such as liturgical rituals, often have a pedagogical function with a central reason for the ritual to be the transmission of knowledge to the participant. In these rituals the sacred cosmos is clearly described so that the participant understands what aspect of a sacred cosmos is being enacted, and what they need to do to become engaged with it.

Since I am specifically observing rituals on the labyrinth to discover how participants engage themselves in their concept of a sacred cosmos, my working definition of ritual is directed towards its cosmic implications. For this reason I define ritual as an intentional act with representational significance that can both transmit and evoke knowledge, resulting in an engagement with one's sacred cosmos, however that is perceived. This engagement is not necessarily intellectually articulated, but can be experienced through non-discursive cognition and embodiment. This definition contains two components I believe necessary to ritual—intention and the engagement in representational action.

Caroline Humphrey and James Laidlaw refer to intention as a key component in ritual. They describe intention as a particular constellation of factors that turn into ritual what under other circumstances would be considered an ordinary action.[66] Intention ranges along a spectrum from the simple to the complex. The simplest intention is deciding to show up to the ritual. However, this simple intent is all that is necessary to turn the ritual into a lens to focus attention so that an ordinary act is turned into an extraordinary one. At the other end of the spectrum, there is the intent to be part of the design and construction of the ritual, a stage which I call formulation. Formulation includes all the components of ritual design including purpose, audience, place, time, symbolic representation and action. In formulation the decision is often made regarding the level of adaptation and innovation that will be allowed or encouraged. For example, the ritual of a wedding can be formulated in a traditional manner with a ritual specialist (priest) following a liturgy in a church setting, or it can become an innovative ritual designed by the participants outside of conventional structures. Hence, one of the key aspects of formulation is whether the ritual is under the auspices of a ritual specialist or developed by a group or individual. Many of the labyrinth rituals at ELPC were formulated by the Labyrinth Committee which consisted of five to eight people. During a process of open dialogue and brainstorming, decisions were made about labyrinth rituals in terms of time, place, theme, symbols, and music. An example of a complex formulation occurred during one such meeting when the Labyrinth Committee designed a six-week program during the season of Lent, the forty-day period of repentance leading up to Holy Week. The intention was to lead people to a more reflective state on their labyrinth walks during Lent. A journal was created with different meditation themes for each week such as repentance and renewal, along with an inspirational scripture and place to write personal insights. These journals were provided for walkers, along with a poster describing their use, at the usual Wednesday walks to deepen the experience of the Lenten season. This formulation process was quite in-depth including hours of work on designing the journal, collection of appropriate scripture, the financial outlay for printing, making the poster, and the labyrinth set-up.

In some innovative and improvisational rituals there is not a specific stage of formulation. But there is still an intent, or purposeful act, to engage in the ritual. I think that intention is central to ritual, and it is intention that distinguishes ritual from habit.

Some scholars disagree that the intent to involve oneself in the ritual is central to the ritual act but instead describe ritual by its repetitive, rather than intentional attributes. Roy Rappaport describes ritual as that which is ordered, invariant, meticulous, and recurring.[67] Rappaport's definition of ritual could include repetitive acts such as walking the same route every day to work. In doing so there is the implication that the walk has become "ritualized" because there is a consistency to the action and it is a routine, done in the same manner at the same time. Likewise eating dinner at 6 PM could be a ritual, or watching the news from 7:30 to 8:30 could be defined as ritualized behavior. I disagree with this overly broad definition. The fact that something has structure and routine does not make it a ritual. Otherwise every activity done on any type of consistent basis could be labeled a ritual. And while calling the morning commute a ritual may make one feel better about the hour spent in traffic, it is not a ritual. It is commuting to work. There is nothing about it other than what it appears to be.

Referring to these types of routinized behaviors as ritual is based on a definition of ritual that comes from research on traditional cultures where rituals are seen as consistent, reliable, and replicable actions linked to tradition. In this way Rappaport's research on the Maring pig exchange of New Guinea directs his definition of ritual as ordered, invariant, meticulous, and recurring, and that which is "characterized by punctilious repetition and are *thus represented as never changing"* (his italics).[68] Rappaport even includes stylized displays by animals, such as a mating dance, as fitting into his definition of ritual. Though he does not refer to it directly, there is no reason to think that the formality of a 9-5 job and all the structures of life that regularly surround and support that lifestyle could easily meet Rappaport's definition of "formal," that is, an adherence to form.[69]

As a relatively new culture, America does not have thousand year-old rituals that maintain a cohesive community, hence we look for acts that we can label "ritual," as if that somehow creates a more rooted sensibility. The "morning commute," the "executive lunch," and "Saturday at the Mall" in many cases sustain the rhythm of our society, and hence may have the feeling of ritual including the by-product of establishing a sense of place and connection. But the problem in calling any activity that is repetitious and formal a ritual is that the usefulness of the term to describe specific activities comes into jeopardy. I agree with J.Z. Smith that ritual is not habitual, and believe that such a broad usage of the term ritual is ultimately unhelpful.[70] It disregards what I view as a central and necessary component of ritual—intent—which I define as the conscious decision to purposely act.

Labyrinth rituals that are directed toward the construction of a sacred cosmos must also include participant "engagement." Engagement in ritual is not limited to a theoretical involvement or a cognitive interpretation of the ritual. Engagement can also occur on a pre-cognitive level or take place in the body. Theodore Jennings states that ritual is a symbolic structure that is a "primary, engaged, bodily way of knowing," and by which humans understand and construct their world. It is through ritual action, the exploratory "doing," by which one becomes engaged and knowledge is gained.[71] The actions engaged in need to be representational, either through symbol or metaphor. Williams and Boyd refer to the representations of symbol and metaphor in their discussion of Virtual time/space.

There are differences between a symbol and a metaphor, and each is a complex topic that has merited scholarly attention. However I am going to keep my use of these terms simple and directed toward how they are used in specific labyrinth rituals. A symbol is a "representation in physical form of ideas, beliefs, actions, persons, events, etc. . . which bring the observer into connection and participation."[72] A metaphor is "a figure of speech in which one thing is likened to another, different thing, by being spoken of as if it were that other."[73] Both symbols and metaphors are representations of something else. A symbol is a physical representation; a metaphor is a figurative representation. The labyrinth is referred to as a symbol when described as Jerusalem, and a metaphor when it is called "the journey of life." Events that happen on the labyrinth often take metaphorical significance. A common example is a woman who is stuck behind a man who is walking very slowly on the labyrinth, and therefore blocking her more rapid progress to the center. She will describe this event metaphorically as similar to the manner in which movement toward her goals in life are blocked by others who get in her way. Ron Grimes states that "a common characteristic of ritualistic activity is the serious use of metaphor" and that perhaps one way to define ritual is as "the enactment of a metaphor."[74]

In describing the representational power of the labyrinth I will use Williams and Boyd's description of metaphor, which they conflate with images and symbols. They state that although metaphors and symbols are central to ritual, this is not because the metaphor itself transmits knowledge and has a special meaning. In fact they contend that metaphors can be meaningless. The meanings gained by symbols and metaphors are complex and come from interplay between the idea, texts, contexts, people, and interpretations. In their words:

> Words used metaphorically have no special features prior to and independent of the context in which they are used. There is not

metaphorical meaning in the words themselves, by themselves. This means that whatever we carry away from an encounter with a metaphor is the result of a cooperation between its creator, the literal meaning of the words, the context, and our imagination. . . Metaphors are heuristic and create new knowledge not because they contain multiple hidden analogies which only need to be discovered, but because the meaning of metaphors are the product of, are generated by, creative collaboration between the image and the interpreter, who may be situated in changing social and theological conditions. . . Metaphors, in this view, always provoke interpretation and, at the same time, defeat any one, settled interpretation.[75]

The labyrinth is given different meanings by different people in different contexts, in part, because of the various interpretations possible for symbols and metaphors. Though the architectural form of the labyrinth may provide a consistency in the Physical space, the Meaning space can change depending on what metaphors are generated by the interpreters. These multiple metaphors create multiple interpretations among the participants, and lead to multiple perceptions of Virtual time/space created in labyrinth rituals.

Conclusion

The labyrinth is a template upon which ideas of a sacred cosmos can be depicted. A sacred cosmos is a socially constructed framework that explains and justifies the seen and unseen world, providing for humans a system of order, placement, and meaning. Ideas of a sacred cosmos change among cultures and exist along a continuum that goes from highly complex theories articulated in doctrines and texts, to general ideas embedded in folklore and social practices, to vaguely defined personally negotiated worlds of meaning.

One of the most important functions of a sacred cosmos is to provide placement in a world of meaning. When connection to a person's world of meaning becomes unstable due to disruptions in life, it is the task of ritual to link the individual to their idea of a sacred cosmos, thus reestablishing their place in the world. Ritual does this in part by connecting humans to communal and cosmic rhythms. Ritual also can reconstruct a sacred cosmos through the creation of a Virtual time/space where the participants act "as if" their experience of the sacred cosmos is real. This act of creating a Virtual time/space is done through a multifaceted interaction of the physical objects and events used in the ritual with the symbolic or metaphorical interpretations of these objects and events. Since the interpretations of symbols and metaphors are complex and situated in changing social and theological conditions, the rituals on the labyrinth are also complex and change depending on their context.

The next two chapters provide examples of labyrinth rituals that highlight some aspects of a sacred cosmos. Chapter 5 uses liturgical rituals to illustrate how very highly complex theories of cosmology, like Christianity, can be constructed through ritual. Chapter 6 demonstrates how more general and less articulated ideas of a sacred cosmos can also be enacted in labyrinth rituals. Whether the framework described in one's sacred cosmos comes from traditional institutional religion or from personally negotiated beliefs, it can still provide a sense of order, placement, and meaning.

5
Church-Based Liturgical Labyrinth Rituals

A sacred cosmos can be evaluated by several different measures, including its history, traditions, ethics, philosophy, sacrality, adherents, integration into the society, and the deceptively simple question: is it the truth? These determinants join together to provide a fuller understanding of the cause and consequences of belief. But my main consideration for evaluating a cosmology, or frame, by which people perceive the world rests on whether it constructs a world that provides order, meaning, and placement.

Order is literally at the root of cosmology (from the Greek *kosmos*, meaning order), and stands in direct contrast to its opposite, chaos, or disorder. A sacred cosmos is what separates the chaos of life into distinct divisions that makes life understandable. Even general distinctions such as good/evil or earth/sky provide an orientation to the world that establishes balance. More specific distinctions are found in a framework consisting of the five structural elements of a sacred cosmos—Who, What, When, Where, and How—that were introduced in Chapter 4. Whether general or specific, the framework of a sacred cosmos provides an order that provides meaning to the events that transpire through life and establishes an individual's sense of his/her place in the world.

Christianity is one of the world's most complex and fully articulated sacred cosmologies. The order of the Christian universe is clearly laid out through its long history, philosophical inquiry, traditional practices, and church doctrine. Christianity provides clear guidelines for adherents to follow so that their life has order, meaning and a sense of place. As discussed in Chapter 4, two central components that provide this place are temporal and spatial, or the "when" and "where" of the world. In

Christianity the "when" and "where" are combined in the liturgical calendar. My church-based research site, East Liberty Presbyterian Church (ELPC) used the labyrinth as part of their celebration of the liturgical calendar.

The Liturgical Calendar

The Liturgical Calendar contains within it an overview of the Christian sacred cosmos. It is based on what I have termed Theological time in that it revolves around events in the life of Christ. For Christians, both the broader and more specific views of time originate with Christ. In the broader spectrum, Christ is God's ultimate intervention in humanity; time is divided into all that occurred and led up to the revelation of Christ (BC—before Christ) and all that has occurred since (AD—Anno Domino, Year of the Lord). Time also stretches into the future with the promise of Christ's eventual return, and even into eternity with the salvation of faithful followers.[1]

However within this broad canvas of time there is a yearly cyclical experience called the liturgical year that revolves around Christ's birth, death, and resurrection. The liturgical year links Christ to the lives of Christians through the celebration of the holy days surrounding the Incarnation (Christmas) and the Resurrection (Easter) as a circular recurring form, creating a closed cycle that turns back on itself at the end of the length of a year to repeat again. Although the liturgical year has some connections to the natural world (Christmas is linked to the winter solstice, for example), it cannot be considered based on occurrences of nature. Rather it was constructed to link society to the events in Christ's life and regulate society by providing a rhythm and temporal ordering.

The Presbyterian publication *Liturgical Year: The Worship of God* states that the use of the liturgical year for Presbyterians is a phenomenon of the twentieth century.[2] Soon after the Reformation there was an attempt by Protestants to use the liturgical calendar of the Catholics by keeping Christmas, Good Friday, Easter, Ascension, and Pentecost; eliminating Advent, Lent, and All Saints Day; and by cutting out Catholic feast and fast days. The attempt did not work and the liturgical calendar was eliminated in its entirety in 1644. Since these early Puritan reformers shaped Presbyterianism as it was practiced in colonial America, there were no Christian festivals observed in the seventeenth century and those who celebrated Christmas were punished by being placed in stocks. By 1789 there was no reference to the liturgical calendar, but after the Civil War ended interest grew in Christmas and Easter.

It was not until the early twentieth century that the liturgical calendar was placed into the Presbyterian Book of Common Worship. In 1906 only Good Friday, Easter, Advent, and Christmas were included; 1932 saw the addition of Lent (called Preparation for Easter), Palm Sunday, Ascension Day, Pentecost, and All Saints Day. In 1946 Maundy Thursday (called Thursday before Easter) and Trinity Sunday were added. The Second Vatican Council (1962-1965) made changes to the Catholic liturgy which led to the creation of an ecumenical liturgical calendar under the creation of Consultation on Common Texts (C.C.T.), of which the Presbyterian Church was a part.

In 1984 a task force was appointed to prepare a book to celebrate the liturgical calendar, resulting in the adoption in 1989 by the Presbyterian Church USA of the *Directory for Worship for the Liturgical Year*. According to this book, in addition to Sunday (the Lord's Day) the liturgical year consists of two constantly repeating cycles: The Incarnation Cycle which includes four weeks of Advent, twelve days of Christmas, and Epiphany; and The Resurrection Cycle which includes forty days of Lent, fifty days of Easter, and Pentecost. These two cycles are separated by Ordinary Time which extends from the day after Epiphany to the Tuesday before Ash Wednesday, and the day after Pentecost through the Saturday before Advent (see fig. 17).

In order to illustrate the ways in which the labyrinth has been combined with the liturgical calendar to engage people in the Christian cosmos, I examine Christian liturgical rituals that were enacted at ELPC. I began my research at ELPC in 1996 at the dedication of their first labyrinth. At the time they were the first church in Pittsburgh to have a labyrinth. By 2003 ELPC had three canvas labyrinths and a permanent labyrinth approved to be built outside in a courtyard. Proudly called the "grandmother" of labyrinths in the area, its lending program had introduced many other denominations in the city and surrounding areas to the ritual of walking the labyrinth.

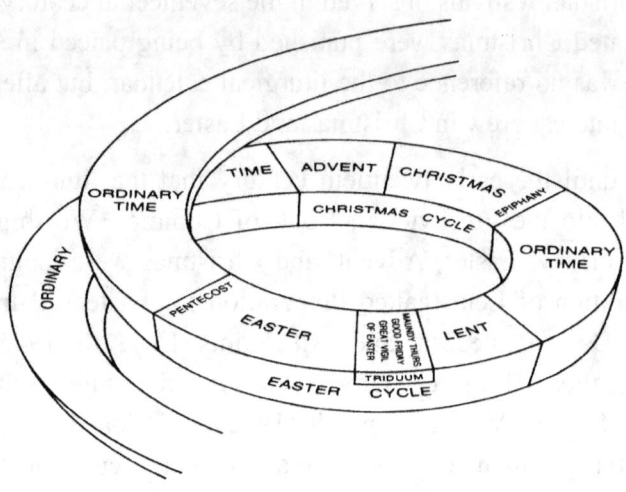

Figure 17: Liturgical Year.

ELPC is a large, liberal Presbyterian church. Its use of the labyrinth is tied to the Veriditas church-based network. Members at ELPC were introduced to the labyrinth in a Seekers class by reading Artress's 1995 book *Walking a Sacred Path*. A group of interested members bought a Veriditas seed kit and created their own Chartres-style labyrinth with volunteer help for a little over $2000 in materials. Heidi, the pastor in charge of the labyrinth ministry, went to Grace Cathedral in San Francisco to take the Veriditas labyrinth facilitator training. She subsequently trained a group of volunteers to help with the labyrinth using the Veriditas material.

Since most of my research on church labyrinths comes from my six years of participant observation at ELPC, I believe an introduction to the church is in order. ELPC is not your typical Presbyterian church. It was built in 1931 by a gift from the Mellons, one of Pittsburgh's steel families, at the cost of $4M during the same period that shanty towns were dotting the city due to the Great Depression. It is a huge church, modeled after a medieval cathedral with flying buttresses and magnificent stained glass. In 2001 the church had an endowment of around $30M (depending on the stock market), the interest of which makes up 90% of its annual budget.

Taking up an entire city block, it was built in what was once an upscale neighborhood and catered to the wealthy; now the neighborhood suffers from years of steady decline and is known as a place best not traveled after dark. One night I remember being somewhat surprised when one of the burly security guards, who are always posted at the entrance, offered to walk me to my car. Since that time I have parked close to and within view of the main entrance. In the middle of the decay of the surrounding neighborhood ELPC, with its intricate architecture and towering steeple, the church stands like a beacon of hope, and is named The Cathedral of Hope.

Bob Chestnut, the head pastor during the years of my research, said the church has been embraced by the community and that there has never been any vandalism. In fact, this juxtaposition of apparent wealth with the inner city has led to a racial, class, and worship diversity that makes ELPC a benchmark church in the Pittsburgh area. In 2002 at the retirement of Chestnut after fourteen years of service, a lifelong member stated: "He helped us see the changing community around us not as a detriment but as an opportunity. Most other churches in similar situations have to search for a mission, for a vision. He let us see that our mission was all around us."[3]

A canvas labyrinth is laid out on Mondays and Wednesdays in either the social hall, gym, or outside courtyard, for the public to engage in unsupervised "open walks." There are also more elaborate "scripted ceremonials" such as rituals to celebrate the liturgical calendar, which are scheduled during special times.

My typical visit to the church labyrinth for an open walk begins with first signing in at the front desk with my name, time of arrival, and intended purpose under the watchful but pleasant eye of the security guard. From there I stride past the daycare center, a study group for the Course in Miracles, an art show consisting of black and white photographs of "non-traditional" families (i.e., gays and lesbians), the café where for $5.88 a tasty lunch is served (dessert is extra), a gym where ten local teenagers are playing basketball (the church even has a bowling alley though I have never seen it used), and down into the bowels of the church to the social hall where, lit only by the pale glow of torch lamps and candles, the labyrinth awaits. Even with large signs marking the way to the labyrinth I still manage to get lost periodically, and without the signs it is easy to end up in entirely the wrong place.

When moving through this variety of activities I feel like I have entered a small city. There is always something going on, and with people coming and going the church feels like a beehive of activity. The facility houses a homeless shelter, food pantry, and soup kitchen. It offers four worship services a week, including a Taizé worship, and one specifically for the homeless men, for a total weekly worship attendance at around 400. The church has opened its doors to the entire city and is used by many groups for meetings and a broad array of offerings that include medicine wheel walks, grief groups, world-beat parties, Handel's messiah, a Jazz mass, and blessings of the animals.

ELPC has embraced its role as a link between worlds which is reflected in its strategic plan:

> Our congregation seeks to promote peace, justice and human dignity; to reflect a spirit of openness, sharing and learning in our ministry and mission; to build a richly diverse faith community that witnesses to oneness in Christ across all boundaries of race, social class, culture, gender and sexual identity.[2]

Based on its size, complexity, and diversity it is not surprising that the bureaucracy is equally complex and that the demands on the administrators, including the pastors, are great. It is a small corporation, with decisions made in the typical Presbyterian manner, by committee. There are no fast decisions but one gets the sense that ELPC is moving toward a tolerant, diverse, and creative future. However it was not always this way and dissention within the church to the increasingly liberal and diverse offerings (including the labyrinth) led to conflict and the eventual loss of one-third of its members. Dr. Chestnut wrote in 2000 about the transition from a conservative mainstream church to its current transformation in his book *Transforming the Mainline Church*.[4]

ELPC is not a typical Presbyterian church, in size, endowment, or congregation. Hence I do not intend to imply that its use of the labyrinth is typical of other churches that include a labyrinth in their worship. The comparative use of labyrinths by churches has not been my area of study, though it would be an interesting topic to pursue. I can say that based on my knowledge of what other smaller churches do with the labyrinth— including Catholic, Non-Denominational Fundamentalist, Episcopalian, and Methodist—ELPC's use of the labyrinth is different more by degree that by content. It is, as would be expected, more extensive and diverse in its offerings than other churches nearby, but it is still firmly rooted in its Christian mission and it views the labyrinth as a ministry.

Even though ELPC includes the labyrinth as part of its Christian ministry, it does so out of the context of the main Sunday service. There is some disagreement in the church over whether the labyrinth is "Presbyterian." Labyrinth history goes back over 4,000 years and is linked to the pagan cultures of Egypt, Greece, and Rome. Therefore it is not unusual for there to be objections to the labyrinth as "pagan," an objection that is easily countered by pointing to a later medieval use of labyrinths by the Catholic Church. In the twelfth to sixteenth centuries, sixteen labyrinths large enough to walk were built in cathedrals and churches, mostly in France but also in Italy, Belgium, and West Germany.[5] The labyrinth that is used most often at ELPC is modeled after the earliest surviving cathedral labyrinth which was built at Chartres, France c. 1200 CE (see fig. 5). This disengages the labyrinth from paganism and places it firmly into Christian territory.

However, there is still the problem that although the labyrinth may be Christian, it is Roman Catholic, and nearly 500 years and a Protestant Reformation separate Catholicism and Presbyterianism. No matter how you contextualize it, liturgical rituals using a medieval catholic icon smacks of the very type of activity that Protestants have shunned. In an open meeting at the church in 2001 to discuss opposition to the decision by the church to build a permanent labyrinth the question was brought up: Is the labyrinth Presbyterian? As a member of the Labyrinth Committee and involved in the preparation for this meeting, I knew the question was expected and the committee came prepared with newsletters from other Presbyterian churches to show that they were using the labyrinth, and teaching material published by the Presbyterian Church that showed how to incorporate the labyrinth into church curriculum. There was even a quote in this material by John Calvin where he metaphorically compared the journey to God with a labyrinth:

> For we should so reason that the splendor of the divine countenance, which even the apostle calls "unapproachable," is for us like an inexplicable labyrinth unless we are conducted into it by the thread of the Word; so that it is better to limp along this path than to dash with all speed outside it.[6]

But ironically, the more the Committee pulled in material to attempt to link this Catholic icon to the Presbyterian Church, the more it provided ample proof that no, the labyrinth is not Presbyterian. At the meeting when the question was in fact raised about the Presbyterianism of the labyrinth, Chestnut did not refer to the data the committee had provided or make any attempt to show the labyrinth was Presbyterian. Instead he stated that the Presbyterians came from Catholic roots. At ELPC there is an interest in accepting the Catholic ancestry of Presbyterians. Many of the services and rituals the church enacts are influenced by Catholicism, including the labyrinth, Taizé, Stations of the Cross, processions, the worship of Mary, and use of the liturgical year.

There is no doubt that something is stirring in Protestant churches, something that has echoes of a Great Awakening, a time when a desire for a lived experience of the sacred was more important than the written word.[7] Chestnut described this desire when he discussed spiritually hungry people not getting nourished by the textual food provided in Protestant churches.

> We're not just minds, sitting on our rumps trying to integrate some concepts. We're on a journey, we're on a quest. It's often in the dark, or in the semi-dark. We're seeking the light. We need the light. We're finding our way but it's not altogether a clearly laid out path either. We have some notion of where we're going but there is

an element of risk and uncertainty and confusion and disorientation in it as well.

One way that ELPC has begun that quest is through the labyrinth. Though the labyrinth is used in varying ways at ELPC, this section will focus on how rituals on the labyrinth and the liturgical calendar combine to construct aspects of the Christian cosmos.

The liturgical calendar structures the ritual season and shapes a major part of the worship services at ELPC. The labyrinth is one of the many ways that ELPC observes and celebrates the liturgical year, and during the six years I have conducted research at ELPC I have seen liturgical rituals on the labyrinth for Advent, Epiphany, Ash Wednesday, Lent, Good Friday, and Pentecost. In addition to providing an opportunity to worship, these rituals have a pedagogical function in that they teach some aspect of the Christian cosmos. For example, they purposely reconstruct some event in Christianity, such as Christ's crucifixion, in elaborate formal rituals that I call "scripted ceremonials."

In providing a description of scripted ceremonials constructed on the template of the labyrinth, I will use the three-part formula I discussed in Chapter 4 to explain how a Virtual time/space was created that enabled participants to feel "as if" they were part of the event being noted. A summary of this formula is as follows: First, the temporal and spatial context for the particular part of the liturgical year being celebrated is established with a narrative which comes from scripture, prayer, text, and hymns. Second, these temporal and spatial contexts are constructed on the labyrinth by means of Physical space, which includes physical objects such as icons, scents, lightings, and images, and Meaning space, which includes the symbolic and metaphorical significance of the physical objects that are used. This leads to the third part of the formula which is the creation of a Virtual time/space where participants feel "as if" the experience is real, allowing them to actively engage in their own idea of the cosmos. The first ritual to consider occurs at Advent.

Incarnation Cycle: An Advent Ritual

The liturgical calendar begins with Advent, the first event in the Incarnation cycle. The Incarnation cycle shifts the focus of Christ's birth from the single day of Christmas to a period of forty days across a span of three months. In 2001 Chestnut stated the following about Christmas where he emphasized the importance of establishing the correct tempo of the season, which when disregarded can lead to disharmony:

> Much of the problem that many people experience with the season of the year we're now entering has to do with bad timing based on spiritual misperceptions. The Christmas season is rushed, largely due to commercial pressure, and everything comes to a screeching halt with a big letdown on the 26th of December. If we get the timing right in our church observances, we can help to counter these unfortunate trends in the secular culture. We're really talking about three seasons here and they are traditionally interrelated in ways that make good sense spiritually and psychologically. First is the season of Advent, beginning the fourth Sunday before Christmas. It is a period for quiet preparation and anticipation, not for premature celebration. Second is the season of Christmas that begins on December 25 and lasts for twelve days—an extended time to celebrate the joy of God's love in the birth of Christ. Third is Epiphany on January 6—a time to share the gift of God's love with all the world (represented by the gentile Magi who came to worship the Christ child). Do you see the sense of it all? First preparation, then celebration, then reaching out to share the gift of God we've received—all of which should lead us into the new year with our faith renewed and our spirits lifted.

A rhythm is set through observance of the liturgical calendar that links personal, communal, and cosmic life. This rhythm begins with Advent, the four weeks of preparation for Christ's birth. Advent is a time filled with expectancy, looking forward with joyful anticipation to Christmas, the time when God incarnates on earth through Christ the Savior, and that "the Word became flesh and dwelt among us, full of grace and truth" (John 1:14).

For three consecutive years at ELPC this quality of expectancy and the preparation of Christ's birth have been observed in association with Mary, his mother, in an Advent ritual called *Walk with Mary*. While Mary is not typically celebrated in Protestant churches, she has become closely associated with the Chartres labyrinth and has been developing a presence at ELPC.

Pamela was instrumental in bringing the labyrinth to ELPC and taught a three-week workshop on Mary at the church at which time she described Mary as the "feminine face of God." In an interview with Pamela she stated the following about the association of the labyrinth with Mary:

> Christianity has been very patriarchal. I've missed the feminine. The labyrinth resonates with me and Mary resonates with me and the feminine. The rose in the center of the labyrinth is the symbol of Mary. It is the womb of Mary. Mary points the way to Christ. Mary is birthing the Christ within us. I was brought up thinking Mary was something for the Catholics. But she's for everyone and can be a role model of faith, trusting in the Holy Spirit. She said yes and never wavered. She is a symbol of wholeness and healing. We are reclaiming our catholic heritage with Taizé and the labyrinth. People need symbols, and people need solitude, meditation and prayer. Presbyterians have always been so head-oriented.

This association of Mary with Advent is easy to understand, once the link has been made between Advent and the experience of preparing for birth. Mary is the one who is preparing, Mary is the one expectant, Mary is the one carrying the seed, and Mary is the one who has within her the "indwelling Christ." The three *Walk with Mary* events in December 2000, 2001, and 2002 were similar and modeled after a pilgrimage of the same name offered by Lauren Artress to the labyrinth at the Chartres Cathedral in France. Pamela and another woman, Rene, went on that pilgrimage and then organized the rituals at ELPC to recreate the same powerful experience they had at France. They described the *Walk with Mary* ritual at Chartres which began at night:

> We started down there—the underground, the oldest part—walking where people had pilgrimaged for years. In past times people joining the church would walk this path. Walking up from the catacombs was like being born again. When down there we burned/released anything negative. . . At the labyrinth Gregorian chants were being sung by men and women in different languages, Latin, Greek, Hebrew. We were given a rose as we entered the labyrinth. . . The whole thing was meant to symbolize a rebirth into Mary. There were all denominations of people that went to this *Walk with Mary*.

I asked if they felt Mary's presence in the labyrinth at Chartres and Pamela said: "I did. I don't know about anyone else. There was a statue of Mary when she was being transformed into heaven—Ascension—I felt like Mary was drawing me to her. Afterwards I put my rose (given to her during the ritual) there." Then I asked if Pamela felt Mary's presence on the ELPC labyrinth and she answered: "Especially with the Mary walk."

In the Advent ritual one part of Christian cosmology—the incarnation of the central deity—is constructed so that participants can fully engage in the process "as if" they, along with Mary, prepare for the birth of Christ. The ritual began in the small chapel led by Catherine, the minister. Seventy-five people were in attendance along with five musicians and singers.[8]

Stage one of the formula, developing the temporal and spatial context, was created using a variety of narrative sources including the Bible, the program booklet, hymns, and an introduction by Pamela. The New Testament story told in Matthew 1:16-25 and Luke 1:27-56 and 2:1-7 set the temporal context of a time when Mary was full of pregnancy soon before the birth of Christ. The spatial context was not a manger in Bethlehem, for this would be the space celebrated at Christmas, but rather the dwelling place of Christ during this time of Advent—Mary's womb.

In the introduction Pamela told the participants that the ritual was inspired by a pilgrimage that Lauren Artress led to Chartres Cathedral in

France entitled *Walk with Mary* and described Mary as the feminine aspect of God. In the chapel songs about "preparing the way for the Lord" were sung and meditation was used to direct participants' thoughts toward Mary as the expectant mother of Christ. The handout for the 2002 *Walk with Mary* stated: "Tonight we celebrate Mary, the Mother of Jesus, the birth mother of God... seeking to know more fully Mary's courage, strength and trust that opened her heart to give birth to the divine. Through her body flowed our salvation."

The second part of the formula involved the creation of the Physical and Meaning spaces. The Physical space was constructed by using a variety of music, lighting, scents, and sounds that will be described shortly. Its associated Meaning space was generated through the symbolic representations attached to those physical components. The central meaning of the ritual was for participants to identify with the pregnant Mary and to act "as if" it was not only Mary, but also themselves that contained the indwelling Christ. There were prayers and chants to bring the participant into closer connection, even association, with Mary. For example, a pink prayer card was provided for each participant during a silent meditation that had a drawing of Mary and baby Jesus. The card stated: "During this silence, please write or draw on the enclosed prayer card some thoughts you might have about Mary and her gifts to us. Thinking about Mary may be new to you. If so, you are encouraged to look at her story through the experiences of your own life."

Throughout the ritual in images, song, and literature the participants were told that they too contained the indwelling Christ and that during this time of Advent they too could give birth to the new. This message was supported throughout the entire event, beginning with the cover of the program which had a drawing of Mary with Christ in her womb and the title "Mary: An Icon of Possibility" (see fig. 18). The program stated: "...we will prepare ourselves in heart, mind and spirit for the indwelling presence of Christ." A quote by Thomas Merton confirmed this: "Christ is born to us in order that he may appear to the whole world through us."

Figure 18: Program for Advent ritual at ELPC. Author's photo.

After song, prayer, and meditation in the chapel the participants, each with a lit candle, processed through the darkened church through the magnificent gothic sanctuary, also illuminated only by candles. At various places along the darkened route were shrines to Mary, lit with candles and draped with scarves, which were made of photos, drawing, icons, or images from various cultures including Native American, Guatemalan, and African (see fig. 19).

Stationed near the shrines at selected intervals throughout the church were male and female vocalists singing medieval chants, which created a beautiful and haunting effect of walking toward and away from the sounds, which echoed throughout the sanctuary. This created an atmosphere of otherworldliness, encouraging participants to leave their everyday world.

Figure 19: Shrine to Mary at Advent ritual at ELPC. Author's photo.

From the sanctuary the participants moved down a rarely used narrow winding stone stairway, also lit only by candlelight. The winding stairway ended in the darkened basement at the social hall where the labyrinth was lit only by candles which encircled it. The symbolic meaning of this journey through the narrow passage was to recreate for the participant the journey through the birth canal. Pamela stated: "The tunnels are like the birth canal and the doorways are shaped liked vesica. The vesica is like a vagina. We entered the part of the vagina. Then we went on to be symbolically re-baptized and then walked up to the labyrinth which was a symbol of our rebirth…"

In the center of the illuminated labyrinth was a wooden baptismal font filled with water. It was unusual to see objects in the center of labyrinths and this rather large baptismal font dominated the space (see fig. 20).

As participants filled the hall, Catherine, the pastor who was leading the event, welcomed them to the labyrinth. She then explained that the waters in the baptismal font could be seen, among other things, as the birth waters of Christ. I was surprised to hear such a graphic representation of birth in association with Christ, whose bodily functions are rarely mentioned. The Bible says only that Mary gave birth to her firstborn son and wrapped him in bands of cloth. There are writings that have more graphic accounts of his birth, but they are not in the Canon.

Figure 20: Baptismal font at Advent ritual at ELPC. Author's photo.

I wondered if I heard Catherine correctly, but the symbolism was repeated in the written program which stated: "The Chartres labyrinth has at its center a baptismal font, to remind you of the waters of creation, the birth waters of Jesus, your own baptism, and the waters of your rebirth." Participants were reminded that in the same way that Mary held the indwelling Christ and prepared to give birth, they too carried the indwelling Christ, and that those waters symbolized their own rebirth. During the labyrinth walk I saw many people pause at the baptismal font, where some placed water on their heads or crossed themselves.

Using the three-part formula of constructing a Virtual space/time, one can see how the narrative in the Bible and in the program set the necessary context for the ritual by linking it both to the temporal and spatial elements of Christ's birth.

The narrative was constructed by the Physical Space which included the shrines, dark and winding hallway, labyrinth, singers, and soft candlelight. The Meaning space was the symbolic representation given to these physical elements: the shrines repeatedly brought participants into full awareness of Mary; the winding hallway was a symbol of the birth canal; the labyrinth as the womb; the baptismal font was the birth waters of Christ. The singing of medieval chants to Mary which reverberated in a candlelit room created an otherworldly atmosphere. The Physical and Meaning space combined to create the Virtual time/space of Bethlehem right before Mary gave birth to Jesus.

Virtual time/space is a subjective awareness brought about by a personal experience that arises from the gestalt of the ritual. One participant's quote gives an example of how the Virtual time/space was perceived:

> I can say that as I was walking the labyrinth I had images I never even previously considered—the womb of Mary swollen with possibility, and at its center, Jesus waiting to be born. I imagined Mary's water breaking, a central indicator of full blown labor and imminent delivery, images of Jesus flowing down the birth waters, images of Jesus wet, bloody, wrinkled and newborn came to me, unbidden. The words and the mental images they evoked were unexpected. And when I got to the center I looked into the waters of the baptismal font and imagined them colored red with blood.

The Christian cosmos is clearly evident in this ritual and can be explicated using the five structural elements of a sacred cosmos. Who, are the central figures of the incarnation, Jesus and Mary; What, is the story of the incarnation of Christ; When, is the temporal period soon before Mary gives birth; Where, is the spatial element of Mary's womb; and How, is the symbolic enactment of the story through ritual, song, prayer, meditation, and procession.

Reflections on Advent: The Recovery of the Feminine

The *Walk with Mary* Advent ritual directs attention to some of the dynamics of the current Labyrinth Movement, particularly its strong connection to Mary in particular and the feminine in general. As stated in

Chapter 3, Mary is associated with the Chartres labyrinth because Chartres Cathedral is dedicated to Mary and because of the six petals in the center of the labyrinth, which is seen by some as a rose, a symbol of Mary. This rose center is so strongly associated with Mary that tensions arose among members of the Labyrinth Committee at ELPC when a Santa Rosa labyrinth was bought as a third labyrinth for the church. The Santa Rosa labyrinth is a modified Chartres style, about twenty-five feet in diameter, with seven-circuits instead of eleven, and no rose-shaped center. The lack of the rose center was seen as reason enough for some members of the Labyrinth Committee to question the use of the Santa Rosa at ELPC. Later when a design for a permanent labyrinth for the church was being discussed, one member made her views clearly known that she only wanted the Chartres labyrinth with the rose-center to be built, due to its association with Mary. The Committee also bought a statue of Mary to place in the labyrinth during some labyrinth walks. Not everyone on the Labyrinth Committee supported this association of the labyrinth with Mary. One member did not attend the *Walk with Mary* ritual, even though the Committee sponsored it, because she did not care for the strong association made between Mary and the labyrinth. She believed instead that the focus should be kept on Jesus and his role as son of God.

Besides the specific connection between the Chartres labyrinth and Mary, there is the more general association with any labyrinth, regardless of style, with the feminine. This is due to the fact that the labyrinth's shape can be seen as resembling a uterus or womb. Women at times refer to their walk into the labyrinth as a metaphor of "walking into the womb of the Mother" (as in Divine Goddess image), and more concretely as their own mother's womb. One woman states that: "Treading the labyrinth for the first time was difficult for me—it felt like I was re-entering my mother's womb, and I could only feel intense grief..."[9]

This visual connection between the form of the labyrinth and the womb is further emphasized by its use in two other cultural contexts. The first is found among the Hopi Indians of the Southwestern United States. Frank Waters's 1963 *The Book of the Hopi* describes the two labyrinth shapes of the Hopi, which resemble the seven-circuit Classical style, as relating to a womb and a mother giving birth. This connects the labyrinths with the Hopi myth of the Emergence into the Fourth World. The symbol is commonly known as *Tapu'at* (Mother and Child) and represents, among other things, the arms of the mother wrapped around the child. Waters states "The two ends symbolize the two stages of life—the unborn child within the womb of Mother Earth, and the child after it is born, the line symbolizing the umbilical cord and the path of Emergence."[10] In India the labyrinth image of the *Chakra-vyuha yantra* also strengthens the link between the womb and the labyrinth. This *yantra* was designed to help the unborn child find its way out of the labyrinthine uterus, thereby easing birth.[11]

Walking the labyrinth is also seen as an intuitive and embodied ritual. It is conceived as more "right-brain, feminine" and is in contrast to the left-brain masculine seen in the intellectually conceived sermons of mainline Protestantism, or the patriarchy of the Catholic Church. As one informant stated: "The labyrinth is a welcome relief, a connection to the feminine means of worship and contrast to the patriarchal foundation of the church."

Artress, at a September 1999 workshop at ELPC, reported: "The labyrinth is a feminine receptive archetype about cooperation, flowing, and allowing. That's what we need on the planet at this time. We need receptivity and community building, a tool for opening our consciousness." A man in the audience agreed with her assessment by saying: "The problem with our culture is we've gone down the masculine analytical path. We're out of balance and need these feminine qualities. We need to be more integrated but the rise of fundamentalism is going against this."

The enhancement of these qualities of receptivity and intuition are part of the labyrinth's appeal at ELPC. Chestnut says:

> Our Presbyterian tradition has been so heavily left-brain, logical, rational, linear, non-emotional, word-oriented. That has its place, but it needs balance and increasingly I think for spiritually hungry people that alone is not enough. There needs to be intuitive, there needs to be the experiential, there needs to be mystical, and there needs to be the full self involved. Not just a sitting and listening to

cognitive concepts. So, the body is involved, obviously, in walking the labyrinth. You're putting your whole being into it.

The experience of walking the labyrinth and partaking in labyrinth rituals has an appeal to women. I have found that approximately 75% of labyrinth walkers are women, the same percentage cited by Artress during a labyrinth retreat at ELPC. Perhaps this is partly because there is very little dogma or clericalism, traits that are linked to the patriarchal aspects of religion, associated with the labyrinth. The experiential interiority found in labyrinth rituals has been largely relegated to the world of women's experience, and therefore it may offer a more feminized approach to the divine. Even the liturgical Christian rituals allow for a great deal of creative expression and could hardly be considered routinized.

Finally, leadership roles in the Labyrinth Movement also tend to be held by women. The Labyrinth Committee at ELPC for the past four years has been almost exclusively female. The two ministers who most often used the labyrinth at ELPC were women. The first President of TLS was also a woman and when it came time to select a new president in 2003 it was considered important that a woman be chosen. The TLS Board of Directors also has a majority of women.

In spite of the strong female presence at TLS it still attracts more males than ELPC. This is likely due to the fact that TLS includes different contexts for the labyrinth than just the church's use as a Christian ministry. TLS members use the labyrinth in corporate, educational, medical, therapeutic, magical, and mathematical venues, as well as spiritual and religious. Many of the men central to TLS are involved in the design and construction of labyrinths, with several operating full-time labyrinth businesses. Other male members are interested in the mathematical qualities of labyrinths, known as sacred geometry. All of these areas are quite different than the intuitive and emotional spiritual *foci* mentioned in association with women.

An Epiphany Ritual: The Magi's Journey

Advent is followed by the twelve days of Christmas. After Christmas comes Epiphany on January 6th. Epiphany comes from the Greek word *epiphaneia*, which means manifestation. It is during Epiphany that the Magi followed the star of Bethlehem and by its light discovered Christ, the "light of the world."[12] The Magi were most likely from Persia and were gentiles, or non-Jews. Their journey across the desert to find the Christ child is considered a demonstration of the importance of Christ and Christianity to all the peoples of the world, regardless of race, religion, or class. The 1998 Epiphany ritual at ELPC re-constructed this part of Christian cosmos so that participants could partake in the Magi's journey.

Using the three-part formula used to create Virtual time/space I will describe the ritual of Epiphany and the Magi's journey. First, the temporal and spatial contexts were established from the narrative. The narrative came from the New Testament, Matthew 2:1-19, which describes the story of the Magi who left their home in the East and followed the star of Bethlehem to find the baby Jesus. Once they found Jesus they honored him with gifts. They warned Mary and Joseph of the dangers of King Herod, whom they had met on their way to Bethlehem, and advised them to escape to Egypt. The Magi did not go back to Herod as he had demanded, but instead returned from whence they came by a different route. The temporal context established was Christ's infancy and the period of the Magi's journey; the spatial context was the path of the journey which began in the East as they followed the star to the town of Bethlehem.

Second, the Physical space of the ritual began at the Chapel where the participants were led in procession by candlelight through the darkened sanctuary, down to the social hall where the labyrinth awaited. The Meaning Space, which is created by the symbolic and metaphorical representations of the Physical space, was articulated in the flyer designed for the event. The flyer symbolically linked the procession through the sanctuary and the walk on the labyrinth to the path of the Magi as they journeyed across the desert in search of Christ. The candles were said to represent not only the light of the Star of Bethlehem, but also the Christ the "light of the world." The flyer stated:

> How do we go forth from Christmas? How do we discern our way? Our Epiphany retreat offers an opportunity to focus on your personal journey, following the three wise ones, the light which leads to Christ, along an illuminated journey throughout the evening using candles to light your way. There will be a candlelit prayer walk and anointing with oil on the labyrinth.

Third, the creation of a Virtual time/space occurred from the integration of the Physical and Meaning Space. In the Virtual time/space the participants acted "as if" they were on the same journey as the Magi. The correlation between the Magi and the participants was made clear in the narrative of the flyers. In 1999 the flyer stated:

> ...when will we have the time to make the long, slow journey across the burning desert as did the magi? Or sit and watch the stars as did the shepherds? Or brood over the coming of the child as did Mary? For each of us there is a desert to travel. A star to discover... And a being within ourselves to bring to light.

Once the Magi met the Christ child they became transformed, and instead of going back to Herod, they "return by a different way." The Magi are on a journey, in the same way that Christians are on a journey, to find Christ and be transformed by his light.

It stated in the 1999 Epiphany flyer: "We are all pilgrims traveling together along God's holy path." Just as the Magi went forward to find the Christ, symbolically represented as the center of the labyrinth, so did the participants go forward to the center of the labyrinth where they were anointed with oil. And just as the Magi "return by a different way," having been changed by their experience, so too did the participants return back along the labyrinth's path, transformed.

The Christian cosmos is again clearly enacted in this ritual and can be understood as being constructed through the five structural elements of a sacred cosmos. Who, are the central figures of Christ and Mary as well as the secondary figures of the Magi, Joseph, and Herod; What, is the Biblical narrative of the discovery of Christ by the gentiles; When, is the time of Christ's early infancy; Where, is the path leading from the East to Bethlehem; How, is through procession and anointing with oil. Through walking the path of the labyrinth the participants act "as if" they were following the Magi in their journey to first find and then be illuminated by Christ.

Reflections on Epiphany: The Three-Fold Path

A frequent metaphor for the labyrinth is a path or journey, and at times the path is directly associated with some specific event, as in this case, the travels of the Magi. But when not used to represent a specific journey, as at an open walk, the path is described in many contemporary Christian settings as a "three-fold path." This description of the labyrinth walk as a three-fold path has become so attached to the Christian use of the labyrinth as to be nearly institutionalized, not only at ELPC but at many other churches as well. ELPC has a large posterboard in purple and gold with the heading "How to Walk the Labyrinth" followed by "There are three stages of the walk: Release, Illumination, and Union," with a description of each. There are also flyers available for visitors which describe the walk in this fashion.

The beginnings of this attachment of the labyrinth walk with the three stages goes back to Artress. The labyrinth was presented in this manner in her 1995 book *Walking a Sacred Path*, at the facilitator training with her organization Veriditas, and at the labyrinth at Grace Cathedral Episcopal Church in San Francisco, which also has a large poster describing the labyrinth walk as a three-fold process. In *Walking a Sacred Path* Artress explains this association by stating that the mystical path in Western Christianity is called the Three-fold Path and is made up of three stages: purgation, illumination, and union. She then describes the labyrinth walk as emulating these stages, which can be seen in the labyrinth's path (see fig.21).

Figure 21: Labyrinth path, ELPC; author's photo

The first stage of the labyrinth walk, from the entrance to the center, is defined as "purgation," and it is during this time that a walker can purge, release, or shed all that stands in the way to communication with God. This could be seen as a process of clearing the mind, and letting go of mental or physical stress. The second stage is "illumination" and takes place when the walker is in the center. After quieting the mind during purgation, the center becomes a place to meditate and pray so one can open to increased awareness, knowledge, or connection with God. It is common for people walking the labyrinth to stop in the center briefly for a prayerful bow, or for an extended time to engage in yoga or meditation. The third stage is when the walker goes from the center back out, and is called "union." Union is the period when people integrate the insights gained on the walk so that these insights can influence their daily life. These could be such things as increased knowledge, a connection to God, a sense of empowerment, increased creativity, compassion, and forgiveness.

This three-fold path can be equated with Victor Turner's notion that ritual is a transformative process that occurs in three stages.[13] Turner describes the first stage of the ritual process as "separation," which is the experience of separating from what is the norm, such as one's place in the society. On the labyrinth this relates to purgation and the movement from the circumference towards the center during which time the separation or release from daily stressors can occur. Turner's second stage is "liminality," where one is "betwixt and between" the life that has been released and the life that has yet to come. On the labyrinth this is found in illumination, the point at the center where the past has been traversed, but the future has not yet been achieved. The center, the point where illumination occurs, is no longer of the world, but a liminal space of prayer and meditation. Turner's third stage of *"communitas"* is described as a new stage in life and a new status in the community. This relates in the labyrinth to the stage of union, which occurs on the walk out. Here one takes the experience of the total labyrinth process and integrates it into a new place in their community, becoming in some way transformed.[14]

The stages of the mystical three-fold path and Turner's ritual process are illustrated in the labyrinth ritual at Epiphany, which symbolically reenacted the journey of the Magi to find Christ. The first stage of purgation/separation was seen in the movement along the path from entrance to center, which represented the extrication of the Magi from their home and religious community in the East—the act of letting go of the past. The second stage of illumination/liminality was the arrival at the center of the labyrinth, a representation of Bethlehem and the place where the star illuminated the baby Jesus. In the center they stood between the world of the old and the world yet to come. The third stage of union/*communitas* was the path back out from the center, representing a path of transformation since the Magi "return by a different way," taking their new knowledge not back from whence they came (Herod), but forward as a witness for the world. By participating in the labyrinth procession of Epiphany the participant had this transformative journey, not across the desert sands, but within themselves.

The labyrinth walk is so often described as the three-fold path that it has given rise to a belief that the three-fold path of purgation, illumination, and union is an integral and historical part of the labyrinth. A member of the Labyrinth Committee at ELPC brought material that she had written to introduce the labyrinth to newcomers. She included a statement of the three-fold path as if it were a traditional part of the labyrinth, not a process that had been recently attached. When I explained to her that it was not material that came out of the medieval use of the labyrinth, but rather that Lauren Artress made the association between the three-fold path and the labyrinth walk, she seemed somewhat surprised but not all that interested. It was as if the association had been so internalized for her that the root of the concept was unimportant.

One of the interesting aspects of working on the Labyrinth Movement has been the ability to watch a religious movement at the early stages of its development, before the nascent rituals and policies have become so integrated that their origination is forgotten. The attachment to the labyrinth of the three-fold path and its accompanying doctrine is an excellent illustration of Berger's three stages of social construction—externalization, objectivation, and internalization. Externalization, the first expression of the idea, occurred when Artress first thought of associating the labyrinth in terms of the Christian three-fold mystical path. Objectivation, when the idea took on a life of its own separate from its originator, happened when Artress described the three-fold path in *Walking a Sacred Path*, followed by its description in newspapers, magazine articles, church literature, posters, and flyers. Internalization, when the idea has been seen and heard so many times that it is taken for granted, was seen in the ELPC member's belief that the three-fold path had always been part of the labyrinth. From internalization, alienation is very close behind. Alienation is the act of forgetting that linking the labyrinth walk to the three-fold path was an artificially constructed concept. Instead it is believed that it is "just the way it has always been," evident by the member's lack of knowledge that the three-fold path was a concept recently attached to the labyrinth by Artress.[15]

It has been fascinating to watch this idea of the three-fold path become attached to the labyrinth in only five years. But my fascination is cause for concern to some informants who do not want the labyrinth to become the sole property of the Christian Church, and who would see this type of internalization as a clear sign that such an ownership is well underway. One informant was talking about all the places that the labyrinth was being used, both in and out of the church, and stated: "Others would prefer that it not be happening any place else other than the church. So once again it that control thing that Christianity cannot seem to unburden itself from." The concern that Veriditas, and by extension, the Christian Church, would begin to dominate the labyrinth and direct its use exclusively toward Christian purposes was part of the reason for the creation of TLS. There was a desire to have a venue for labyrinth work that was not exclusively Christian. Though TLS does include Christian use, it also supports the labyrinth in other venues, such as educational, medical, corporate, and psychological.

One of the reasons that the labyrinth is utilized in so many arenas, sacred and secular, is because it is relatively easy to create a variety of metaphors to link the labyrinth to any intended audience by using whatever language and imagery that will work best within that context. In her facilitator training Artress states that it is important to know your audience and use the language that will make the labyrinth familiar and comfortable to them. Artress stated in her lecture during the 2000 Arkansas TLS Gathering that she has made a conscious attempt to link the labyrinth with Christianity to make it palatable to the Christian audience at her church. She realized that although the labyrinth is a medieval Christian icon and part of the Catholic symbolism and architecture, that it is also, and for a longer time, a pagan icon and part of pagan culture. Artress believes that the labyrinth is such a valuable tool that it would be regrettable for churches not to use it due to its pagan past. Therefore it is her work to make the labyrinth as "Christian" as she can. She clearly stated that the church is her arena and the Christianization of the labyrinth is her mission. She did not imply exclusivity of the labyrinth. Rather she acknowledged that others would have different venues in which to introduce the labyrinth, and therefore different missions.

One way to control the use of the labyrinth is to control the choice of what language is used to metaphorically describe it. The issue over the choice of language was evident when a fundamentalist Christian church in Pittsburgh borrowed an ELPC labyrinth for an all-day retreat. They specifically asked that the ELPC Committee member who accompanied the labyrinth and would normally provide an introduction, not to talk or introduce the labyrinth to their congregation. They wanted to provide their own introduction, concerned that the wrong words, possibly too liberal in context since ELPC is known as a liberal congregation, would link the labyrinth to liberal Christianity.

Ordinary Time

Most of the liturgical year is constituted as Ordinary Time which stands in contrast to the extra-ordinary time celebrated as Christ's birth/incarnation and death/resurrection. Ordinary Time is time that is standard, typical, or the norm. The standard services included in the weekly service such as the Doxology are termed "ordinaries," meaning they are the usual occurrence. When the passage of time is termed "Ordinary" it puts the focus on the week-by-week Sunday worship instead of the special holy days that celebrate major festivals such as Christmas and Easter. Ordinary Time is not totally without its special days and there are festivals celebrated on some Sundays in Ordinary Time, such as Baptism of the Lord. But for the most part Ordinary Time acts as a divider between the two major cycles—resurrection and incarnation—that are celebrated in the Christian liturgical calendar. [16]

The Resurrection Cycle: An Ash Wednesday Ritual

After Ordinary Time concludes, the Resurrection cycle begins. The Resurrection cycle is ninety days beginning with Lent, continuing through Easter, and ending with Pentecost. Lent most likely began in the Early Church as a period of preparation for those who would be baptized on Easter; beginning as a two-day fast it later became modeled after Christ's forty days in the desert where he faced and resisted the temptation of the devil. For the Christian it is an opportunity to face the "devil" within and engage in self-examination and repentance. Out of this struggle with the darkness one emerges to the new light, analogous to Christ's resurrection at Easter. Bob Chestnut said in a 1998 sermon at Lent that:

The good news as we begin Lent is not that there is no sin or evil within us, no darkness in ourselves or in our world. The good news is that Jesus our Savior has faced the darkness for us. He has faced it and faced it down—not so that we won't have to, but so that we can face it with him. So that we can move into and through the darkness to the light that lies beyond. So that we can move through the Lent of life into God's Easter of new life.

Not all rituals are as elaborately formulated as *Walk with Mary* yet still can construct some aspect of the Christian cosmos. An example is the ritual of Ash Wednesday. Ash Wednesday is the first day of Lent and occurs on the day the labyrinth is usually set up in the social hall for the weekly open walk. Therefore the ritual needed no special formulation and only required giving the day a special context.

The Biblical narrative upon which Lent is based is Matthew 4:2 where "Jesus was led up by the Spirit into the wilderness to be tempted by the devil. He fasted forty days and forty nights and afterwards he was famished." The central ritual act of Ash Wednesday, having ashes placed on one's forehead in the shape of a cross while the words "You are dust and to dust you will return," comes from Genesis 3:19, "From the earth you were taken; dust you are and to dust you shall return." These narratives set the temporal context of some point in the future when each participant will face his/her own death. The spatial context is the physical body, which is simply flesh and bones and one day will decay into dust. On Ash Wednesday one is reminded that it is through the act of physically dying that one can experience the rebirth of resurrection.

The Physical space is created by placing ashes on the forehead, and the Meaning space is the symbolic representation of those ashes. The ashes symbolically represent the brokenness of life, physical mortality, and a reminder that nothing in this physical world lasts forever and that it is only through Christ that eternal life is possible.

The Virtual time/space created from this combination of Physical and Meaning Space was an "as if" perception of release of the attachments of the material world and a recommitment to the life of Christ. The labyrinth became the journey through life, with its twists and turns of both lightness and dark. The labyrinth is the *metanoia* (turning around), "of changing directions from self-serving toward the self-giving way of the cross."[17]

The idea of Lent as a journey similar to that that taken by Christ in the desert is supported in the ELPC Ash Wednesday flyer which encourages participants to consider "what burdens we need to set aside in order to begin our wilderness journey...This is a journey for you and your soul. All else falls away, only your spiritual journey survives."

In 1999 my volunteer night for the labyrinth at ELPC fell on Ash Wednesday and when I arrived the mood at the labyrinth was pensive and the music was somber and somewhat depressing Gregorian chants. I considered changing the music to something lighter when I thought perhaps that since it was Ash Wednesday that the music was chosen because it was somber, reminding people, along with the ashes, that life was temporary. Though ashes have been offered from the center of the labyrinth at other years, they were not that year and so the labyrinth in the social hall had no formal ritual formulated and no ritual leader or scripts to follow. There were twenty-three people at the labyrinth when I arrived and at one point thirteen people were walking at once. One woman lay in the center, another woman got on her knees once she arrived at the center and bent at her waist until her head touched the floor. Several people walked with their arms lifted as if in supplication. The Virtual time/space associated with death was in full force with an "as if" mood of heaviness and pondering, a very different feeling than the usual Wednesday night walk.

Reflections on Ash Wednesday: Embodiment and Gestures

The pensive mood that was tangible on the labyrinth was partially due to the music that was playing, slow ponderous Gregorian chants which matched the meaning of Ash Wednesday. Helen Raphael Sands, labyrinth facilitator and author of a "how to" book on the labyrinth called *The Healing Labyrinth* describes the power of music and how much music can change the tenor of an event.[18] As a dancer and choreographer she has traveled around different sites in Western Europe with a portable canvas labyrinth creating different rituals and performances. She found that the music she chose had a large influence in matching the experience to the place. For example, traditional Irish music was a good complement for Celtic Christian sites, whereas she played Greek music when focusing on the Cretan myth of the Minotaur. From my experience with labyrinth rituals I have also seen a difference in how people act on the labyrinth based on whether the music is native American drumming, soft new age instrumentals, Gregorian chants, or lively rhythms. Live music is usually part of the more formulated rituals at ELPC and ranges from New Age crystal bowls to a women's choir. The music chosen for a walk sets the rhythm, and the pace of the walk will change midway if the music shifts from slow to lively. I have heard from several informants that the music was significant to their walk, with a change in music partway through the walk often representing some concurrent shift in their consciousness. An interesting follow-up study for the labyrinth would be the effect of music on the experiences people have during labyrinth rituals.

In addition to the effect of the music, the actions of the participants in the center of the labyrinth—lying down, kneeling, prostrating, and arms raised in supplication—were also reflective of the day in that they expressed a submissive stance. Though these gestures are not uncommon in labyrinth walks, they are not usually as widespread among participants and are often balanced with more joyful expressions of other walkers, like skipping or dancing, which were not evident that night.

The physical actions associated with the labyrinth direct our attention to the notion of "embodiment," a concept which has become central in the discussion of ritual. Embodiment is often used as a way to contrast the sensuous body engaged in physical activity, such as ritual, to the intellectual mind engaged in the cognitive aspects of religion, such as sermons and texts. This distinction gives embodiment the appearance of defining an opposition between the physical human body and the rational human mind, a distinction which is expressed through polarities such as female/male, culture/nature, and mind/body. However, as Andrew Strathern points out, embodiment is actually a unification of such a perceived dichotomy since the body contains within it the mind, making it the home of cognitive insights as well as physical sensations and emotions.[19] Ritual is an embodied act since it stimulates the total body—physical, mental, and emotional—through an interplay of modalities that includes music, sounds, scents, symbols, words, and movement. Embodiment is the act of being in the present "here and now" and using the human body as a way to mediate the world.[20] "Here and now" are other terms for "Space and Time," making embodiment central to the idea of locating oneself in a world of meaning.

Embodiment is the physical movement that in the act of doing actually creates a change, both in the body and in consciousness. On Ash Wednesday the woman in the act of kneeling does not just communicate the idea of subordination to herself and others, but kneeling produces a subordinated kneeler in and through the act itself.[21] Embodiment can also reflect the inner states of the person. For example, hands folded in prayer can be indicative that the person has an interior focus, while arms held high can reflect entreaty, or request to receive.

In addition to the general act of walking, which is part of almost all labyrinth rituals, there are also the more specific and often spontaneous acts of embodiment such as dancing, *mudras*, hugging, kneeling, yoga postures, and salutations. One of the reasons people respond positively to the labyrinth is the physical action seems to calm down their minds and let them become more aware of their whole self. One woman stated: "When I got there [to the labyrinth] I found out I didn't have to think at all, I just let myself experience it," and a man reported: "It was powerful because I could personally just feel it in my body and I just felt grounded, it's not really the word I'm looking for, just the oneness of the energy was very powerful, that I could feel the energy, I could feel it on all sides of me."

Holy Week Ritual: Stations of the Cross

The central focus of the Resurrection Cycle is Holy Week, which includes Maundy Thursday, Good Friday, Holy Saturday, and Easter. In a sermon in 1996 Chestnut said of Holy Week:

> If you want new life you will have to taste death, the death of the old self to give birth to the new self. You will have to undergo a

turn-around in your life, an inner cleansing of your own spirit like the cleansing of the temple. Are you able? That is the question the events of Holy Week pose for us. Are we able to go through in our own lives all that tough stuff that follows Palm Sunday in order to get to Easter with Jesus? Will we be with him through the agony of Maundy Thursday, the pain of Good Friday, the grief of Holy Saturday? If not, can we really expect to arrive at Easter Sunday's gift of new life?

In 2001 and 2002 the Stations of the Cross were combined with the labyrinth to create a ritual during Holy Week that reminded participants of the suffering and death of Christ. The Stations of the Cross are a retelling of the story of the final three days of Christ's life using fourteen different scenes, or stations. Moving through the events chronologically from one station to the next is specifically meant to create a mental representation, a Virtual time/space, where the participant can experience the crucifixion of Christ. Though the Stations of the Cross are associated with Catholicism, the Presbyterian *Liturgical Year* states that on Good Friday it is appropriate to have representations of the way of the cross.

The Stations of the Cross at the labyrinth were open to the public from 9 AM to 9 PM on Friday and Saturday of Holy Week to allow people to come whenever it was convenient. There were no specialists leading the ritual, but the ritual had been clearly formulated so that participants were self-directed with instructions written on a posterboard and in a personal booklet that guided them through the ritual.

The narrative came from events in the New Testament Gospels of Matthew, Mark, Luke and John, which tell the story of Christ's crucifixion and resurrection. This narrative sets the temporal context of the final three days of Christ's life, and the spatial context of different sites around Jerusalem including where he was betrayed by Judas, arrested by the Romans, crucified, and buried.

The Physical space was a darkened room where the thirty-six-foot labyrinth was surrounded by candles that were placed on the floor, each nestled in colored scarves. At the head of the labyrinth was a white cross, seven feet high, draped with a purple shawl, and there were three candelabras holding multiple candles. At the entrance of the labyrinth was a poster placed on a tripod that illustrated the fourteen Stations. There was also a basket of handmade booklets that had one page for each Station, accompanied by a biblical scripture describing the Station. For example: "Station #8: Simon of Cyrene Helps Jesus. As they led him away, they seized a man, Simon of Cyrene, who was coming from the country, and they laid the cross on him, and made him carry it behind Jesus (Luke 23:26)." The labyrinth was surrounded by fourteen small tables covered in purple cloth, each one representing a Station of the Cross (see fig. 22). At each table there was an illustration of the events that took place at the site represented by the Station accompanied by a plaster case and piece of charcoal so each participant could do a charcoal rubbing of the Station in the handmade booklet provided.[22] The ritual involved each person taking a booklet and moving from table to table, where he/she would make a charcoal rubbing of an illustrated drawing of the event on its corresponding page.

Figure 22: Holy Week - Stations of the Cross, ELPC. Author's photo.

The Meaning Space was constructed through the symbolic representation of the tables which held the Stations of the Cross. The plaster casts were not placed there just as an opportunity to be artistic, but rather provided a means to take the symbolic journey through each of the fourteen events leading to Christ's crucifixion, providing a place for reflection and meditation along the way. The Virtual time/space was developed through a combination of the Physical and Meaning space. The low lighting, white cross, purple draped tables, quiet surrounding, and moving through the Stations both scripturally and artistically all set the stage for an "as if" perception of placing one's self with Christ during the period surrounding his death.

Reflections on Holy Week: Procession

One quality of the labyrinth that is well illustrated by this particular event is that at the most fundamental level the labyrinth contains the rules for the ritual; there is one entrance, and once a person enters the labyrinth there is one path to follow, which leads to only one place, the center. Once in the center the only real option is to follow the path back out and exit the labyrinth. In my six years of observation of over 100 labyrinth rituals only one time did I see participants break these embedded rules and meander around the labyrinth crossing paths in an apparent chaos. That occasion was a ritual called "The Hero's Journey" sponsored by mental health therapists at a New Age center. The leader of that event told the thirty participants that the labyrinth was to represent the hero's journey and that as individual "heroes" they could follow that path any way they choose, including not following it at all.

The pre-imposed rules from the limited structural design of the labyrinth (entrance, path, center) bring to mind Humphrey and Laidlaw's analysis of ritual as the repetition of rules imposed from the past. In *Archetypal Actions of Ritual* they analyzed the traditional ritual of morning *puja* in a Jain temple and concluded that the repetitive rules of the past ensured the maintenance of social continuity in the present.[23] The labyrinth, with its limited size and singular path, constitutes its own set of rules that has maintained continuity for centuries, if not millennia. Once a participant has decided to enter the labyrinth, following the path to the center and back out again is the only obvious resolution, making the structural design of the labyrinth imposing and invariant.

In the Holy Week ritual of Stations of the Cross this is doubly so. In addition to the labyrinth's path, the ordinal layout of the fourteen Stations around the circumference of the labyrinth also directs the participant's behavior. The journals, plaster casts, and charcoal rubbings are set out with a poster showing their completed state, again implying what actions are to be completed at each Station. The ritual of moving through the Stations of the Cross is reminiscent of what Ronald Grimes refers to as a procession: "the linear ordered, solemn movements of a group through charted space to a known destination to give witness, bear an esteemed object, perform a ritual, fulfill a vow, gain merit, or visit a shrine."[24]

Though the path of the labyrinth is not linear, since it winds circuitously in a circular structure, it still has a definite beginning and end. It is clearly not a circumambulation in that it does not entail continuous movement around a sacred object, but rather is directed by a path to a special place—the center—and back out again. The labyrinth, like a procession, has a clear beginning and end and people know what is expected of them in the process. Though at times some people will walk the labyrinth multiple times in a row, typically the return to the entrance is considered the end of the journey. Walking the labyrinth also fits with Grimes's assertion that processions are solemn events and that they take place at a slower rhythm than normal walking.

Grimes states that processions often have stations where processants perform rituals or rest. Even though the Stations were placed around the circumference of the labyrinth, they were still experienced linearly starting with #1 and ending with #14. Once the fourteenth Station was reached the end of the procession had occurred. The procession linked spatial orders, as Grimes suggests processions do, in that each Station constituted a specific space and time. For example, Station #1 reenacts Jesus praying alone in the Garden, and from there the participant moved from one Virtual time/space to another until at Station #14 where Jesus is buried in the tomb.

Though procession may describe the act of walking the labyrinth, the labyrinth has also been referred to as pilgrimage, and certainly as a "journey," which is one of the most common metaphors ascribed to the experience. As far as a pilgrimage is concerned there is historical evidence suggests that the early medieval pavement labyrinths were used as virtual substitute pilgrimages to Jerusalem after its fall to the Muslims.

However, the short distance of the path (1/3 mile) and the short time for the journey (1/2 hour), and the lack of sacrifice needed to embark and continue the walk, make walking the path of any single labyrinth unlikely to be considered a pilgrimage. There is speculation that medieval pilgrims would traverse the labyrinth on their knees to increase the sacrifice required, but this story is not substantiated. However, even if walking an individual labyrinth does not constitute a pilgrimage, this is not to say that people do not take pilgrimages to particular labyrinths around the world that do entail sacrifice, extended time, and traversing far distances. The labyrinth at Chartres, France, is a major destination for pilgrims and there are "pilgrimages" offered to labyrinths in England, France, or Germany for example.

Conclusion

Christianity is a highly developed and clearly articulated sacred cosmos. For 2,000 years it has been thoroughly considered, reconsidered, and debated by churchmen across the centuries. At times there has been disagreement in doctrine leading to divisions within the church that have emerged with even more finely honed distinctions. Overall the organization of Christianity is structurally complex and the expectations of its adherents are coherent and clearly expressed in doctrines and texts.

Christians are part of this sacred cosmos and join in it through a variety of methods. One of these is by living in accordance with the rhythm of the liturgical year where one's individual and communal life moves in cadence to the life of Christ. The liturgical calendar also provides tempocosms, or points of access between individual worshipers and their sacred world. Another method is the labyrinth, used in ritual since the twelfth century when it was built in the nave of cathedrals inviting pilgrims and parishioners to walk its winding path.

Today, the liturgical calendar and labyrinth are being combined to provide the opportunity for participants to actively engage in the Christian world through ritual. Rituals designed to celebrate Advent, Epiphany, Ash Wednesday, and Good Friday demonstrated how the Christian cosmos is reconstructed using a three-part process. First, the temporal and spatial elements are established through a narrative. Second the Physical space and corresponding Meaning space are constructed through a combination of material objects and events, such as icons, lighting, costumes, music, scents, physical props, and actions, and the symbolic representations of what these physical objects are supposed to mean. Third, a Virtual time/space is created through an integration of the Physical space and Meaning space. In Virtual time/space the participant engages in a sense of the ritual "as if" it were real. Virtual time/space is a liminal space in that it mediates between the known and unknown, the mundane and sacred.

In the next chapter, rituals from the nature-based branch of the Labyrinth Movement will be explained that describe a view of the world that is not as organized and clearly articulated as Christianity. Yet even without a highly comprehensible view of the world and a well-established institution, the labyrinth can still act as a template upon which participants can engage in their idea of a sacred cosmos.

6
Nature-Based Labyrinth Rituals

The church-based branch of the Labyrinth Movement does not represent the beginning of recent labyrinth use nor does it define the recent labyrinth revival, though it may appear to the general public that it does both for several reasons. First, the replica of the twelfth-century Chartres labyrinth, often referred to as the Christian labyrinth, is the main labyrinth used by the churches. This association with the Chartres labyrinth provides a clearly defined point of origin, a well-respected Christian lineage, and even a pilgrimage site for Christians. Second, there is a consensus among the church-based branch that the labyrinth is ministry of Christ, a vehicle for prayer, and a method of bringing people into the church. Third, the boundaries between various churches that could normally be seen as divisive become fluid with regards to the labyrinth. For example ELPC frequently loans their canvas labyrinths to other churches in the area regardless of denomination, including fundamentalist, Methodist, Episcopalian, and Catholic. In 2002 and 2003 when ELPC had full day introductions to the labyrinth it sent a mailing out to all the Christian churches within fifty miles of Pittsburgh. Fourth, Veriditas, housed at Grace Cathedral Episcopal Church in San Francisco, acts as focal point and an organizational agent for church-based use and has a wide reach in terms of marketing and networking. It sells the Chartres-style labyrinth and trains facilitators on how to use the labyrinth in their churches. Lauren Artress, founder of Veriditas, has become the *de facto* spokesperson for the church use of the labyrinth and travels extensively giving presentations.

In contrast to the organization and appearance of unity that the church-based branch confers, there is the loosely connected nature-based branch of the Labyrinth Movement that is much less known to the general public, even though it is the oldest branch and very well established in its own right. The labyrinth style often used is the seven-circuit Classical labyrinth which dates from 2000 BCE (see fig. 1 on pg. 3). This labyrinth is often built outdoors in a place chosen by dowsing, a type of intuitive sensing of energies that are present in the earth. At times these labyrinths are temporary and made from objects found in the natural environment, for example the labyrinth made from pinecones (see fig. 23).

*Figure 23: Pinecone seven-circuit labyrinth in Massachusetts, 2001.
Photo by Sara Penn-Strah.*

I have documented labyrinths made from rock, ice, snow, leaves, grass, surveyor's flags, string, and outlined on a sandy beach. At other times the labyrinths in nature are made to be permanent, as the rock labyrinth at a healing center in California (see fig. 24).

Figure 24: Rock seven-circuit labyrinth in California, 2003. Photo by Jan Bradley.

Many people are unaware that dowsers are connected with the labyrinth, or that there is an older labyrinth style than Chartres (by 2400 years) that is being created all across the country. One reason for this lack of general knowledge is that nature-based labyrinth users do not have the same singular Christ-focus as church-based, and utilize the labyrinth for multiple reasons. Some examples include a Summer Solstice ritual, a healing metaphor for children whose parents have terminal illness, an art installation, a solitary walk in winter, a farewell ritual to a woman with cancer, a geometry lesson at a school, an energy pharmacy, and a forgiveness ritual. And while they often use the same seven-circuit Classical labyrinth and are aware of each other, they have no *de facto* spokesperson or historical ownership of the labyrinth. In the nature-based branch, though the Classical labyrinth is often the labyrinth of choice, the users of it do not identify themselves as Cretan, or Greek, or pagan in the way that many users of the Chartres labyrinth in the churches think of themselves as Christian.

Additionally the nature-based branch does not have the organization that Veriditas offers. Although the American Society of Dowsers were building labyrinths at their conventions as early as the mid 1980s, they have not defined labyrinths as central to their organization. A look at their website (dowsers.org) in September 2023 showed no evidence of labyrinths as a "category." *The Labyrinth Society* (TLS) could be seen as an organizational tool for the nature-based branch since it was conceived, at least in part, to act as a balance to Veriditas by offering public exposure to the wide variety of uses for the labyrinth. It also has a strong contingency of dowsers and a search in 2023 for "dowsers" brought up 49 results. Yet while TLS offers a venue for nature-based use (along with just about every other use of the labyrinth) it does not provide an organizational structure just for dowsers.

In this chapter I am going to explain the nature-based branch of the Labyrinth Movement using Catherine Albanese's theory of nature religion. In doing so I contend that while the nature-based branch of the labyrinth does not have the institutional structure or clearly defined cosmology of the church-based, that it does in fact express a belief in a sacred cosmos that participants engage in through rituals and practices on the labyrinth.

The Labyrinth and Nature Religion

As a way to understand and contextualize the nature-based branch I turn to Catherine Albanese's contention that people observe a nature-based religiosity.[1] Albanese maintains that behaviors and practices that often seem unrelated are a way of organizing reality around the concept of "nature." She views nature as an organizing, encompassing, and consistent construct, and terms the beliefs and practices associated with nature as "nature religion." She concurs that people would not likely describe themselves as practitioners of nature religion; nonetheless she believes it is a helpful construct and that using the term nature religion:

> . . . throws light on certain aspects of our history that we have only haphazardly seen—or even failed to see—religiously. By thinking of these manifestations as nature religion, we begin to discover the

links and connections among them, we gain a sense of their logic, and we come to a sense of their power.[2]

Albanese points out that a listing of religious experiences that have occurred in nature would be so varied and vast that to catalog them would be nearly impossible. Yet in spite of this ubiquitous quality there has been very little effort to create a nature "church" and in fact, one of the hallmarks of nature religion is its failure to organize or institutionalize. She remarks that in spite of our desire to have exactitude in religious identification, that with nature religion we must be content with a somewhat murky world made up of spectrums and continuums. Yet this does not mean that nature religion does not provide meaning and order to one's world.

Albanese would likely see the diverse and unorganized behavior of the nature-based branch of the Labyrinth Movement as typical for those who look to nature as a guide. In the same way that this lack of structure makes nature religion hard to identify, label, and discuss, it makes the nature-based branch of the Labyrinth Movement widespread and changeable. The nature-based branch is not clearly developed, has no organizational structure or leader, and offers a broad spectrum of beliefs and rituals—many that are one-time events. Albanese states that the main reason for such a lack of organization is that most experiences in nature are solitary and personal, with a "lone wolf" archetype most representative of a devotee of nature. The practitioner of nature religion has privatized his/her experiences, which often occur outside of religious institutions and their accompanying plausibility structures. This is opposite the social, cultural, and historical community involvement which is needed to stabilize congregations. Hence while "an experience within nature can shape and orient a life. . . the experience of sacrality in nature does not usually move congregationally."[3]

Ray Billington believes that there is a need for a religious sensibility divorced from a god-based model that he contends is often dogmatic and limited. In describing a new religious sensibility he turns strongly toward a mystical experience of the numinous that can occur when one is in harmony with nature.[4] He surmises that the new religious person "will probably be a lover of nature, and will seek out particular places whenever he can. . . He will view nature not just as something to be enjoyed as a thing of beauty, but, somehow, as a spirit with which to be engaged."[5]

Martin Marty refers to this "protean, enduring, viscous form of spirituality and religion as a 'countercovenant' which stands in contrast to the highly masculine, often institutional, and transcendent covenants of the biblical Judeo-Christian and the reasoned Enlightenment." This countercovenant has a history that includes Native Americans, Transcendentalists, women, healers, and naturalists who "urge that we keep contracts only with nature, produce only what harmonizes with it, achieve without grim competition, and live within a natural and human universe."[6]

Of these countercovenant groups, Albanese looks toward the Transcendentalists as having the most influence on shaping popular mentality in regard to ideas about nature religion. The Transcendentalists were guided by the thoughts of Ralph Waldo Emerson and Henry David Thoreau. They peaked in influence in the 1840s and 1850s and had both an idealist and embodied view of nature. Albanese believes the Transcendentalists contained the germ of nature religion and are largely responsible for "producing a lasting template for what might count as nature religion in the United States."[7]

From the Transcendentalists, Albanese tracks three trends in nature religion that diverge, yet are still related to and influenced by one other. I call these trends Environmental, Metaphysical, and Mind/Body Healing.[8] The first trend, Environmental, arises from Emerson, Thoreau, and John Muir. This trend looks to nature as sacred (divine in its own right), alive (flowing with channels of energy), and sentient (able to receive love and capable of imparting wisdom). This trend also believes that a connection with nature can lead one to have inner intuition, mystical experiences, and a deeper wisdom. Today this attitude is seen in the environmental movement and those who view the earth as alive and sacred. The environmental movement was influenced by John Muir who was founder of the Sierra Club and the national park system. He had a sacramental vision of nature that was combined with a social activism and directed toward environmental ethics.

The second trend is Metaphysical. It arises from Emanuel Swedenborg's doctrine of correspondences and Franz Mesmer's contention that there is a universal fluid that flowed in all things, and that this fluid could be harnessed and directed. The metaphysical trend is based on the idea of a connection between the physical and spiritual worlds, and is found in Spiritualism and Theosophy. Today it includes dowsing, magic, astrology, parapsychology, and much of the New Age.

The third trend is Mind/Body Healing. This trend is based on an understanding of nature as it is manifested in the physical body. The laws of nature were believed to also apply to the human body; if the laws were kept, the body would be healthy, if broken the body would be diseased. This trend is found in the practice of homeopathy, osteopathy, and chiropractic, where the trapped energies of the body could become released. There was also the contention that matter was malleable and could be shaped by thoughts in the mind. This included mental healing approaches that used affirmations and visualizations, such as in Christian Science and New Thought. This trend also encompassed a variety of healing practices that dealt with the effects of food on healing, including herbalism. Today this trend is evident in alternative medicine, mind/body therapies, and the effect of visualization on healing.

By examining the Labyrinth Movement along these three trends I maintain that the nature-based branch is an expression of nature religion, and that nature religion can provide a framework of order, meaning, and significance found in more institutional religions. Albanese's acceptance of the power of nature to provide a sense of meaning and order in an individual's life is well stated in the following:

> ...nature functions as an absolute that grounds and orients life. It transforms and reinvests each person's life project, and it operates in a realm that, arguably, is best described as religious. Here (with nature religion) the religious concerns ways of framing what is thought to be both ground and absolute for meaningful life, and it concerns, as well, ways of interacting with that ground/absolute consistently and comprehensively. It means too, the ways that people orient themselves with reference to ordinary as well as extraordinary aspects of their worlds—to the powers, meanings, and

values that give them something substantive to think and do on Planet Earth as they await their deaths.[9]

Nature religion involves more defined and delineated concepts about the world and how to relate to it than would be found in the more generalized term "worldview" as discussed in Chapter 4. As will be seen in the following rituals that expound the three trends, some ideas about nature are quite specific.

Environmental Trend

The first trend is Environmental and depicts a divinity of nature outside of any theological concept of God. Nature is divine in a *sui generis* sense and not as a consequence of any other action, such as that it was created by God. This trend, which has similarities to the Native American view of the earth as sacred, was defined by John Muir (1838-1914), founder of the Sierra Club and instigator of the forest preservation movement and the national park system. Muir carried the writings of both Emerson and Thoreau with him on his journeys and had a rapturous belief in the divinity of nature and saw nature as a replacement to God.

Today a similar belief is expressed as the "Gaia hypothesis," which views the earth as a living organism. Put forth by British scientist James Lovelock in 1968 at the American Astronautical Society, this thesis states that the earth is alive and an interlocking, interconnected, and self-regulating system. Lovelock named the hypothesis after Gaia, the Greek Earth Goddess, creating mythical and religious connotations.

For Lovelock the Gaia hypothesis was both a scientific and religious concept. He stated that: "Thinking of the Earth as alive makes it seem on happy days, in the right places, as if the whole planet were celebrating a sacred ceremony. Being on the Earth brings that same special feeling of comfort that attaches to the celebration of any religion when it is seemly and when one is fit to receive."[10] Lovelock reminded his readers that in ancient times there was belief in a living Earth and a living Cosmos and that the Goddess was (and still is) worshipped in many religions, both as a fruitful giver of life and a destructive bringer of death.[11]

The belief that the earth is both sacred and alive can be found in the following labyrinth rituals. These rituals are based on a conviction that nature is conscious and alive with energy, and the subsequent notion that nature can be "energetically" damaged by actions done to her, and by extension, also be healed. To illustrate this more completely I will describe two different labyrinth rituals that convey this view of the world.

Trail of Tears Ritual

The first ritual was spontaneously created one evening at the November 2000 TLS Gathering in Fayetteville, Arkansas, and was designed to heal the Trail of Tears. The Trail of Tears was an illegal relocation of the Cherokee Indians that took place in the winter of 1838-39 as over 18,000 men, women, and children were forced to march from their lands in the southeastern United States to lands west of the Mississippi. It is estimated that over 4,000 deaths occurred during the forced relocation due to exposure and disease.[12]

I want to use this ritual to revisit the idea of constructing a sacred cosmos on the labyrinth through the creation of virtual time/space. In doing so I intend to show that even if a sacred cosmos does not come from a well-organized and clearly articulated belief structure such as Christianity, it can still be constructed in labyrinth rituals. A sacred cosmos is a framework that orders the world and gives one's actions meaning. Since the ideas inherent in nature religion are "coherent and encompassing," nature religion can provide a framework for a sacred cosmos even if it lacks the institutional structure of an organized religion. This can be seen in Taoism, a belief of being in harmony with nature that in spite of having no deity or institutional structure, still provides order and meaning to its adherents. Many labyrinth rituals express a belief that the earth is alive, sacred, filled with energy, able to be damaged by the actions of people, and consequently healed by the actions of people. These rituals are a syncretic blend of many traditions such as Native American, dowsing, Goddess worship, eco-feminism, geomancy, environmental movement, and even physical healing techniques such as mind/body therapies.

The first step to re-construct a cosmos is in setting the temporal and spatial context through a narrative. The narrative of the Trail of Tears ritual was not part of a text, but was verbally given by three women who were central in the implementation of the ritual—Vicki, Virginia, and Toby. The ritual began at 8 PM and fifty people attended. It began with everyone sitting around the circumference of a Classical seven-circuit labyrinth that was forty feet in diameter that had been laid out on the floor of a large carpeted room using masking tape. Vicki, who first had the idea to do the ritual, began by telling about her friend who had recently walked the Trail of Tears which had made her very aware of its historical significance. Vicki had driven to the TLS conference in Arkansas from her home in North Carolina along the route of the Trail of Tears while listening to recorded songs of a Native American grandmother to her son about her Trail of Tears experience. Vicki was aware that the site of the Gathering, the Mt. Sequoia Conference Center, was located along the route of the forced walk and suggested that as a group TLS do a healing ceremony for the Cherokees who were subjugated or died while in transit, and for the land, which bore the burden of their deaths and held the graves. She had suggested it over dinner and that night the conference center was abuzz with word-of-mouth announcements of the ritual.

After Vicki finished, Virginia, a woman with a Native American background, continued the narrative. She told of her work with a Cherokee Medicine Clan and her five years of working with mending the land and healing the ancestors who had suffered on the Trail of Tears. She said that as a Medicine Woman she interceded with the Spirits of the Land and had been shown how the "old ghosts" still lingered. She stated that when a traumatic event happens on the land that there is emotional residue ingrained in the land, and that the land suffers as well as the people. Virginia told a story where she went with a friend to part of the Trail of Tears near a bridge and a cornfield. She walked by herself down to the water and saw in a vision an old woman and a young woman with a child who had died on the walk and been buried on that land. In the vision the woman and child told her to create healing. In telling this story, Virginia established the idea that the earth can be injured by the actions of people, and that it can be healed by the actions of people.

Toby spoke third and gave the instructions for the ritual. She said that participants should get up to walk the labyrinth as they felt moved to do so. She suggested that during the walk each person make a gesture as if they were holding something, just as the Cherokees would have as they walked the Trail of Tears. When participants got to the center of the labyrinth, Toby suggested that they let go of whatever they were holding into the sky for release. She then instructed each person to walk back out from the center with a sense that comes from the joy of healing.

From these three narratives the temporal and spatial contexts were set. The temporal context was 1838-1839, the duration of the forced march. The spatial context was the path taken by the Cherokees across the southeastern states, through Arkansas to Oklahoma.

The second part of the formula was the creation of the Physical and its corresponding Meaning space. The Physical space included a large forty-foot diameter seven-circuit Classical labyrinth. The lighting was dim and there was recorded music of Native American chanting. Drums and rattles were available for participants to use. The dim lighting and the native music set the tone of the walk that first was slow and serious, but got more intense as more people began their walk to the accompaniment of the rhythm of rattles and drums. Many people were walking to the beat of the music, like an Indian dance, and using gestures to represent their burdens. The Meaning space was the representational interpretations of these physical actions.

The third step was the creation of a Virtual time/space that comes from the integration of the Physical Space and the Meaning space. The embodied gestures of the participants as they mimed their actions while walking to the center created the "as if" feeling that each was carrying a burden on the Trail of Tears. I saw one woman with her arms cradled like she was holding a baby. Another had her hands cupped like she was holding a basket. When people got to the center they released their burdens into the air, arms lifted high. As the ritual progressed, the music built and the drums and rattles, which set the tempo, got faster and faster. By the time all participants were on the labyrinth the tempo was very fast and the people from the center started walking quickly out. Some people started making whooping sounds and chanting. It was a cacophony of sounds held together by the drums and the rattles. As people finished the walk they circled the circumference of the labyrinth shaking their rattles until everyone had walked and joined the large circle. The last four people to walk were alone on the labyrinth and by then the tempo was very rapid and celebratory. The people were dancing, running, quickly following the path with the appearance of freedom.

After everyone was off the labyrinth, Toby suggested for people to sense the electric energy that had been created by the experience. She then talked for about ten minutes about the importance of healing ourselves, clearing the *chakras,* and committing to be healing forces for the planet. She even discussed the significance of the number of people who attended according to numerology. As people were dispersing when the ritual ended I heard comments like "awesome" or "wow," and they seemed genuinely moved by the experience. In later comments to me about the ritual Toby also remarked on healing the pain of the people and earth which also suffered.

> I was interested from the standpoint of knowing the energetic trail that is left in the earth when a traumatic incident occurs. Given the number of people who died along this walk, I knew we were dealing with earth bound souls who were wanting help to move on. It made sense that as a collective we could assist them using the labyrinth pattern with intent. The intent was to walk, honoring their human dignity willing to allow them to walk in us in a celebration of release.

Just as in the Christian labyrinth ritual of Epiphany, the labyrinth was seen as a path. At Epiphany it was the path the Magi took to Bethlehem to see the Christ child. In the Trail of Tears ritual it was the journey the Cherokees took from Tennessee to Oklahoma.

Aspects of the Environmental trend in nature religion were seen in this ritual, especially that the land is in some fashion alive and suffers when injustice is done. Parts of the Native American idea of a sacred cosmos were also visible. For example the ritual included the importance of ties to the land, the subjugation of the Native peoples into Reservations, the pain and suffering they have endured, the significance of ancestors, and the belief in the lingering spirit of ancestors.

Canadian Relocation Ritual

Another example of a labyrinth ritual which illustrates the Environmental trend of nature religion also involves a forced relocation. The narrative set the temporal context of 1755 and spatial context of a small town in Canada. Many of the ancestors of the town were deported by the King of England when they refused to fight in the Colonies. The ritual's goal was to use the labyrinth as a tool for healing the people in the town, who still held anger at the loss of their ancestral lines and for a healing of the earth, which was also damaged. Virginia, who led the ritual, writes:

> I've used this tool (the labyrinth) with healing and mending of the land and the people. I've just completed co-building a seven-circuit (labyrinth) in New Brunswick, Canada. I was able to sit in circle with these people and facilitate the letting go of all the emotional, etheric, and amazingly past life "stuff." I found the residue was very ingrained in the "matrix" of the area as well. That is to say, the land was suffering as well.

The Physical space included a Classical seven-circuit stone labyrinth that the group of twenty-five people had made with stones that had been gathered for months along the Atlantic shores. Before the participants built the labyrinth Virginia talked to the land to be sure they were putting it in the right place. She related that what she did to find the right place for the labyrinth was similar in intent to what a dowser does, but follows a different process. She wrote:

> . . . it came time for me to talk to the land, or what a Dowser does with a 3D tool. I go within the dimensions and create a sympathetic alliance and agreement because this labyrinth is going to remain long after we are gone. I prayed with the stones and gave corn meal, rice, tobacco, and lavender not because it asked for it by name, but because of the humility of the offering. Then I walked the land where the labyrinth was to be and it began to awaken. . .

immediately when I was finished a big tom cat came running over, they always sense it, then the birds began to sing louder, those are the measurements I sense and recognize.

This description clearly refers to the land as alive and capable of having an "alliance." Through the animals and natural elements she experiences the land as able to respond to her requests.

The ceremony itself involved a syncretic blend of traditions that included Native American, Tibetan, Peruvian, and Christian. The Meaning space was created through the symbolic and metaphorical representations of the physical elements. The participants built a Peruvian cleansing fire and they imagined the fire as "burning away" the anger that they still carried over the relocation. They used crystal bowls to "tone" the land and break up "energy" that was stuck in the people and the earth from past events. As a group they sanctified the land so that the labyrinth would be a place where people could continue to come to "worship, heal, and be reborn." In the center of the labyrinth they dug a hole and placed objects that symbolized the transformation that was occurring. They included an old textbook that symbolized the British forcing their ideas on the people, and holy water from shrines to represent healing. When the ceremony was over the images of "angel clouds" in the sky confirmed that the ritual was a success.

This ritual demonstrates the ideas of a sacred cosmos as it relates to the environment. The ideas expressed are complex and quite specific; the earth is seen as alive and the energy of the earth is seen as affected by events that occur upon it. The earth is a receptor for pain and can suffer. But the same "aliveness" of the earth that allows it to suffer, also allows it to heal. Stuck energy of the earth can be "broken loose" by such methods as vibrations created by toning crystal bowls. The labyrinth was used as a tool to heal the suffering, and to make it the most effective.

Virginia "talked" to the land to "create a sympathetic alliance and agreement" for its correct placement. She prayed to the land and made offerings and received messages from the land, through animals and birds, that the offerings had been accepted. The labyrinth was then built as a "living place" for healing. The center of the labyrinth was a receptacle of symbolic objects to represent healing of the pain from the past. At the end of the ritual the earth gave a confirmation that the building of the labyrinth and the healing ceremony had gone well through the appearance of a certain type of cloud. In building the labyrinth, and in the subsequent ceremony, the earth was treated as fully alive, even to the point of being treated as a co-creator who gave blessings to the site and confirmations for the healing of the land.

Reflections on the Environmental Trend: Improvisation

The Trail of Tears and Canadian Relocation rituals illustrate the multi-layered quality that Roof, Lippy, and Wuthnow contend are central to the self-conscious creation of religious identity commonly found in popular and lived religion. Both of these rituals were constructed (i.e., invented) by those who participated in them. And both rituals most likely will never occur again.

The Trail of Tears ritual was a spontaneous eruption of expressive dancing and gestures. In fact, the ritual was very unlike what Vicki had in mind when she suggested the group do it. After the ritual ended and during everyone's amazement and comments of how "awesome" it was, Vicki appeared taken aback and a bit confused. She told me she had thought the ritual would be slower, more subdued, and serious. The wild and celebratory nature had surprised her; she said it was fine, just not what she had expected. This disjuncture between what was expected and what the actual results were brings up the issue of improvisation in ritual and is an opportunity to consider the contentious dichotomy in ritual—ritual as repetition or ritual as invention. While some scholars, such as Rappaport, line up on one side of the issue, I do not think it is useful to suggest that there is a correct answer to this question. It seems clear that ritual can be either repetitive or inventive depending on the historical and cultural context. But since I am examining labyrinth rituals in contemporary American society, my interest is on the improvisational and inventive nature of ritual.

The Trail of Tears ritual had never been done before, and it did not turn out like the woman who initially originated the ritual thought it would. What she had envisioned as a serious and solemn event turned out to be full of energy and joy. Additionally it was an eclectic combination of factors that went way beyond homage to a Cherokee way of life. While it included American Indian beliefs, drumming, chanting, dancing, prayer, body movements, and storytelling, it also brought into the mix labyrinths, *chakras*, celestial timing, and even numerology as the date of the event and the number of people who participated were seen as significant. The participants who were involved ranged from a Native American Medicine woman to an Episcopalian priest.

This improvisational and syncretic nature of ritual goes against Roy Rappaport's definition of ritual as ordered, invariant, meticulous, recurring and that which is "characterized by punctilious repetition and *thus represented as never changing*" (his italics).[13] Though I cannot affirm if the stated intention of the ritual was accomplished (i.e., that the earth and the spirits of the Cherokees were healed), it was deemed successful by the participants. The apparent success of the ritual goes against Rappaport's notion that while "new rituals do appear from time to time" the conscious formation of such a ritual would be forced or false and "not so much a ritual as a charade."[14] He is so certain of the falsity and failure of new rituals that have been consciously constructed, that his only exception is if the inventers can claim some type of revelatory access to the divine. For Rappaport, a mere mortal invention of ritual could not possibly be a success. I have seen this limited and ultimately dismissive attitude toward newly invented rituals proved wrong again and again in successful labyrinth rituals, including rituals that were constructed for one-time use.

This is not to imply that labyrinth rituals have no formal structure and are never repetitive. Some, such as the liturgical rituals of ELPC, have a noticeable structure that is repeated from year to year. Yet even these could hardly be referred to as "invariant." One of the hallmarks of labyrinth rituals is what Lauren Artress refers to as the ability of participants to "trust the labyrinth." In other words, trust that whatever action occurs on the labyrinth is appropriate and best suited for the occasion. This attitude is in marked contrast to the idea that ritual needs to follow a formal order.

Labyrinth rituals can be described as "performance ritual," but not because they are performed in a theatrical fashion to an audience. Quite the opposite, there is typically no distinction between the performers and the audience. Labyrinth rituals are performative in the sense that the question asked when they are over is "Has it worked?"[15] Whereas liturgical rituals, which are more concerned with maintaining social continuity through the reinforcement of rules and doctrine, ask the question "Did we do it right?" A successful labyrinth ritual is based not so much on correct performance, but on the final act of transformation. Even in its most constrained and formal use, as in liturgical rituals, the labyrinth is still open to personal improvisation.

An examination of emerging rituals on the labyrinth brings greater import to the question of what constitutes a ritual, since many labyrinth rituals are non-traditional, improvisational, creative, never repeated, and enacted without ritual specialists. The Trail of Tears or the Canadian Relocation ritual did not comprise a ritual because they met the criteria of being traditional, repeated, never changing, and part of a doctrine. I contend the Trail of Tears ritual is a ritual because it is the self-conscious intent of the participants that the actions they take have meaning beyond the surface appearance. Participants are not simply walking; they are walking in the path of the Cherokees who were forced from their homes and into reservations. They are not simply folding their arms; they are folding their arms to hold a baby, as one of the Cherokee women may have done. Though there was direction of what to do in the ritual (i.e., act as if you are holding something as you walk to the center and then release it), the variety of actions were based on individual proclivities. This challenges Rappaport's contention that ritual acts are encoded by those other than the performers and that "performers of rituals. . . follow, more or less punctiliously, orders established or taken to have been established by others."[16] When all is said and done in labyrinth rituals the only real rule is to "trust the labyrinth."

Metaphysical Trend

The Metaphysical trend of nature religion takes the Environmental trend one step further. The Metaphysical trend states that not only is nature alive with energy lines and forces, but that this energy can be affected by humans through an inner/outer or "as above, so below" connection. In the Metaphysical trend nature is not *sui generis* a sacred thing, but rather, nature is sacred because it is a reflection of some greater spiritual reality that can be tapped into and utilized by people for specific purposes. The Metaphysical trend arises from the Transcendentalists, particularly as seen in Emerson's *Nature*. In *Nature*, Emerson discusses a vision of nature influenced by the neo-Platonic belief that the world of matter is really a reflection of some ideal forms that exist on a spiritual plane. Matter is really just a denser version of a more refined spirit, a microcosm of the macrocosm. Emerson spoke of a correspondence between humanity and nature and said that "the greatest delight which the fields and woods minister, is the suggestion of an occult relation between man and vegetable" and that this connection could be utilized by humans for various purposes.[17]

Emanuel Swedenborg's eighteenth-century doctrine of correspondences, Frantz Anton Mesmer's late-eighteenth century theory of universal magnetic tides, and esoteric philosophies such as Theosophy are part of the Metaphysical trend. The belief in communication with the dead, as in Spiritualism, is also Metaphysical in that ghosts are perceived as a more refined form of matter, and hence part of nature.[18] Albanese links the Metaphysical trend to beliefs such as the New Age Movement, Wicca, and Neo-Pagan groups. These groups look to nature as a "law and a guide." If one is able to connect the mind to that greater source behind nature, then many things become possible, even magical.[19]

This Metaphysical trend can be seen in the nature-based branch of the Labyrinth Movement in the many rituals that use the power of mental ideas to connect people to larger spiritual/magical energies. The two relocation rituals just discussed employed these metaphysical ideas when the participants believed that the actions taken by them in ritual could make a positive change. However, in those rituals the earth was seen as alive and sacred in its own right, and not a reflection of some greater reality. The Environmental and Metaphysical trends converge and blend in places, making them at times hard to distinguish. But an examination of the importance of dowsing to labyrinths is one good example of the belief that there is a correspondence between nature and humans that can be known, experienced, and utilized.

Dowsing

In Becker and Eisland's 1999 book, *Contemporary American Religion,* dowsing is listed as a largely unorganized and family-taught method of sensing earth energies, particularly the presence of water, which became more organized with the establishment of the *American Society of Dowsers* (ASD) in 1961.[20] Dowsers are an integral part of the Labyrinth Movement and are founding members of TLS, labyrinth builders, keynote speakers, workshop leaders, and book authors.

In brief, dowsing involves sensing the energies of water, minerals, earth, or unknown sources through tools, such as rods or pendulums, or without tools, through intuition. Dowsing is used in two main ways with labyrinths. The first is to decide where to place a labyrinth so that it is in correct alignment with the earth; in this way the labyrinth will be in greatest harmony with its surroundings and most efficacious, not only for the person using the labyrinth, but also for the earth. The second way is to discover what type of energy pattern the labyrinth generates once it has been built; in this way the labyrinth can be correctly utilized for specific functions.

I want to examine the juncture of dowsing, nature religion, and labyrinths through the ritual work of several dowsers. The first is Alex Champion. Champion earned a doctorate in Bio-chemistry from UC Berkeley. In 1987, after twenty years working in science, he combined his love of gardening with an interest in labyrinths and started a full-time business of creating labyrinths and other geometric earth sculptures. He has made over seventy installations, what he calls "earth symbols," around the United States, many of his own design, including thirty-five large earthworks (see fig. 25).

Figure 25: Alex Champion's dowsed Classical seven-circuit labyrinth in Mendocino County, California, 1987. Photo by Cindy Pavlinic.

Champion is a member of the American Society of Dowsers, a frequent lecturer at their West Coast conferences, and a founding member of TLS. Champion is particularly interested in the types of energy that labyrinths generate and understands the energy to come largely from the geometry of the symbol, as opposed to emanating from the earth. He states:

> I see labyrinths and some mazes as another example of a complex geometric symbol based on sacred geometry, which means the archetypal patterns of nature. For example, the circle, square, triangle, golden mean proportion, spiral, hexagon, wave, the vesica piscis, etc.—there are only a couple of dozen. Other examples of these symbols are rose windows, stone henges, medicine wheels, stone circles, and crop circles. . . With labyrinths you are inside the symbol, walking in its energy, which is the way I think the labyrinth does its magic, besides self-hypnosis. I see the labyrinth and other symbols as tools that bring in their own energy, and they are

analogous to a small orchestra of tuning forks, depending on what the pattern is.[21]

His investigations, which he admits are very subjective, involve a daily record where he reports what happens while he is creating an earthwork. He dowses his earthworks, what he describes as "to actively intuit," for various types of energy. These energies often run in straight lines through the land, called ley lines, as well as create a variety of other energy patterns. For the first eight earthworks Champion built he dowsed the sites at three stages: before the project was started, after the symbol was drawn on the land, and when the project was completed, which included moving soil so that the final structure was three-dimensional. He says that when dowsing, "I looked for primary water lines, solar energy lines, power spots, yod lines, and zones; other male energy lines, from the earth or spirit world; and mound energy." What Champion discovered was that there was a correspondence between the earth symbol he built and the type of energy which emanated from it; with different designs creating a different type of "energy signature" (see fig. 26).

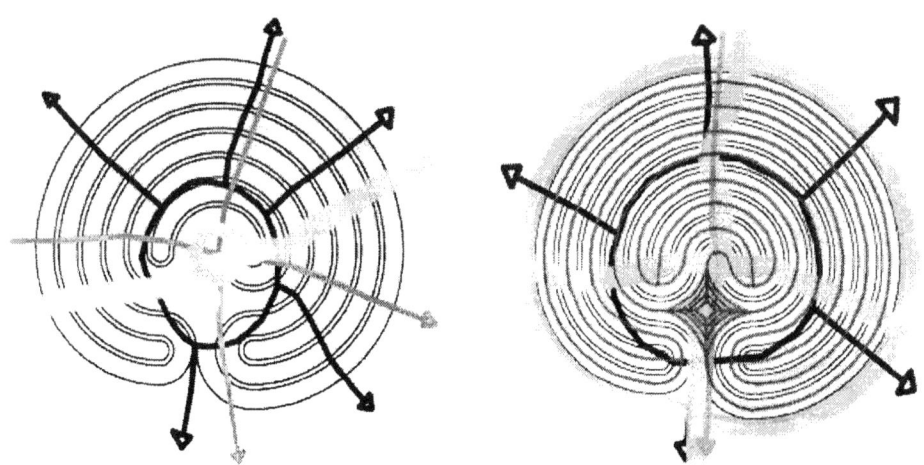

Figure 26: Alex Champion's illustration of labyrinth energy.

Champion promotes the energy signature of eight of his designs, stating that based on his investigation a particular design may provide the type of energy a person may need. For example, one design may have an energy signature that would be energizing, others may be transformative, balancing, soothing, relaxing, peaceful, integrating, healing, or alleviating depression. He states:

> So people, who are also based on sacred geometry, want to harmonize or resonate with the energy of the symbol. If you are in there (the symbol) long enough, you will start to vibrate in unison with the symbol, which is good primal energy. . . Anything inconsistent with your true nature will be challenged and with sufficient exposure to the (symbol's) energy, the incompatible energy is transformed or released. This is what I call passive healing, which is based on the raw energy of the pattern. Once you acclimatize to a pattern you can still use it for healing purposes by working actively with the energy, something I am just beginning to investigate.

In addition to the energy that a particular geometric form will emanate, Champion also calls on energetic help from other, more spiritual, sources. He uses the following prayer to God, local spirits, and Mother Earth before he begins an earthwork:

> We ask that the energy that comes in as this symbol is made to be of the highest and purest type, and that the energy remains as long as at least 50% of this earthwork is still here. We ask that any energy present here now or in the future that is not of the highest and purest type to be transformed and recycled by spirits present. We ask that all experiences of those who use this symbol be for their highest good.

Champion's sacred geometry, dowsing, and prayer, are used to "create a meeting place between heaven and earth," and are a clear example of the metaphysical belief in a connection between the macrocosm and the microcosm, between spirit and matter. His work also demonstrates that the energy believed present in the earth can be manipulated, in this case through construction of symbols and prayers to deities. The energy can also be used for specific results, as in creating certain types of energy for specific forms of healing.

Another dowser, Marty Cain, MFA, has "co-created with nature" over seventy labyrinth installations. She uses a "Prayer for Assistance" in dowsing for labyrinths and for diverting energy that may be detrimental to a person or a place. Her prayer is as follows:

> Mother/Father/God, thank you for hearing me. I request that you come to this house and clear it of any entities, demons, spirits, negative thought forms, and critters. Please lead each and every one of them into the Christ light and on to their next appropriate place or level of development. I ask that you do this with the greatest compassion of the Divine Plan, filling this home with love and light from above. I ask that you do this now. Thank you.

Again, this is an example of the Metaphysical trend of nature religion to use mental ideas to create changes in the physical world.

Dowsers are interested in doing research on the accuracy of their work but since dowsing is an intuitive art, and not a hard science, varied results are expected. Sig Lonegren mentions that different dowsers sensing the same sacred site or power spot can have different results depending on how the dowser was trained, who trained him/her, and the level of expertise. Like the metaphorical story of the three blind men who each describe different parts of the elephant (trunk, leg, tail) quite differently, dowsers can also report based on their own perception. Another example of a labyrinth ritual that illustrates the metaphysical view of a sacred cosmos is the Trapped Souls ritual, which contains beliefs that are closely aligned to the ideas of Spiritualism, the ability to communicate with the dead.

Trapped Souls Ritual

The idea that there are non-physical entities and spirits that can be influenced by prayer is also part of the Metaphysical trend of nature religion. Spirits are understood to be a more highly refined form of matter and are ruled by the same laws as any other form of matter. The following ritual for Trapped Souls is based on the belief that it is possible to communicate with the dead and to influence what happens after their death. It is not unusual for labyrinth walkers, whether in church-based or nature-based settings, to have a "sense," or even a vision, of a deceased loved one in the labyrinth. However, more elaborate rituals involving the dead are not common. For this reason I want to focus on a ritual coordinated by Toby Evans that was centered around her Prairie Labyrinth (see fig. 27). The Prairie Labyrinth is a 166-foot diameter seven-circuit Classical labyrinth which she mowed into prairie grasses outside Kansas City, Missouri, on the Spring Equinox of 1995. The Prairie Labyrinth was dowsed to establish the placement of the fourteen-foot center, as well as to establish the size of the paths. Evans is a founding member of TLS, as well as an artist, teacher, past life therapist, and ordained minister.

Figure 27: Prairie labyrinth outside Kansas City, MO. Photo by Toby Evans.

According to her website she facilitates labyrinth experiences on her Prairie Labyrinth and on a portable "Chakra Aligned" seven-circuit Classical labyrinth.[22] *Chakras* are energy center or portals into the sacred cosmos and part of the beliefs of Hinduism. However, the connection between the seven circuits of the Classical labyrinth and the seven main *chakras* is a fairly common association. Often the seven circuits of the labyrinth will each be a different color to correspond to the associated *chakra*. For example the first circuit will be red, which is the color associated with the base *chakra*, and so on. At other times the paths are lit with colored lights of the associated *chakra*, or symbols representing each *chakra* are placed on the labyrinth in their associated path. An entire workshop was offered at a TLS Gatherings using colored lights, streamers, and chanting to make the connection between the labyrinth paths and the *chakras*.

Evans describes the *chakras* as "energetic force centers of our spiritual bodies" that are each associated with a particular color, sound, vibration and function. In keeping with this, Evans has deliberately made a correspondence between each of the seven paths of the Prairie Labyrinth to one of the seven *chakras* by placing poles, called Gateway posts, at the beginning of each path to inform the walker of the correlation between the path and the *chakra*. The poles are identified with the *chakras* using *Chakra* Angels that Evans made out of clay in the corresponding color of the *chakra* (first chakra is red, second is orange, and so on). The corresponding musical note is supplied by wind chimes that go through the C Major scale (see fig. 28). Evans writes of the connection between the Prairie Labyrinth and the *chakras*:

> Entering the labyrinth is a commitment to rebalance body, mind, and spirit. Walking through the labyrinth is akin to walking through your own energy bodies. At each Gateway post you may stop and reflect asking, "What do I most need to release or receive from my Root *Chakra*? My Sacral *Chakra*? My Solar Plexus, etc.[23]

Evans sees the labyrinth as a spiritual tool that can be helpful for people during major transitions, including death. She states: "Over the years, many people who came to walk the paths shared experiences of sensing their deceased loved ones as they walked the design. I also became aware of entities that arrived asking for help to move on."

The Prairie Labyrinth was the focal point of a transformational ritual on September 17, 2001, that was to help those who had died during the September 11th terrorist attack to "complete their journey of passing over." Through discussions with individuals who were concerned about the state of their deceased loved ones and Toby's "experiences working with the disincarnate" she came to realize that when someone dies an automatic "portal" is opened that allows them to "move on," or transition from earth to heaven. Some souls may not "move on" due to unfinished business and strong emotional ties. Instead they can stay linked to the person who is still living, adding to the burden and grief the living already carries. Other souls may want to "move on" but are unable because they do not know how, or because they are confused by a death of unexpected violence, as in 9/11. Evans states that she communicates with earth-bound souls in order to help them move through the portal and transition from being earth-bound, to being set free.

Figure 28: Chakra post at Prairie Labyrinth. Photo by Toby Evans.

After the terrorist attack of 9/11 Evans began to "see" a huge dome of light over New York and Washington, D.C., that she interpreted as a "holding pattern" of all the souls who died on 9/11 who were too stunned and confused to move on after their death. A friend of Evans suggested using the image of the labyrinth as a portal to assist these trapped souls to move on. September 17, 2001, was chosen as an auspicious day for the ritual and she sent out an e-mail to invite anyone who had a labyrinth to join. She wrote:

> I ask that those of you who have access to labyrinths please walk them on this day with the intent to use the double spiraling energy to create and activate a portal above their dome. Hold the image of the spirit (of the trapped soul) escorted by their "Higher selves" in the presence of the angels. Envision them easily moving through the opening energized with your love and prayers. Finger-walking a labyrinth design or simply focusing on a labyrinth pattern can also be used.

While this ritual offers a complex idea of the soul's journey after death, it is not so different from other religious beliefs, such as the Tibetan belief that a soul can get stuck in the "*bardo*" and hence the need for instructions given in *The Tibetan Book of the Dead*, or the Catholic belief in the possession of the body by a spirit, that can be released through exorcism. But when such an idea of trapped souls who need help to "move on" is offered outside of a formal or organized religious institution it is often looked upon with disbelief and even distain.

Once again, Peter Berger's theory of the social construction of religion explains why an idea in one context is acceptable, when a similar idea in another context is not. He refers to the "plausibility structure" which creates the consensus in society that something is legitimate, or plausible, by extent of the idea's integration in society through systems such as religion and education. America has a highly developed plausibility structure that Christ rose from the dead and that a place outside of the physical world exists, and that place is called heaven. Likewise Tibetans have a well-established plausibility structure that the soul continues to exist after death of the physical body, and will reappear in another physical form through reincarnation. But with ideas that are less embedded in society, such as those found within nature religion, the plausibility structure is weak, or non-existent. When viewed in the light of nature religion however, souls are a denser form of matter that need to transition to a more refined form, so they can "move on." Concepts of Neo-Platonism are evident in this idea that souls need to move to higher levels of being in order to return to their spiritual home. This ritual demonstrates the Metaphysical trend of nature religion in that a relationship between the physical and spiritual worlds exists, and that a ritual on a labyrinth, or by only thinking about a labyrinth, has an effect on the trajectory of the deceased.

Mind/Body Healing Trend

I refer to the third major trend that Albanese discusses in nature religion as Mind/Body Healing. In Mind/Body Healing the universal laws of nature are acted out on the human body. Albanese states: "Nature became to stand for the physicality of the human body itself. Here . . . matter remained subject to universal natural laws, and violations of which automatically brought disease and ill health, and the observances of which, by contrast, guaranteed health and blessing."[24] This trend views the body as a microcosm of nature, subject to nature's same laws, which when kept, allow the body to live in health. Historically, Albanese puts Christian Science in this trend since it contained the belief that the body could be healed by adhering to divine truth. New Thought belongs here as well as matter was viewed as a "plastic substance that could be shaped and changed by the power of the mind." [25]

Today these ideas that the body responds to natural laws, and that by adhering to these laws the body will stay healthy, are part of the holistic health and alternative medicine movements. In alternative health modalities, such as chiropractic, acupuncture, and yoga, the body is thought to have channels which are conduits for energy. In much the same way that nature has energy lines that can be effected by physical manipulation and mental thoughts, the body also has lines of energy that can be similarly affected. Richard Feather Anderson is a dowser and geomancer who founded the *West Coast Institute of Sacred Ecology* in

1985. He is also a founding member of TLS and helped Grace Cathedral Episcopal Church with their first labyrinth design. In the 1986 *Yoga Journal* he compared geomancy and yoga, stating that the two systems maintain the flow of energy in earth and humans, respectively.[26]

The Mind/Body Healing trend also includes Psychoneuroimmunology, a branch of behavioral medicine which studies the relationship between the mind and the immune system. The use of visualization on combating cancer as well as the effect of prayer on recovery from disease is part of this rubric of Mind/Body Healing. A TLS member and cancer survivor stated she is "interested in the role of the labyrinth on healing, particularly in cancer alternative therapies." She is considering a research proposal to study the "health benefits of mind/body interventions using the labyrinth."

More hospitals are acknowledging that the body and the mind are connected and the increase of labyrinths in hospital settings is part of this trend.

The San Francisco Chronicle reports that the California Pacific Medical Center in San Francisco, California, was the first hospital to install a labyrinth in 1997. In 2004 there are nearly twenty hospitals that have labyrinths. The Chronicle reports that: "Patients often walk it (the labyrinth) before their chemotherapy treatments. Doctors use it as part of their prescriptions. Families walk it while waiting for their relatives to come out of surgery, and nurses use it to decompress during breaks."[27]

Marty Kermeen, a labyrinth builder, was installing an outdoor labyrinth at The University of Texas, Medical Branch, a medical school with 10,000 students and doctors. As he was working on the labyrinth a doctor walked by with his students and stopped by the labyrinth. Marty reported hearing the doctor tell his students that the labyrinth is a new tool in medicine, and that the students are to remember that there is a human being in the medical scan. He told them that taking care of the soul is as important as the physical wound and said that: "if you want to be doctors of the future you better get on the bandwagon."

One informant, Julie, described a physical healing that occurred on a seventy-foot seven-circuit Classical labyrinth on top of a hill in

Pennsylvania. Julie has had rheumatoid disease for fifteen years, which is very painful. She says that walking the labyrinth is good for her health and depending on the ease or difficulty of the walk she can ascertain the status of her rheumatoid disease. One day she walked to the hilltop labyrinth when it was very cold and she was in pain. It was hard for her to walk up the hill, and when she arrived at the labyrinth she went quickly to the center, where on a clear day you can see three states. At the center she felt her body straighten up and for ten minutes she was pain free. Julie comes from a Quaker background, and in the center of the labyrinth she could hear that "still small voice" say, "I am healed."

Annette Reynolds is a Registered, Board Certified Art Therapist, a nurse, and a founding member of TLS, as well as The Labyrinth Project of Alabama. She uses the labyrinth as a tool for emotional healing with clients and she states: "People are attracted to the labyrinth for many reasons, but especially when they need help. . . On the labyrinth we 're-member' who we are by connecting to ourselves, to our bodies, to the earth, to each other, and to the Divine." She co-created "Maggie's Labyrinth" a seven-circuit Classical on the beach at Hilton Head, South Carolina, for a "blessings ceremony for a woman in her final stages of the heroine's journey through cancer. It was made by using a piece of nearby driftwood and decorated with sea oats, shells, and seaweed. Maggie's roommate played the flute as Maggie walked the labyrinth with her woman friends."

In another instance Reynolds co-created a seven-circuit Classical labyrinth out of pine straw at a two-day bereavement camp for children and teens who have lost loved ones due to terminal illness. She named the labyrinth "The Circle of Life" and it was used as the centerpiece for group processes and activities as children shard their grief, danced, and sang on the labyrinth. The following poem titled "True Blessing" was written and recited by the teen group at the closing ceremony:

> The first day we arrived at camp
> We all had a different feeling.
> Some were excited, some were nervous
> But all in need of healing...

At the Circle of Life we walked the path
We began our journey to the middle.
We didn't know each other at first,
People's pains were such a riddle.

Huddled under a blanket we began to talk
We learned about one another.
Some had lost mothers, others had lost fathers
We shared like sisters and brothers.

In two short days we've come so far
Our hearts did much confessing.
With all its pain and all its sorrow
The Circle of Life gives us true blessings.

These examples of how the labyrinth is used in both physical and emotional healing are a few of many. It has been used for parents of AIDS victims, after the Oklahoma City Bombing for the survivors, and as a place of support and healing in the aftermath of the massacre at the Columbine High School of Colorado. Grace Cathedral in San Francisco offers "Labyrinth Peace Walks" every Friday. Artress says that these are troubling times and "You get all bent out of shape with the terror of things like going to war, and walking the labyrinths just seems to give you some inner peace. . . We need labyrinths desperately and we need them everywhere."

At Washington, D.C., in 2000, there was a three-day labyrinth walk on the lawn of the Capital called "Labyrinths for Peace." During this event hundreds of people walked five portable labyrinths, which were removed when the event ended (see fig. 28).

And a coalition of labyrinth organizations joined together to submit a proposal for a Ground Zero memorial that included a labyrinth. All of these are examples of rituals on the labyrinth that represent the trend of Mind/Body Healing where nature is found within the human body, mind, and spirit.

Figure 29: Labyrinths for Peace at Washington, D.C., 2000.

Conclusion

The nature-based branch of the Labyrinth Movement represents a varied group of people with multiple agendas and methods who use the labyrinth as a way to enact their beliefs and make sense of their world. Using Catherine Albanese's notion of nature religion, these beliefs and practices form a sacred cosmos in that they provide meaning and order to the world. While not a cosmology in a formal sense, nature religion is seen as having coherency and providing an orientation to life. The three trends of Environmental, Metaphysical, and Mind/Body Healing are seen as a way to frame a religious worldview that may otherwise be overlooked. Nature religion, diffuse and unorganized, illustrates that there can be a spiritual presence without theology, and that religious experiences do take place outside of institutional structures.

7
Endings and Beginnings

The labyrinth has sparked the imagination of millions of Americans who walk its path in search of the sacred. Its design is simple—a circle with a path to the center—but within its circumference it contains a complexity of thought and action. Topics as far ranging as Christianity, nature religion, goddesses, Christ, Mary, Osiris, Isis, Theseus, Ariadne, dowsing, lost souls, hell, heaven, earth, time, and space have all been discussed in these chapters as having been enacted in ritual within the labyrinth. How is this possible? That is the question with which I began my exploration. How is it possible that a geometrical form that is at least 4,000 years old can be used by people of such diverse beliefs? And what does this say about American religion?

More than twenty percent of the American population has spiritual sensibilities that are not being expressed in the context of organized religion. They are called "spiritual but not religious" and they have been seeking the sacred in a spiritual frontier outside the parameter of institutional religion. Even though these seekers are mostly from the large and influential baby boom generation, their spiritual quest has been largely ignored by scholars. This is partly due to the fact that most scholarship on American religion revolves around the "major religions," partly because it has been hard to document their practices, and partly because their beliefs have not fit into acceptable categories and so have been considered "fringe" and not worthy of study.

But the religious climate in America has changed. Religious diversity is a fact of life due to the large numbers of immigrants who have brought Hinduism, Jainism, Buddhism, and folk traditions with them to American soil. Increased education has led to a more exploratory and tolerant populace. Secularism has moved people from the churches, and the transient nature of our society has moved them out of town. People no longer dwell only in stable religious communities, but rather are searching, often alone, for that which matters most. Workshop leaders and therapists are taking the place of rabbis and priests, yoga classes take the place of Sunday services, bookstores provide religious texts, and rituals take place in nature rather than the sanctuary.

The labyrinth is part of this change. Since 1986 the labyrinth has crossed the boundaries of religion and been used for rituals in environments as different as cathedrals, hospitals, schools, backyards, and beaches. It arose independently from two branches—in the churches as a ministry for Christ and with dowsers as a way to connect to the earth—and then spread to link a network of individuals who use it in rituals of prayer, meditation, centering, and healing. The labyrinth has been embraced by such a broad spectrum of Americans, both in and out of the churches, both spiritual and religious, for a number of the following reasons.

One of the most significant reasons is that it allows people to worship in any manner they please. Aside from the dictates of the geometrical form—a circle with a path to the center—there are no rules to the labyrinth. Though its origins go back millennia, it has managed to make it through history without becoming the sole property of any single religion or nation. It does not have a definitive ritual associated with it, nor does it have religious elite to dictate action, no sacred text to interpret, no dogma or doctrine. The labyrinth provides a place for individual worship. This is especially important in a society where so many people are finding their own worlds of meaning outside the context of organized religion. The rituals on the labyrinth are part of this religious reframing in that people are consciously "inventing" ritual by renegotiating religious language and adapting religious symbols.

Labyrinth rituals are an eclectic mix of many traditions as people create a textured quilt of religions, beliefs, and ethnic practices that cross religious boundaries. The importance is not on whether practices are consistent with traditional beliefs, but rather if they are coherent to the individual, even if to outsiders they may look false. The labyrinth provides a place where people can explore their spiritual nature on their own terms.

The labyrinth is able to be an arena for such diverse rituals because it acts as a template upon which people overlay their idea of the world. The labyrinth is like a spiritual Rorschach test, where people see in it a reflection of themselves. The labyrinth has been described as the road to Jerusalem by a Christian, circumambulating the Ka'ba by a Muslim, the Tree of Life by a Jew, the womb of the Mother by a feminist, and the Hero's Journey by a psychologist. The symbol of the labyrinth can be overlaid with any number of metaphors, each describing some aspect of the world according to the believer. The labyrinth is a liminal object that moves between worlds, both secular and sacred. This amorphous quality of the labyrinth is one of its great appeals and practitioners refer to it as "universal," "containing all symbols," and "free of dogma." Even in the Christian church, where the symbolism applied to the labyrinth is the most consistent, it still slips easily between descriptions that alternate between the journey to Bethlehem and the womb of the Virgin Mary.

This ability to be metaphorically adaptive is part of the labyrinth's long history. For over 4,000 years the labyrinth has been used to represent the central beliefs of various cultures and religions as ideas and symbols have been selectively appropriated from one tradition to the next. It began with the Egyptian story of the death and rebirth of Osiris, which was transfigured by the Cretans into the triumph of Theseus over the Minotaur. Theseus's tale was taken by the medieval Christians as a prefiguration of Christ's defeat of the Devil in the Harrowing of Hell. The medieval labyrinth at Chartres Cathedral is said to have had Theseus and the Minotaur at its center, and the only known Christian labyrinth ritual to come from medieval Christendom is the reenactment during the Harrowing of Hell. The importance of the Goddess to the labyrinth has also made the transition through time as Isis, Ariadne, and Mary are still part of labyrinth symbolism.

Another reason the labyrinth is so well received is its transient nature. Like many Americans, it is portable, transports easily, can be found in all fifty states, and if necessary, can be temporarily set up until it is time to be dismantled and move on. There are even small three-foot labyrinths that can be packed in a suitcase to be used on the go. An internet search engine will locate a labyrinth around the country, providing a contact number and times it is available to walk. The most common metaphor of the labyrinth is a "journey," and people often talk of walking the labyrinth in terms of following their spiritual path.

Yet in spite of the individualized, transient nature of society there is still a desire for community. One of the reasons the labyrinth is successful in churches is because it draws in spiritual seekers looking for a place to dwell. And outside of churches there is a network of "labyrinthians" held together by popular books, conferences, tours, internet, and e-mail who provide support without dictating action. The labyrinth allows individuals to maintain their private beliefs while walking the path together.

Another important quality of the labyrinth is that it provides an embodied, physical way to experience the divine. I heard from many informants that they wanted a spiritual *experience*, something more than an intellectual approach to God. The labyrinth is a place where a person can be totally engaged—body, mind, and spirit. People tell of their bodies becoming relaxed and their minds slowing down. They often feel more present in the moment and report an increased awareness and new insights. Americans are becoming increasingly stressed with the high speed of life and the over stimulus of technology and media. The labyrinth is slow, easy, undemanding, and, as one informant stated, "only has one moving part." The labyrinth seems to offer a respite from the rush of the world and is available anytime, for any reason. This "lived" experience of the sacred is one of the appeals the labyrinth offers Protestant churches, who find it balances their dependence on sermons and texts.

The labyrinth provides this lived experience because it is an arena for ritual. Its geometric form—a circle with a path to the center—is a template upon which countless rituals representing many different beliefs have been enacted. I contend that such a broad array of rituals—in secular, spiritual, and religious settings—can occur on the labyrinth because people overlay their idea of the world upon this template and then act out these beliefs through ritual. Since these beliefs go beyond what could be termed religious, I have used the term sacred cosmos to describe them. A sacred cosmos is a socially constructed belief that explains and justifies the seen and unseen world, and that creates an overarching frame of reference that provides order, placement, and meaning. Ideas of a sacred cosmos change among cultures and exist along a continuum that ranges from highly complex theories articulated in doctrines and texts, to general ideas embedded in folklore and social practices, to vaguely defined personally negotiated worlds of meaning.

One of the most important functions of a sacred cosmos is to locate or place a person in a world of meaning. When connection to a person's world becomes unstable due to disruptions in life, it is the task of ritual to link individuals to their idea of a sacred cosmos, thus reestablishing their place in a world of meaning. Ritual does this in part by connecting to communal and cosmic rhythms. But ritual can also re-construct a sacred cosmos through the creation of a Virtual time/space where the participants act "as if" their experience of the sacred cosmos is real. The act of creating a Virtual time/space is done through a multifaceted interaction of the physical objects and events used in the ritual with the symbolic or metaphorical interpretations of these objects and events.

Since the use and interpretation of symbols and metaphors change based on context, the rituals on the labyrinth also change. Chapter 5 described rituals that constructed the highly complex and well-articulated Christian cosmos through events of the liturgical calendar. Rituals of Advent, Epiphany, Ash Wednesday, and Holy Week described the ways in which labyrinth rituals on the eleven-circuit Chartres labyrinth connected Christians to events surrounding the incarnation and resurrection of Christ.

Chapter 6 studies nature religion as an example of less formulated ideas of a sacred cosmos and demonstrates how these ideas can also be purposely constructed in ritual. Nature religion consists of protean and diffuse beliefs and practices that at first may seem unrelated, but that are organized around the concept of nature. I use three trends in nature religion—Environmental, Metaphysical, and Mind/Body Healing—to explain rituals on the seven-circuit Classical labyrinth to demonstrate that what at first may seem to be idiosyncratic beliefs, actually fit into a larger understanding of the world as interconnected and sacred.

An examination of the Labyrinth Movement tells a story about what is currently happening in American religion. The baby boomers who are on a spiritual quest are redefining what it means to be religious outside of traditional, orthodox, or "major" religious traditions. The boundaries that have defined religions in the past are breaking down. Religious symbols are being mixed into eclectic combinations to create individual worlds of meaning. There is very little consideration given to the effect a religious concept may have when taken out of its traditional context and religious ideas are being sold on the marketplace, to the chagrin of many. An examination of rituals being enacted on the labyrinth is like a mirror of the changing face of American religion. The rituals range from the ultra-traditional—traversing through the labyrinth on one's knees as a form of penitence—to the novel idea of using the labyrinth as a landing site for UFOs.

The religious composition of America is changing partly because of the millions of immigrants who have arrived in America with their traditional religions intact. Unfortunately, Americans are all too aware of the problems caused by the clashing of religious beliefs and there is a general agreement that there is a need for greater tolerance, acceptance, and understanding among various religious traditions. The labyrinth has shown itself to be a ritual arena where various religious beliefs can interact. Further research may be useful to understand how the labyrinth could be used as a way to possibly build bridges between religions. A very preliminary morphological analysis points to several themes present on the labyrinth that could cut across religious divides. For example, two common metaphors to describe the labyrinth are that it is a religious path and the journey through life. These are concepts present in many religions and may help in finding common ground among those of different faiths. The labyrinth is also being used in the peace and social justice movement, as well as alternative medicine, psychological therapy, and stress reduction. Scholars in these various disciplines may find this study on the use of the labyrinth in religion as a point of departure for their own research.

The fact that people are constructing rituals which enact a sacred cosmos is indicative that having a connection with the cosmos is important to them. It is important enough for some people that if they are not part of an institutional religion where a sacred cosmos is pre-existing and clearly articulated, they will invent one for themselves by reframing religious symbols. I have discussed three main reasons why a sacred cosmos is important to people. The first is that it provides a sense of order; second, it provides a world of meaning; and third, it provides a sense of location or place. Until fairly recently people had a belief that they were part of something larger than themselves in which they could find meaning. The secularization of American society has left many people without a religious framework that provides that sense of meaning and placement. And the disruption in people's lives caused by war, terrorism, unstable economic times, crime, broken families, and our transient society leaves many people feeling adrift. This study suggests that ritual can be used as a way for people to reconnect to a sense of meaning and placement in their lives. And since many people are not getting their rituals in religious institutions, they are inventing rituals themselves.

Ritual can no longer be understood only as traditional, repetitive, and formal events that occur under the auspices of religious specialists. That description of ritual is still applicable in certain cultural and religious settings, but it is inadequate in describing the state of ritual in American contemporary society. Ritual is now in the hands of lay people who are inventing it by mixing and matching religious symbols with abandon. The result is an eclectic, syncretic event that is often never repeated. These rituals put more focus on the importance of invention, rather than tradition, on intent rather than repetition, and on improvisation rather than formality. Contrary to what many scholars think, these invented rituals are meaningful to the people who engage in them, and that alone makes them worthy of study.

Will interest in the labyrinth last? Is it only a passing trend? Since the Labyrinth Movement is still young it is hard to predict its trajectory. But from the time when I began my study in 1996 I have seen it grow. This is evidenced by an increase of labyrinths in the United States and the world, an increase in the people who have walked labyrinths, the use of the labyrinth in a larger variety of settings, publication of popular labyrinth books, a stabilizing of organizational structures, and the mainstreaming of labyrinths in American popular culture. It is possible that the geometrical form of the labyrinth is sufficiently amorphous that it can adjust to match the changing conditions of American religion. If not, it still provides a mirror into religious trends at the turn of the millennium, and that in itself is a substantial contribution.

NOTES

Chapter 1

[1] Laurie Goodstein, "Reviving Labyrinths, Paths to Inner Peace," *New York Times* 10 May 1998:1

[2] Heather Knight, "Peaceful Path: In troubled times more people turn to the labyrinth to walk their worries away." *San Francisco Chronicle* 28 Feb. 2003: <http://www.sfgate.com>

[3] Internet search on July 6, 2011 and Sept 16, 2023 at www.labyrinthlocator.com, which lists only the labyrinths that are reported to it, and does not include every labyrinth in existence.

[4] This earliest accurately dated depiction is graffito on the back of the Pylos tablet, a clay tablet from Pylos in western Messenia.

[5] In addition to Lonegren's labyrinth, Paul Devereux built a labyrinth at Omega Institute in NY and Nigel Pennick built one in CA during the mid 1980"s.

[6] Definitions by Alex Champion, *Earth Mazes* (Emeryville: Bacchus Press, Inc., 1990) 21.

[7] Sig Lonegren, *Spiritual Dowsing* (Glastonbury: Gothic Image Press Publications, 1986) 1.

[8] Lonegren, *Spiritual Dowsing* 4.

[9] Lonegren, *Spiritual Dowsing* 5.

[10] Sig Lonegren, *Labyrinths: Ancient Myths and Modern Uses*, 2nd ed. (Glastonbury: Gothic Image Publications, 1996) 22.

[11] These holidays are capitalized by those who celebrate them and will therefore be capitalized throughout this work.

[12] See Ruth Prince and David Riches, *New Age in Glastonbury: The Construction of Religious Movement* (San Francisco: Harper, 1993) for their discussion of the New Age culture in Glastonbury.

[13] Lauren Artress, *Walking a Sacred Path: Rediscovering the Labyrinth as a Spiritual Tool* (New York: Riverhead Books, 1995) 2.

[14] *Source*, A *Veriditas* Publication. Winter 1996.

[15] Adrienne Morello from *Veriditas*, 26 June 26, 2003. personal e-mail.

[16] http://www.gracecathedral.org/labyrinth/aboutus

[17] Heather Knight, "Peaceful Path: In troubled times more people turn to the labyrinth to walk their worries away." *San Francisco Chronicle* 28 February 2003: <http://www.sfgate.com>

[18] The two distinct branches of the Labyrinth Movement have been noted by others. David Gallagher, past Corresponding Secretary of TLS in May 2000 at a TLS Gathering in Glastonbury England spoke of the Labyrinth Movement in the United States as starting from two threads that were chronologically concurrent but unaware of each other. He termed these threads the Geomantic Pagan, which used mostly the Classical labyrinth, and the Western Hermetic, which was more related to the Chartres style. The current labyrinth revival is also noted as having taken "two parallel tracks" in *Through the Labyrinth* (2000), the translation of Herman Kern's monumental *Labyrinthe: Ercheinungsformem und Deutungen; 5000 Jahre Gegenwart eines Urbilds* (1982), p. 311.

[19] J.Z. Smith, *To Take Place: Toward a Theory of Ritual* (Chicago: The University of Chicago Press, 1987).

Chapter 2

[1] Lindner, Eileen, Ed. *The Yearbook of American and Canadian Churches* (Nashville: Abingdon Press, 1998) 5.

[2] "Religious Adherents in the United States of America, AD 1900-2000," *Britannica Online*. http:www.britannica.com.

[3] Lindner 5.

[4] Diana Eck, Ed. *On Common Ground* CD-ROM (New York: Columbia University Press, 1998).

[5] Robert Wuthnow, *Restructuring American Religion: Society and Faith Since World War II* (Princeton: Princeton University Press, 1988) 147.

[6] Wuthnow, *Restructuring American Religion* 151.

[7] Wuthnow, *Restructuring American Religion* 154.

[8] Wuthnow, *Restructuring American Religion* 157.

[9] Wuthnow, *Restructuring American Religion* 168-169.

[10] Wuthnow, *Restructuring American Religion* 167.

[11] Diana Eck, *A New Religious America* (San Francisco: Harper San Francisco, 2001) 5.

[12] Wade Clark Roof, *A Generation of Seekers: The Spiritual Journeys of the Baby Boomers* (San Francisco: Harper San Francisco, 1993) 2.

[13] Roof, *A Generation of Seekers* 2.

[14] R. Laurence Moore, *Religious Outsiders and the Making of Religion* (New York: Oxford University Press, 1986).

[15] Robert Ellwood, *Alternative Altars: Unconventional and Eastern Spirituality in America* (Chicago: University of Chicago Press, 1979).

[16] Jon Butler, Magic, Astrology, and the Early American Religious Heritage, 1600-1760," *American History Review*. Vol. 84. (April 1979) pp. 317-346.

[17] Jon Butler. *Awash in a Sea of Faith: Christianizing the American People* (Cambridge: Harvard University Press, 1990).

[18] www. fas.harvard.edu/~pluralism.

[19] For overview on American pluralism see Chuck Lippy, *Pluralism Comes of Age* (Armonk: M.E.Sharpe, 2000).

[20] Diana Eck, *A New Religious America* 5.

[21] Wade Clark Roof, *Spiritual Marketplace* (Princeton: Princeton University Press, 1999) 6.

[22] John Eade and Michael Sallnow, *Contesting the Sacred: The Anthropology of Christian Pilgrimage* (London: Routledge Press, 1991) 15.

[23] Bronislaw Malinowski, *Magic, Science, and Religion* (Garden City: Doubleday, 1954).and Robert Redfield, *The Little Community and Peasant Society and Culture* (Chicago: University of Chicago Press, 1967).

[24] Keith Thomas, *Religion and the Decline of Magic* (New York: Charles Scribner's Sons, 1971).

[25] Peter Williams, *Popular Religion in America: Symbolic Change and the Modernization Process in Historical Perspective* (Urbana: University of Illinois Press, 1989) 5.

[26] Laura Stark, "Popular Religion in Southern Europe: A survey of Recent Anthropological Research" *Suomen antropologi* 19/3 (1994) 40.

[27] Natalie Davis, "From 'Popular Religion' to Religious Cultures," *Reformation Europe* (St. Louis: Center for Reformation Research, 1982); Natalie Davis, "Some Tasks and Themes in the Study of Popular Religion." in *The Pursuit of Holiness in Late Medieval and Renaissance Religion*. eds. Charles Trinkaus and Heiko Oberman (Leiden: E.J. Brill, 1974) pp. 307-336.

[28] Catherine Albanese, "The Study of American Popular Religion: Retrospect and Prospect," *Explore* (Fall 1984) 7 12.

[29] William Christian, *Local Religion in Sixteenth-Century Spain* (Princeton, Princeton University Press, 1981) 178.

[30] Robert Fuller, *Spiritual but not Religious: Understanding Unchurched America* (Oxford: Oxford University Press, 2001) 8.

[31] Robert Bellah, *Habits of the Heart: Individualism and Commitment in American Life* (New York: Harper and Row, 1985) 198.

[32] Williams 17-18.

[33] Roof, *Spiritual Marketplace* 41.

[34] Roof, *Spiritual Marketplace* 41.

[35] Roof, *Spiritual Marketplace* 41.

[36] Roof, *Spiritual Marketplace* 9.

[37] Roof, *Spiritual Marketplace* 203.

[38] For more on recovery as religion see: Kathleen Lowney, *Baring Our Souls: TV Talk Shows and the Religion of Recovery* (New York: Walter DeGruyter, 1999).

[39] Roof, *Spiritual Marketplace* 169.

[40] See Robert Ellwood, "UFO Religious Movement," *America's Alternative Religions*, Ed. Timothy Miller, (Albany: State University of New York Press. 1995) pp. 393-399.

[41] Roof, *Spiritual Marketplace* 115.

[42] Robert Wuthnow, *After Heaven: Spirituality in America since the 1950's* (Berkeley: University of California Press, 1998) 11-15.

[43] Roof, *Spiritual Marketplace* 77.

[44] Laurence Moore demonstrates that linking religion to commerce has a history far longer than the current quest culture's entrance into the marketplace in *Selling God: American Religion in the Marketplace of Culture* (New York: Oxford University Press, 1994).

[45] *Source*. A Veriditas Publication. Number 6, (Spring 1998).

[46] Roof, *Spiritual Marketplace* 163.

[47] Robert Wuthnow. *Experimentation in American Religion* (Berkeley: University of California Press. 1978) 190-191.

[48] Robert Fuller, *Spiritual but not Religious: Understanding Unchurched America* (Oxford: Oxford University Press, 2001) 9; Roof, *Spiritual Marketplace* 10.

[49] Wuthnow, *After Heaven* 1-6.

[50] Wuthnow, *After Heaven* 8.

[51] Wuthnow, *After Heaven* 169.

[52] Wuthnow, *After Heaven* 17.

[53] http://www.labyrinthsociety.org/html/365club

[54] Wuthnow, *After Heaven* 178-193.

Chapter 3

[1] Catherine Bell, *Ritual Perspectives and Dimensions* (New York: Oxford Press, 1997) 210-223.

[2] Tom Driver, *The Magic of Ritual* (San Francisco: Harper San Francisco, 1991) 50.

[3] Bell 145.

[4] Hermann Kern, *Through the Labyrinth: Designs and Meanings over 5000 Years* (Munich: Prestel, 2000) 21.

[5] For a full historical analysis see Hermann Kern, *Through the Labyrinth* (2000); Jeff Saward, *Ancient Labyrinths of the World* (1997); Penelope Doob, *The Idea of the Labyrinth: From Classical Antiquity through the Middle Ages* (1990); W.H. Matthew, *Mazes and Labyrinths: Their History and Development* (1970, 1922); S.H. Hooke, *The Labyrinth: Further Studies of the Relation of Myth and Ritual in the Ancient World* (1935).

[6] Samuel Henry Hooke, *The Labyrinth: Further Studies in the Relation of Myth and Ritual in the Ancient World* (London, 1935) vi. Kern disagrees that the images of

the mortuary seals are labyrinths but states instead that they are spiral forms. See image in Kern p. 35.

[7] "Egyptian Mythology." *New Larousse Encyclopedia of Mythology*. 21st ed. (New York: Crescent Books, 1986) 17.

[8] C. N. Deedes, "The Labyrinth," *The Labyrinth: Further Studies in the Relation of Myth and Ritual in the Ancient World*. Ed. S. H. Hooke (London: 1935) 22-26.

[9] Deedes 22.

[10] Deedes 9.

[11] The earliest mention of Crete was in the Homeric saga dated 750 BCE, followed by the historians Herodotus and Thucydides who wrote in the fifth century BCE that King Minos of Crete ruled the Aegean. Plutarch's (c. 45-120 CE) biography of Theseus tells specifics of the classic tale including all of its inconsistencies and alternate explanations. Though there are many versions of this myth the most famous references are Vergil (70 BCE-19 BCE) in the *Aeneid* and Ovid (43 BCE-18 CE) in the *Metamorphoses*.

[12] At the time of this myth there was no apparent distinction between the maze and labyrinth, a distinction that is common today.

[13] There is debate as to whether there was an actual labyrinth at Crete. Arthur Evans claimed the labyrinth was the Palace at Knossos; others say it was cave outside of Knossos. Hermann Kern does not believe the labyrinth was a building at Knossos but supports the idea that the labyrinth was the outline of a dance performed at Crete.

[14] Penelope Reed Doob, *The Idea of the Labyrinth: From Classical Antiquity through the Middle Ages* (Ithaca: Cornell University Press, 1990) 126.

[15] Rodney Castleden, *The Knossos Labyrinth: A New View of the 'Palace of Minos' at Knossos* (London: Routledge, 1990) 7-15; Kern 41-42.

[16] Deedes 27.

[17] Catullus, *Poems 61-68*. trans. John Godwin (Wiltshire: Aris & Phillips Ltd., 1995).

[18] Mike Dixon-Kennedy, *Encyclopedia of Greco-Roman Mythology* (Santa Barbara: ABC-CLIO, 1998).

[19] Robert Graves, *The Greek Myths* (London: Penguin Books, 1955) 110.

[20] John Chadwick, *The Decipherment of Linear B* (Cambridge: Cambridge University Press, 1967) 125.

[21] Chadwick 125

[22] Deedes 31

[23] Simon Davis, *The Decipherment of the Minoan Linear A and Pictographic Scripts* (Johannesburg: Witwatersrand University Press, 1967) 175.

[24] For more on the goddesses and priestesses of Crete see Norma Lorre Goodrich, *Priestesses*. (New York: Franklin Watts, 1989).

[25] As quoted in Kern 45.

[26] John Kraft, *The Goddess in the Labyrinth* (Abo: Abo Akademis, 1995) 15.

[27] Kraft 21.

[28] Michael Grant and John Hazel, *Who's Who in Classical Mythology* (New York: Oxford University Press, 1993) 153.

[29] Adrian Fisher and Georg Gerster, *The Art of the Maze* (London: Weidenfeld and Nicholson, 1990) 40.

[30] Janet Bord, *Mazes and Labyrinths of the World* (London: Latimer New Dimensions Limited: 1976) 13. There are labyrinth-type drawing in rocks in northwest Europe as early as 2000 B.C.E, but the earliest datable labyrinth in the British Isles is a classical type called the Hollywood Stone, c. 500 C.E.

[31] Jeff Saward, *Ancient Labyrinths of the World* (Thundersley: Caerdroia, 1997) 8.

[32] Kern 106, 144.

[33] Fisher 40.

[34] Kern 145

[35] Saward, *Ancient Labyrinths of the World* 10; Fisher 41; The location and date of creation of these eleven labyrinths are: Arras 1160; Sens 12th century; Chartres 1194-1235; Amiens 1288; Reims 1287-1311; Beyeux 13th century; Poitiers 13th century; Orleans 13th century; Auxerre 1334; St. Omer 14th century; St. Quentin 1495.

[36] Matthews places it c.1190; Villette at 1200; Saward c. 1202; Fisher at 1235; Kern after 1220.

[37] Jean Villette, "The Enigma of the Labyrinth at Chartres Cathedral" *Notre-Dame de Chartres* trans. Malcolm Miller. 11

[38] Doob 131.

[39] Edward Grant, "Cosmology" in *Science in the Middle Ages*. Ed. David Lindberg. (Chicago: University of Chicago Press, 1978) 266.

[40] Peter Ellard, "The Sacred Cosmos: A Study of the Twelfth Century School of Chartres," Diss. Fordham University, New York, 1999.

[41] David C. Lindberg, *The Beginnings of Western Science: The European Scientific Tradition in Philosophical, Religious, and Institutional Context, 600 B.C. to A.D. 1450* (Chicago: The University of Chicago Press, 1992) 247.

[42] Lindberg 246.

[43] William Harris Stahl, *Commentary on the Dream of Scipio by Macrobius* (New York: Columbia University Press, 1952) 103.

[44] Otto von Simson. *The Gothic Cathedral: Origins of Gothic Architecture and the Medieval Concept of Order*, 3rd. ed. (Princeton: Princeton University Press, 1988) xxi.

[45] Anne Prache, *Chartres Cathedral: Image of Heavenly Jerusalem*, trans. Janice Abbot (Paris: CNRS Editions, 1993) 12, 76.

[46] Edward Grant, "Cosmology," *Science in the Middle Ages*. Ed. David Lindberg. (Chicago: University of Chicago Press, 1998) 266.

[47] Simson, 13; George Lesser. *Gothic Cathedrals and Sacred Geometry* (London: Alec Tiranti, 1957) 1.

[48] Simson 27, 35.

[49] Emile Mâle *The Gothic Image: Religious Art in France of the Thirteenth Century*. trans. Dora Nussey. (New York: Harper & Brothers, 1958) originally published in France 1913 under the title *Religious Art in France of the Thirteenth Century* 1-22.

[50] For a further explanation of the geometry of the labyrinth see Keith Critchlow, Jane Carroll and Llewelyn Raughn Lee. "Chartres Maze: A Model of the Universe?" *Architectural Association Quarterly*, 5,2, (1973) 11-22.

[51] Craig Wright in *The Maze and the Warrior: Symbols in Architecture, Theology, and Music* (Cambridge: Harvard University Press, 2001) relates the labyrinth to the realm of purgatory.

[52] Villette 6.

[53] Kern 153.

[54] Woodward 44

[55] Kern 137

[56] Woodward 46

[57] Kern 112

[58] Kern 156.

[59] John Bowker, Ed. *The Oxford Dictionary of World Religions*. Oxford: Oxford University Press. 1997. 82.

[60] Woodward 52-53.

[61] as quoted in Woodward 56.

[62] as quoted in Woodward 57.

[63] Woodward 142.

[64] as quoted in Woodward 147.

[65] Doob 123.

[66] Woodward 64.

[67] Woodward 65.

[68] Woodward 66-77.

[69] Woodward 68-70.

[70] Doob 125; Woodward 82.

[71] Woodward 82.

[72] Jean Gimpel, *The Cathedral Builders*, Trans. Teresa Waugh, 1983 (New York, Grove Press, Inc., 1981) 41.

[73] Kern 160.

[74] Doob 121.

[75] Daniel Connolly, "Imagined Pilgrimages in Gothic Art" Diss. University of Chicago, 1998. 245.

[76] Connolly 32-166.

[77] John Demaray, *Dante and the Book of the Cosmos* (Philadelphia: The American Philosophical Society, 1997) 58.

[78] Kern 106, 207.

[79] Kern 128-135.

[80] Connolly 243.

[81] Connolly 240.

[82] Demaray 21-39.

[83] A story written in 1609 by Sebastien Roulliard and another written in 1671 by Vincent Sablon are found in Robert Branner, ed. *Chartres Cathedral: Illustrations, Introductory Essay, Documents, Analysis, Criticism* (New York: W. W. Norton & Company, Inc, 1969) 71-111.

Chapter 4

[1] Louis Frederic, *Borobudur* (New York: Abbeville Press, 1996).

[2] Norriss Hetherington, *Cosmology: Historical, Literary, Philosophical, Religious, and Scientific Perspectives* (New York: Garland Publishing, Inc., 1993) 23.

[3] Jonathan Z. Smith, *Map is Not Territory* (Leiden: Brill, 1978) 290.

[4] See Peter Berger, *The Sacred Canopy: Elements of a Sociological Theory of Religion* (New York: Doubleday, 1967) for a full discussion of how a cosmos becomes socially constructed.

[5] Berger's definition is similar to the definition in the *Oxford Dictionary of World Religions* (1997) which states that the cosmos is a meaningful whole that expresses order in a harmonious universe that contains both terrestrial and celestial realms "Cosmology," *The Oxford Dictionary of World Religions*, Ed. John Bowker (Oxford: Oxford University Press, 1997) 238-9.

[6] Berger 51.

[7] Berger 27-28.

[8] Berger 34.

[9] Berger 32.

[10] Gregory Schrempp, *Magical Arrows: The Maori, The Greeks and the Folklore of the Universe* (Madison: The University of Wisconsin Press, 1992) xv.

[11] Berger 41.

[12] Smith, Map is Not Territory 292.

[13] Berger 151.

[14] Kees Bolle, "Cosmology," *The Encyclopedia of Religion* Ed. Mircea Eliade (New York: Macmillan, 1987) vol. 4. p. 101.

[15] Berger 26, 35.

[16] Plato, *Timaeus*. Trans. Francis Cornford (New York: Macmillan Publishing Company, 1959).

[17] N. Max. Wildiers, *The Theologian and His Universe: Theology and Cosmology from the Middle Ages to the Present* (New York: The Seabury Press, 1982) 1.

[18] Alexandre Koyre, *From the Closed World to the Infinite Universe* (Baltimore, The John Hopkins Press, 1957) 1.

[19] Berger 112.

[20] Berger 107.

[21] Harry Coffin Stafford, *Culture and Cosmology: Essays on the Birth of a World View* (Washington, University Press of America, 1981).

[22] Hetherington 581.

[23] Daniel de Coppet and Andre Iteanu, *Cosmos and Society in Oceania* (Oxford: Berg Publishers Limited, 1995)1.

[24] Berger 40.

[25] Mircea Eliade, *Cosmos and History: The Myth of the Eternal Return* (New York: Harper Torchbooks, 1959).

[26] E. Adamson Hoebel, *Anthropology: The Study of Man*. 1972. 4th ed. (New York: McGraw-Hill Book Company, 1982).

[27] Gerald Weiss, *Campa Cosmology: The World of a Forest Tribe in South America*. 52/5. Anthropological Papers of The American Museum of Natural History. New York: 1975.

[28] For more information see Christopher Carr and Jill Neitzel, Eds. *Style, society, and person: archeological and ethnological perspectives* (New York, Plenum Press, 1995); Christopher Carr, Ed. *Gathering Hopewell: Society, Ritual, and Ritual Interaction* (New York: Kluwer Academic, Plenum Publishers, forthcoming 2004).

[29] Stephen Toulmin, *The Return to Cosmology: Postmodern Science and the Theology of Nature* (Berkeley, University of California Press, 1982) 5.

[30] Sam Gill, *Beyond the 'Primitive': The Religions of Nonliterate People* (Englewood Cliffs: Prentice-Hall, Inc., 1982) 12.

[31] Rappaport 183.

[32] Clothey, *Rhythm and Intent* 16.

[33] Clothey, *Rhythm and Intent* 78.

[34] Clothey, *Rhythm and Intent* 78.

[35] "Easter," *The Oxford Dictionary of World Religions*. Ed. John Bowker. (Oxford: Oxford University Press, 1997) 301.

[36] Clothey, *Rhythm and Intent* 78.

[37] Clothey, *Rhythm and Intent* 47.

[38] Clothey, *Rhythm and Intent* 77.

[39] Anthony Good, "Congealing Divinity: Time, Worship and Kinship in South Indian Hinduism." *Journal of the Royal Anthropological Institute*. (June 2000) 2 273.

[40] Rappaport 177.

[41] Deborah Rose Bird, "To Dance with Time: A Victoria River Aboriginal Study." *Australian Journal of Anthropology* (2000) 22. 7.

[42] Rose 7.

[43] Rose 1-7.

[44] Rose 3.

[45] Rose 4.

[46] Sam Gill, *Native American Traditions* (Belmont: Wadsworth Publishing Co., 1983) 20.

[47] Clothey, *Rhythm and Intent* 13-15.

[48] Rappaport 210.

[49] Rappaport 210.

[50] Jonathan Z. Smith, *To Take Place: Toward a Theory in Ritual* (Chicago: The University of Chicago Press, 1987) 92.

[51] Smith, *To Take Place* 90

[52] Smith, *To Take Place* 94.

[53] Smith, *To Take Place* 117.

[54] Daniel Connolly, "Imagined Pilgrimages in Gothic Art: Maps, Manuscripts and Labyrinths," Diss University of Chicago, 1998.

[55] Connolly 5.

[56] J. Kenneth Hyde, "Italian Pilgrim Literature in the Late Middle Ages," Bulletin of the John Rylands Library, (1990) 72; 13-33 as quoted in Connolly 2.

[57] Bernard de Clairvaux as quoted in Connolly 11.

[58] Ron G. Williams and James W. Boyd, *Ritual Art and Knowledge: Aesthetic Theory and Zoroastrian Ritual* (Columbia: University of South Carolina Press, 1993) 15.

[59] Williams and Boyd 16.

[60] Williams and Boyd 16.

[61] Williams and Boyd 17.

[62] Williams and Boyd 18.

[63] Ronald Grimes, *Beginnings in Ritual Studies* (Lanham, University Press of America: 1982) 59.

[64] Williams and Boyd 25.

[65] Williams and Boyd 61.

[66] Caroline Humphrey and James Laidlaw, *The Archetypal Actions of Ritual* (Oxford: Clarendon Press, 1994).

[67] Rappaport 64.

[68] Rappaport 187.

[69] Rappaport 35.

[70] Smith, *To Take Place* 103.

[71] Theodore Jennings, "On Ritual Knowledge," *Readings in Ritual Studies*. Ed Ronald Grimes (Prentice Hall, Upper Saddle River, 1996) 325.

[72] "Symbols, symbolism," *The Oxford Dictionary of World Religions*, Ed. John Bowker (Oxford, Oxford University Press, 1997) 934.

[73] "Metaphor," *Webster New Twentieth Century Dictionary Unabridged* (Collins World, 1977) 1132.

[74] Ron Grimes. *Deeply into the Bone: Re-inventing Rites of Passage* (University of California Press. Berkeley. 2000) 343.

[75] Williams and Boyd 90

Chapter 5

[1] I. P. Dalmais, *Introduction to the Liturgy* (Baltimore, Helicon Press, 1961).

[2] *Liturgical Year: The Worship of God* (Westminster: John Knox Press, 1991).

[3] Ann Rodgers-Melnick, "Pastor retires after 14 years at East Liberty Presbyterian," *Pittsburgh Post Gazette*, April 14, 2002, B-1.

[4] Robert Chestnut, *Transforming the Mainline Church* (Louisville, 2000).

[5] According to Adrian fisher and Georg Gerster in *The Art of the Maze* (1990) these labyrinths are as follows: Arras Cathedral, France, 1160; Rome, Italy church of Sta Maria-in-Aquiro, c 1189; Sens Cathedral, France, twelfth century; Chartres Cathedral, France, c. 1200; Cologne, West Germany in St. Severin Church, c. 1200; Amiens Cathedral, France, 1288; Rheims Cathedral, France 1287; Rome, Italy in church of Sta Maria-di-Trastavera, late twelfth century; Bayeux Cathedral, France, thirteenth century; Poitiers, France, thirteenth century; Orleans, France in the church of S. Euverte, thirteenth century; Auxerre, France in the Cathedral of Saint-Etienne, 1334; St Omer, France in the Abbey of St. Bertin, fourteenth century; St. Quentin parish church, France, 1495; Ravenna, Italy, in church of San Vitale, 1584.

[6] John Calvin, "Knowledge of God the Creator" as quoted in: *Hungryhearts* (Summer 2000) (Office of Spiritual Formation, Presbyterian Church (U.S.A).

[7] William McLoughlin, "The Fourth Great Awakening, 1960-19(?)," *Revivals, Awakenings, and Reform: An Essay on Religion and Social Change in America, 1607-1977* (Chicago: The University of Chicago Press, 1978) 179-217; Phillip Lucus, "The New Age Movement and the Pentecostal/Charismatic Revival: Distinct Yet Parallel Phases of a Fourth Great Awakening?" *Cults in Context: Reading in the Study of New Religious Movement*, Ed. Lorne Dawson (Toronto: Canadian Scholars Press, 1996).

[8] Since all three rituals were very similar, for convenience I will collapse them into one description.

[9] Sands 20.

[10] Frank Waters, *Book of the Hopi* (New York: Viking Press, 1963) 23.

[11] Sands 29.

[12] *Liturgical Year*, 44.

[13] Turner was influenced by the work of Arnold Van Gannep, *The Rites of Passage* (Chicago: University of Chicago Press, 1960).

[14] Victor Turner, *The Ritual Process: Structure and Anti-Structure*. 1969. (New York: Aldine de Gruyter, 1995).

[15] Berger, Peter. *The Sacred Canopy: Elements of Sociological Theory of Religion* (New York: Doubleday, 1967).

[16] *Liturgical Year* 49-50

[17] *The Liturgical Year* 31

[18] Helen Raphael Sands, *The Healing Labyrinth* (Hauppague: Barron's Educational Series, Inc., 2001) 16.

[19] Andrew Strathern, *Body Thoughts* (Ann Arbor University of Michigan Press, 1996) 3.

[20] Margaret Lock, "Cultivating the Body: Anthropology and Epistemologies of Bodily Practice and Knowledge." *Annual Review of Anthropology* (1993) 22: 133.

[21] Catherine Bell, *Ritual Theory, Ritual Practice* (New York: Oxford University, 1992) x.

[22] In the booklet handed out at the ritual, passages were quoted which described each of the fourteen stations. They are in order: Station #1 Jesus Prays in the Garden-Luke 22:41-46; Station #2 Jesus is Betrayed and Arrested-Mark 12:43-46; Station #3 Jesus is Condemned-Matthew 26:62-66; Station #4 Peter Denies Knowing Jesus-Matthew 26: 69-75; Station 5 Jesus is Condemned by Pilate-Luke 23: 13-15, 23-24; Station #6 Jesus is Scourged and Crowned with Thorns- Mark 15:16-19; Station #7 Jesus Takes up His Cross- John 19-16b-17; Station #8 Simon of Cyrene Helps Jesus- Luke 12:26; Station #9 Jesus Meets the Weeping Women- Luke 23:27-31; Station #10 Jesus is Crucified- Luke 23:33-38; Station #11 Jesus Promises Paradise to the Crucified Thief-Luke 23:39-43; Station #12 Jesus Cares for His Mother- John 19:25-27; Station #13 Jesus Dies-Luke 23:44-47; Station #14 Jesus is Buried- Luke 23:53-56.

[23] Caroline Humphrey and James Laidlaw, *The Archetypal Actions of Ritual* (Oxford: Clarendon Press, 1994).

[24] Ronald Grimes, *Reading, Writing, and Ritualizing* (Washington DC. The Pastoral Press, 1993) 63-67.

Chapter 6

[1] Catherine Albanese, *Nature Religion in America: From the Algonkian Indians to the New Age* (Chicago: The University of Chicago Press, 1990) p. 6; Catherine

Albanese, *Reconsidering Nature Religion* (Harrisburg: Trinity Press International, 2002).

[2] Albanese. *Nature Religion in America* 13

[3] Albanese, *Nature Religion in America* 32. Though some may see neo-pagans as offering a type of community, Albanese views them as a quickly changing movement that fractures and is not highly organized.

[4] Ray Billington, *Religion Without God* (London: Routledge, 2002) 104.

[5] Billington 137.

[6] Martin Marty in Albanese, *Nature Religion in America*, forward xii-xiii.

[7] Albanese, *Reconsidering Nature Religion* 10.

[8] Albanese, *Reconsidering Nature Religion* 1-20.

[9] Albanese, *Reconsidering Nature Religion* 29-30.

[10] James Lovelock, *The Ages of Gaia: A Biography of Our Living Earth* (Oxford: Oxford University Press, 1988) 205. While this idea has empirical support, such as the ability of the Earth to regulate its temperature known as homeostasis, the idea is controversial within the scientific community.

[11] Lovelock 208-9.

[12] "Cherokee," *The New Encyclopedia Britannica*. 15th ed. 1981. 808.

[13] Roy Rappaport, *Ritual and Religion in the Making of Humanity* (Cambridge: Cambridge University Press, 1999) 187

[14] Rappaport 32

[15] Caroline Humphrey and James Laidlaw, *The Archetypal Actions of Ritual* (Oxford: Clarendon Press, 1994) 11.

[16] Rappaport 32

[17] Ralph Waldo Emerson from Nature as quoted in Albanese, *Nature Religion in America* 83.

[18] Albanese, *Reconsidering Nature Religion* 12

[19] Albanese, *Reconsidering Nature Religion* p. 12-16

[20] Wade Clark Roof, *Contemporary American Religion* (New York, Macmillan Reference USA,1999).

[21] e-mail dated November 20, 1998, and "The Mystery of Labyrinths: Dowsing studies and interesting experiences during the construction of earth symbols."

[22] www.prairielabyrinth.org

[23] www.prairielabyrinth.com/chak-lab.htm

[24] Albanese, *Reconsidering Nature Religion* 19

[25] Albanese, *Reconsidering Nature Religion* 19.

[26] Richard Feather Anderson, "Divining the Spirit of the Place," *Yoga Journal* (Sept.-Oct. 1986) 27-31.

[27] http://www.sfgate.com/cgi-bin/article.cgi?file+/chronicle/archive/2003/02/28

Bibliography

Albanese, Catherine. *Nature Religion in America: From the Algonkian Indians to the New Age.* Chicago: The University of Chicago Press, 1990.

Albanese, Catherine. *Reconsidering Nature Religion*, Harrisburg: Trinity Press International, 2002.

Albanese, Catherine. "The Study of American Popular Religion: Retrospect and Prospect," *Explore* 7 (Fall 1984): 7-15.

Altheide, David and John Johnson. "Criteria for Assessing Interpretive Validity in Qualitative Research." In *Handbook of Qualitative Research,* edited by N. K. Denzin and Y. S. Lincoln. Thousand Oaks: Sage Publishing, 1994.

Arens, W. and Ivan Karp, eds. *Creativity of Power: Cosmology and Action in African Societies.* Washington: Smithsonian Institutional Press, 1989.

Artress, Lauren. *Walking a Sacred Path: Rediscovering the Labyrinth as a Spiritual Tool.* New York: Riverhead Books, 1995.

Attali, Jacques. *The Labyrinth in Culture and Society: Pathways to Wisdom*, translated by Joseph Rowe. Berkeley: North Atlantic Books, 1999.

Barbour, Ian. *Religion in an Age of Science.* San Francisco: Harper and Row, 1990.

Becker, H. *Tricks of the Trade: How to Think About Your Research While You're Doing It.* Chicago: University of Chicago Press, 1998.

Becker, Penny and Nancy Eiesland. *Contemporary American Religion: An Ethnographic Reader.* Walnut Creek: AltaMira Press, 1998.

Behar, Ruth. *The Vulnerable Observer: Anthropology that Breaks Your Heart.* Boston: Beacon Press, 1996.

Bell, Catherine. *Ritual Perspectives and Dimensions.* New York: Oxford University Press, 1997.

Bell, Catherine. *Ritual Theory/Ritual Practice.* New York: Oxford University Press, 1992.

Bellah, Robert. *Habits of the Heart: Individualism and Commitment in American Life.* New York: Harper and Row, 1985.

Berger, Peter. *The Sacred Canopy: Elements of Sociological Theory of Religion*. New York: Doubleday, 1967.

Bernard, Russell, ed. *Handbook of Methods in Cultural Anthropology*. Walnut Creek: AltaMira Press, 1998.

Bernard, H. Russell. *Research Methods in Anthropology: Qualitative and Quantitative Approaches*. Walnut Creek: Altamira Press, 1995.

Deborah Rose Bird. "To Dance with Time: A Victoria River Aboriginal Study." *Australian Journal of Anthropology* 22 (2000): 1-7.

Blacker, Carmen and Michael Loewe. *Ancient Cosmologies*. London: Ruskin House, 1975.

Bochner, Arthur and Carolyn Ellis. "Talking Over Ethnography." In *Composing Ethnography: Alternative Forms of Qualitative Writing*, 13-45. Walnut Creek: AltaMira Press, 1996.

Bolle, Kees. "Cosmology." In *The Encyclopedia of Religion,* ed. Mircea Eliade, et. al. New York: Macmillan, 1987.

Bord, Janet. *Mazes and Labyrinths of the World*. London: Latimer New Dimensions Limited, 1976.

Bowker, John, ed. *The Oxford Dictionary of World Religions*. Oxford: Oxford University Press, 1997.

Branner, Robert, ed. *Chartres Cathedral: Illustrations, Introductory Essay, Documents, Analysis, Criticism*. New York: W. W. Norton & Company, Inc. 1969.

Brooke, John L. *The Refiners Fire: The Making of Mormon Cosmology, 1644-1844*. Cambridge: Cambridge University Press, 1994.

Butler, Jon. "Magic, Astrology, and the Early American Religious Heritage, 1600-1760." *American History Review*, 84 (April 1979): 317-346.

Butler, Jon. *Awash in a Sea of Faith: Christianizing the American People*. Cambridge: Harvard University Press, 1990.

Carr, Christopher and Jill Neitzel, eds. *Style, Society, and Person: Archeological and Ethnological Perspectives*. New York: Plenum Press, 1995.

Carrasco, David. *Religions of Mesoamerica: Cosmovision and Ceremonial Centers*. Prospect Heights: Waveland Press, 1998.

Castleden, Rodney. *The Knossos Labyrinth: A New View of the 'Palace of Minos' at Knossos*. London: Routledge, 1990.

Chadwick, John, *The Decipherment of Linear B*. Cambridge: Cambridge University Press, 1967.

Champion, Alex. *Earth Mazes*. Emeryville: Bacchus Press, Inc. 1990.

Champion, Alex. "Re: labyrinths." E-mail to author 20 November 1998.

Champion, Alex. "The Mystery of Labyrinths: Dowsing studies and interesting experiences during the construction of earth symbols."

Chance, Jane, and O. Wells, Jr., eds. *Mapping the Cosmos*. Houston: Rice University Press, 1985.

Chance, Jane. *Medieval Mythography: From Roman North Africa to the School of Chartres, A. D. 433-1177*. Gainesville: University Press of Florida, 1994.

Chenail, R. Presenting Qualitative Data. *The Qualitative Report*, 2, 3 (December 1995). (http://www.nova.edu.ssss/QR/QR2-3/presenting.html)

Chestnut, Robert. *Transforming the Mainline Church*. Louisville, 2001.

Christian, William, *Local Religion in Sixteenth-Century Spain*. Princeton: Princeton University Press, 1981.

Clothey, Fred. *Rhythm and Intent: Ritual Studies from South India*. Madras: Blackie & Sons Publishers, 1983.

Clothey, Fred. "Ritual, Nature and Theories," In *The Perennial Dictionary of World Religions,* ed. Keith Grim, 624-628. San Francisco: Harper San Francisco, 1989.

Conford. Francis. *Plato's Cosmology: The Timaeus of Plato*. 1935. Indianapolis: Hackett Publishing Company, 1997.

Connolly, Daniel K. "Imagined Pilgrimage in Gothic Art: Maps, Manuscripts and Labyrinths." Diss. University of Chicago, 1998.

"Cosmology," *Oxford Dictionary of World Religions,* edited by John Bowker, 238-39. Oxford: Oxford University Press, 1997.

Critchlow, Keith, Jane Carroll and Llewelyn Vaughn Lee. "Chartres Maze: A Model of the Universe?" *Architectural Association Quarterly* 5, 2 (1973): 11-22.

Curry, Helen. *The Way of the Labyrinth: A Powerful Meditation for Everyday Life.* New York: Penguin Compass, 2000.

Curry, Helen. "Re: September 11." E-mail to TLS members. 12 Sept. 2001.

Davis, Natalie Zemon. "Some Tasks and Themes in the Study of Popular Religion." In *The Pursuit of Holiness in Late Medieval and Renaissance Religion*, edited by Charles Trinkaus and Heiko Oberman. Leiden: E.J. Brill, 1974.

Davis, Natalie Zemon. "From 'Popular Religion' to Religious Cultures." In *Reformation Europe*, edited by Stephen Ozmont. St. Louis: Center for Reformation Research, 1982.

Davis, Simon. *The Decipherment of the Minoan Linear A and Pictographic Scripts*. Johannesburg: Witwatersrand University Press, 1967.

de Coppet, Daniel and Andre Iteanu. *Cosmos and Society in Oceania*. Oxford: Berg Publishers Limited, 1995.

Demaray, John G. *Dante and the Book of the Cosmos*. Philadelphia: The American Philosophical Society, 1987.

Deedes, C.N. "The Labyrinth." In *The Labyrinth: Further Studies in the Relation of Myth and Ritual in the Ancient World*, edited by S. H. Hooke. London, 1935.

Denzin, Norman and Yvonna Lincoln. *Handbook of Qualitative Research*. Thousand Oaks: Sage Publication, 1994.

DeWalt, Kathleen and Billie DeWalt. *Participant Observation: A Guide for Fieldworkers*. AltaMira Press, 2010.

Dixon-Kennedy, Mike. *Encyclopedia of Greco-Roman Mythology*. Santa Barbara: ABC-CLIO, 1998.

Doob, Penelope Reed. *The Idea of the Labyrinth: From Classical Antiquity through the Middle Ages*. Ithaca: Cornell University Press, 1990.

Douglas, Mary. *Natural Symbols: Explorations in Cosmology*. London: Routledge, 1970.

Driver, Tom. *The Magic of Ritual*. San Francisco: Harper San Francisco, 1991.

Durkheim, Emile. *Elementary Forms of Religious Life*, translated by J.E. Swain. Glencoe: Free Press, 1954.

Eade, John and Michael Sallnow. *Contesting the Sacred: The Anthropology of Christian Pilgrimage*. London: Routledge Press, 1991.

Eck, Diana L. *A New Religious America: A "Christian Country" Has Now Become the World's Most Religiously Diverse Nation*. San Francisco: Harper San Francisco, 2001.

"Egyptian Mythology." In *New Larousse Encyclopedia of Mythology*, 21st ed. New York: Crescent Books, 1986.

Eliade, Mircea. *Cosmos and History: The Myth of the Eternal Return.* New York: Harper Torchbooks, 1959.

Eliade, Mircea. "Sacred Architecture and Symbolism." In *Symbolism, the Sacred, and the Arts*, edited by Diane Apostolos-Capadona. New York: Crossroad, 1985.

Eliade, Mircea. *The Sacred and the Profane: The Nature of Religion.* 1957. Translated by Willard Trask. San Diego: Harcourt Brace and Company, 1987.

Ellard, Peter. "The Sacred Cosmos: A Study of the Twelfth Century School of Chartres." Diss. Fordham University, 1999.

Ellwood, Robert. *Alternative Altars: Unconventional and Eastern Spirituality in America.* Chicago: The University of Chicago Press, 1979.

Ellwood, Robert. "UFO Religious Movements." In *America's Alternative Religions*, edited by Timothy Miller. Albany: State University of New York Press, 1995.

Fisher. Adrian and Georg Gerster. *The Art of the Maze.* London: Weidenfeld and Nicholson, 1990.

Frederic, Louis. *Borobudur.* New York: Abbeville Press, 1996.

Fuller, Robert. *Spiritual, but not Religious: Understanding Unchurched America.* Oxford: Oxford University Press, 2001.

Gahan, C. & Hannibal M. *Doing Qualitative Research Using QSR NUD*IST.* London: Sage Publications, 1998.

Geertz, Clifford. *The Interpretation of Cultures.* New York: Basic Books Inc., 1973.

Gill, Sam. *Beyond "The Primitive": The Religions of Nonliterate People.* Englewood Cliffs: Prentice-Hall, 1982.

Gill, Sam. *Native American Traditions.* Belmont: Wadsworth Publishing Co, 1983.

Gimpel, Jean. *The Cathedral Builders*, translated by Teresa Waugh. New York: Harper & Row, 1983.

Good, Anthony. "Congealing Divinity: Time, Worship and Kinship in South Indian Hinduism." *Journal of the Royal Anthropological Institute* (June 2000): V.

Goodrich, Norma Lorre. *Priestesses.* New York: Franklin Watts, 1989.

Goodstein, Laurie. "Reviving Labyrinths, Paths to Inner Peace." *New York Times* (10 May 1998): 1.

Grant, Edward. "Cosmology." In *Science in the Middle Ages*, edited by David Lindberg. Chicago: University of Chicago Press, 1978.

Grant, Edward. *Planets, Stars, and Orbs: The Medieval Cosmos, 1200-1687.* Cambridge: Cambridge University Press, 1994.

Grant, Michael, and John Hazel, *Who's Who in Classical Mythology.* New York: Oxford University Press, 1993.

Graves, Robert. *Greek Myths: Volume 1.* London: Penguin Books, 1955.

Grimes. Ronald. *Beginnings in Ritual Studies.* Washington: University Press of America, 1982.

Grimes, Ronald. *Reading, Writing, and Ritualizing: Ritual in Fictive, Liturgical, and Public Places.* Washington: The Pastoral Press, 1993.

Grimes, Ron. *Deeply into the Bone: Re-inventing Rites of Passage.* Berkeley: University of California Press, 2000.

Hall, David, ed. *Lived Religions in America: Toward a History of Practice.* Princeton: Princeton University Press, 1997.

Hammersley, M and P. Atkinson. *The Process of Analysis: Ethnography Principles in Practice.* London: Routledge, 1992.

Hetherington, Norriss. *Cosmology: Historical, Literary, Philosophical, Religious, and Scientific Perspectives.* New York: Garland Publishing, Inc., 1993.

Honecort, Wilars de. (Villard de Honnecourt) *Sketch-Book,* edited by Robert Willis. London: John Henry and James Parker, 1859.

Hooke, Samuel Henry. *The Labyrinth: Further Studies in the Relation of Myth and Ritual in the Ancient World.* London: Society for Promoting Christian Knowledge, 1935.

Hubert, Jane. "Sacred belief and beliefs of sacredness." In *Sacred Sites, Sacred Places*, edited by David Carmichael, Jane Hubert, Brian Reeves and Sudhild Schanche. London: Routledge, 1994.

Humphrey, Caroline and James Laidlaw. *The Archetypal Actions of Ritual.* Oxford: Clarendon Press, 1994.

Jennings, Theodore. "On Ritual Knowledge." In *Readings in Ritual Studies*, edited by Ronald Grimes. Upper Saddle River: Prentice Hall, 1996.

Kern, Hermann. *Through the Labyrinth: Designs and Meanings over 5000 Years.* Munich: Prestel. 2000. Translated by Abigail Clay. (Originally published in Munich in 1982 as *Labyrinthe: Erscheinungsformen und Deutungen; 5000 Jahre Gegenwart eines Urbilds.*)

Knight, Heather. "Peaceful Path: In troubled times more people turn to the labyrinth to walk their worries away." *San Francisco Chronicle* (28 Feb 2003).

Koyre, Alexandre. *From the Closed World to the Infinite Universe*. Baltimore: The John Hopkins Press, 1957.

Lang, Mabel. "The Palace of Nestor Excavations of 1957: Part II." *American Journal of Archaeology* 62 (1958).

Lesser. George. *Gothic Cathedrals and Sacred Geometry*. London: Alec Tiranti, 1957.

Lewis, C.S. *The Discarded Image: An Introduction to Medieval and Renaissance Literature*. Cambridge: University Press, 1964.

Lindberg, David C. *The Beginnings of Western Science: The European Scientific Tradition in Philosophical, Religious, and Institutional Context, 600 B.C. to A.D. 1450*. Chicago: The University of Chicago Press, 1992.

Lindner, Eileen, ed. *Yearbook of American & Canadian Churches 1998*. Nashville: Abingdon Press, 1998.

Lippy, Charles and Peter Williams, eds. *Encyclopedia of the American Religious Experience: Studies of Traditions and Movements*. New York: Scribner, 1988.

Lippy, Charles. *Modern American Popular Religion: A Critical Assessment and Annotated Bibliography*. Westport: Greenwood Press, 1996.

Lock, Margaret. "Cultivating the Body: Anthropology and Epistemologies of Bodily Practice and Knowledge." *Annual Review of Anthropology* 22 (1993): 13-155.

Lonegren, Sig. *Labyrinths: Ancient Myths and Modern Uses*. 1991. Somerset: Gothic Image Publications, 1996.

Mâle, Emile. *The Gothic Image: Religious Art in France of the Thirteenth Century*. 1913. Translated by Dora Nussey. New York: Harper & Brothers, 1958.

Malinowski, Bronislaw. *Magic, Science and Religion*. Garden City: Doubleday, 1954.

Marty, Martin. *Modern American Religion*. Chicago: University of Chicago Press, 1986.

Marty, Martin. "Where the Energies Go." In *The Annals of the American Academy of Political and Social Science: Religion in the Nineties*, edited by Wade Clark Roof. Newbury Park: Sage Periodicals Press: 1993.

Matthews, W.H. *Mazes and Labyrinths: Their History and Development*. 1922. New York: Dover Publications, 1970.

McGuire, Meredith. "Health and Spirituality as Contemporary Concerns." In *The Annals of the American Academy of Political and Social Science: Religion in the Nineties*, edited by Wade Clark Roof. Newbury Park: Sage Periodicals Press, 1993.

Merchant, Carolyn. *The Death of Nature: Women, Ecology, and the Scientific Revolution*. San Francisco: Harper & Row, 1980.

"Metaphor." In *Oxford Dictionary of World Religions*, edited by John Bowker. Oxford: Oxford University Press, 1997.

Moore, R. Laurence. *Religious Outsiders and the Making of Americans*. New York: Oxford University Press, 1986.

Moore, Laurence. *Selling God: American Religion in the Marketplace of Culture*. New York: Oxford University Press, 1994.

Morello, Adrienne. "Re: labyrinth." E-mail to the author. 26 June 2003.

N4 Classic User's Guide. Third Edition. PDF version of QSR N4 Manual.(2000). QSR International Pty Ltd.

Narayanan, Vahudha. "From Angkor to Atlanta: Hindu Migrations and Culture," from the *Symposium on Hinduism* June 22, 23 2002 and the Presidential address at the AAR Toronto, November 2002.

Needham, Joseph. *Science, Religion and Reality*. 1925. New York: George Braziller Inc. 1955.

Newman, William and Peter Halvorson. *Atlas of American Religion: The Denominational Era, 1776-1990*. Walnut Creek: AltaMira Press, 2000.

Neitz, Mary Jo. "In Goddess We Trust." In *In Gods We Trust: New Patterns of Religious Pluralism in America*, edited by Thomas Robins and Dick Anthony. New Brunswick: Transaction Publishers, 1990.

Paul, Erich Robert. *Science, Religion and Mormon Cosmology*. Urbana: University of Illinois Press, 1992.

Pennick, Nigel. *Mazes and Labyrinths*. London: Robert Hale, 1990.

Plato. *Timaeus*. Translated by Francis Cornford. New York: Macmillan Publishing Company, 1959.

"Pluralism Project." http://www.fas.harvard.edu/~pluralism/

Prache, Anne. *Chartres Cathedral: Image of Heavenly Jerusalem*. Translated by Janice Abbot. Paris: CNRS Editions, 1993.

Prince, Ruth and David Riches. *The New Age in Glastonbury: The Construction of Religious Movement*. New York: Berghahn Books, 2000.

Rappaport, Roy. *Ritual and Religion in the Making of Humanity*. Cambridge: Cambridge University Press. 1999.

"Religious Adherents in the United States of America, AD 1900-2000." Britannica Online. http://www.eb.com

Richards, T. & Richards L. "Using Computers in Qualitative Research." In *Handbook of Qualitative Research*, edited by N. K. Denzin and Y. S. Lincoln. Thousand Oaks: Sage Publishing,1994.

Roof, Wade Clark. *A Generation of Seekers: The Spiritual Journeys of the Baby Boom Generation*. San Francisco: Harper, 1993.

Roof, Wade Clark. *American Contemporary Religion*. New York, Macmillan Reference USA, 1999.

Roof, Wade Clark. *Spiritual Marketplace: Baby Boomers and the Remaking of American Religion*. Princeton: Princeton University Press, 1999.

Rubin, H. J. and I. S. Rubin. *Qualitative Interviewing: The Art of Hearing Data*. Thousand Oaks: Sage Publishing, 1995.

Sanjek, Roger, ed. *Fieldnotes: The Making of Anthropology*. Ithaca: Cornell University Press, 1990.

Saward, Jeff. *Ancient Labyrinths of the World*. Thundersley: Caerdroia, 1997.

Schechner, Richard. *The Future of Ritual*. London: Routledge Press, 1993.

Schrempp, Gregory. *Magical Arrows: The Maori, the Greeks and the Folklore of the Universe*. Madison: The University of Wisconsin Press, 1992.

Simson, Otto von. *The Gothic Cathedral: Origins of Gothic Architecture and the Medieval Concept of Order*, 3rd ed. Princeton: Princeton University Press, 1988.

Smith, J. Z. *Map is Not Territory*. Leiden: Brill, 1978.

Smith, Jonathan Z. *To Take Place: Toward Theory in Ritual*. Chicago: The University of Chicago Press, 1987.

Source. A Veriditas Publication (Winter 1996).

Stafford, Harry Coffin. *Culture and Cosmology: Essays on the Birth of World View*. Washington, D.C.: University Press of America,1981.

Stahl, William Harris. *Commentary on the Dream of Scipio by Macrobius*. New York: Columbia University Press, 1952.

Stark, Laura. "Popular Religion in Southern Europe: A Survey of Recent Anthropological Research." *Suomen antropologi* 19/4 (1994): 34-50.

Strauss, A. and J. Corbin. *Grounded Theory and Practice*. Thousand Oaks: Sage Publishing, 1995.

Tambiah, Stanley. "A Performative Approach to Ritual." In *Readings in Ritual Studies*. Upper Saddle River: Prentice Hall, 1996.

Tedlock, Barbara. "From Participant Observation to the Observation of Participation: The Emergence of Narrative Ethnography." *Journal of Anthropologcal Research* 47 (1991): 69-94.

Thomas, Keith. *Religion and the Decline of Magic*. New York: Charles Scribner's Sons, 1971.

Toulmin, Stephen. *The Return to Cosmology: Postmodern Science and the Theology of Nature*. Berkeley: University of California Press, 1982.

Trimble, Shawn Michael. *America's Alternative Religions*, edited by Timothy Miller. Albany: State University of New York Press, 1995.

Turner, Victor and Edith Turner. *Image and Pilgrimage in Christian Culture: Anthropological Perspectives*. New York: Columbia University Press, 1978.

Turner, Victor. *The Ritual Process: Structure and Anti-Structure*. 1969. New York: Aldine de Gruyter, 1995.

Tweed, Thomas. *Our Lady of Exile: Diasporic Religion at a Cuban Catholic Shrine in Miami*. New York: Oxford University Press, 1997.

Villette, Jean. "The Enigma of the Labyrinth at Chartres Cathedral." In *Notre-Dame de Chartres*, translated by Malcolm Miller. 1983.

Waters, Frank. *Book of the Hopi*. New York: Viking Press, 1963.

Weatherbee, Winthrop. *Platonism and Poetry in the Twelfth Century: The Literary Influence of the School of Chartres*. Princeton: Princeton University Press, 1972.

Weiss, Gerald. *Campa Cosmology: The World of a Forest Tribe in South America*. 52/5. Anthropological Papers of The American Museum of Natural History. New York: 1975.

Wentz, Richard. *The Culture of Religious Pluralism*. Boulder: Westview Press, 1998.

West, Melissa Gayle. *Exploring the Labyrinth: A Guide for Healing and Spiritual Growth*. New York: Broadway Books, 2000.

Wildiers, N. Max. *The Theologian and His Universe: Theology and Cosmology from the Middle Ages to the Present*. New York: The Seabury Press, 1982.

Williams, Peter. *Popular Religion in America: Symbolic Change and the Modernization Process in Historical Perspective*. 1980. Urbana: University of Illinois Press, 1989.

Williams, Ron and James Boyd. *Ritual Art and Knowledge: Aesthetic Theory and Zoroastrian Ritual*. Columbia: University of South Carolina Press, 1993.

Wright, Craig. *The Maze and the Warrior: Symbols in Architecture, Theology, and Music*. Cambridge: Harvard University Press, 2001.

Wolcott, Harry. *Transforming Qualitative Data: Description, Analysis, and Interpretation*. Thousand Oaks: Sage Publications, 1994.

Wolcott, Harry. *The Art of Fieldwork*. Walnut Creek: AltaMira Press, 1995.

Woodward, Kathryn. "Error Labyrinthi: An Iconographic Study of Labyrinths as Symbolic of Submission and Deliverance in Manuscripts and on Pavements Dating from Late Antiquity Through the High Middle Ages." Diss. for Bryn Mawr College, 1981.

Wuthnow, Robert. *Experimentation in American Religion*. Berkeley: University of California Press, 1978.

Wuthnow, Robert. *Restructuring American Religion: Society and Faith Since World War II*. Princeton: Princeton University Press, 1988.

Wuthnow, Robert. *After Heaven: Spirituality in America since the 1950s*. Berkeley: University of California Press, 1998.

www.ingramcontent.com/pod-product-compliance
Lightning Source LLC
Chambersburg PA
CBHW052138070526
44585CB00017B/1882